FOCUSING

THE

WHOLE BRAIN

Other Books by Ronald Russell

The Vast Enquiring Soul

Using the Whole Brain (ed.)

Swimming for Life: The Therapy of Swimming

The Country Canal

and 11 other titles

FOCUSING

THE

WHOLE BRAIN

Transforming Your Life with
Hemispheric Synchronization

EDITED BY RONALD RUSSELL

HAMPTON ROADS
PUBLISHING COMPANY, INC.

Hampton Roads Publishing Company, Inc.
1125 Stoney Ridge Road
Charlottesville, VA 22902
434-296-2772
fax: 434-296-5096
e-mail: hrpc@hrpub.com
www.hrpub.com

The following are registered trademarks of The Monroe Institute:
Metamusic
Gateway Voyage
Gateway Experience
Mind Food
H-PLUS
Human Plus
Hemi-Sync
Going Home
Exploration 27
Guidelines
Lifelines

If you are unable to order this book from your local
bookseller, you may order directly from the publisher.
Call 1-800-766-8009, toll-free.

Library of Congress Cataloging-in-Publication Data

Russell, Ronald.
  Focusing the whole brain : transforming your life with hemispheric
synchronization / Ronald Russell.
     p. cm.
Includes bibliographical references and index.
  ISBN 1-57174-378-2 (alk. paper)
  1. Cerebral hemispheres. 2. Sound--Psychological aspects. 3. Mind
and body therapies. 4. Imagery (Psychology) 5. Brain. I. Title.
QP381.R876 2004
158.1--dc22

                              2003021781

                      ISBN 1-57174-378-2
                      10 9 8 7 6 5 4 3 2 1
          Printed on acid-free paper in the United States

Table of Contents

Foreword
Laurie Monroe

Robert Monroe was a leader in the production of radio network programs in New York City in the forties and fifties. In 1956, he became interested in the feasibility of learning during sleep. He was curious about that third of our life in which our time and energy might be wasted. Since he was an expert in sound, he began to experiment with frequency patterns that could evoke various stages of sleep. As a child, I remember being one of the subjects for a learning experiment.

In 1958, my father began to experience states of consciousness that were totally unfamiliar to him. He experienced himself as totally separate and apart from his physical body. Since he had no formal religious training or spiritual background, he looked to Western science to find the reason for these occurrences.

Through the years, his work was diverted into the exploration of consciousness. Researchers, engineers, scientists, educators, psychotherapists and many others joined him in this quest. Their interest and participation have brought the Hemi-Sync process to its current level of development. Many books now reference Robert Monroe's work as a pioneer in the exploration of the non-locality of consciousness.

Using the Whole Brain, edited by Ronald Russell, M.A., and originally published in 1993, contained a wealth of information pertaining to the use of the Hemi-Sync technology as a tool that has benefited thousands of people in understanding more deeply the conscious mind. I am eternally grateful to him for the enormous amount of time and energy he has invested in compiling this new edition. Russ was a friend and colleague of my father's for many, many years. He is dedicated to the work of The Monroe Institute and to sharing the many practical applications and benefits of the Hemi-Sync process. This book is a measure of his support and commitment to our work and a testament to the effectiveness of the Hemi-Sync technology.

Thank you, Russ, for your contribution, assisting others to better understand how they may use Hemi-Sync to further their own personal growth and develop their unlimited potential.

The Way of Hemi-Sync
Robert A. Monroe (1915–1995)
Reprinted from the preface to *Using the Whole Brain, 1993*

The inescapable law of cause and effect can't be ignored, whatever the situation or the reaction. We may or may not like or anticipate the result. Yet there will be one, even many years later.

That is the case in Hemi-Sync, our acronym for hemispheric synchronization. Back in 1956, our New York-based company had been a leader in the production of radio network programs, using voices, music, and specialized sound. With the rising power of television, a decision had to be made whether to convert to this new medium or to try something else.

A possibility came to our attention: learning during sleep, that third of our lives over which we had little or no control and where much of our time and energy may well be wasted. We set up a research and development program to explore the prospect and immediately ran into the basic problem. We couldn't get our subjects to go to sleep when we needed them to do so for test periods, and the use of sleep-inducing drugs seemed contradictory to our basic purpose.

Using our area of expertise, we began testing subjects with various sound patterns to find those that would evoke various stages of sleep. It was slow work, but we did have just enough early success to lure us to continue.

When EEG testing of subjects showed waveforms similar if not identical to the sound patterns we were using, we began to call the result frequency-following response (FFR). Later, as we began using binaural beat sound, we found similar waveforms in both sides of the brain at the same moment. This synchronization of the brain's hemispheres came to be known as Hemi-Sync.

I had been one of the leading subjects in our tests. In 1958, I began to experience states of consciousness totally unknown to me. They seemed both dangerous and exciting. Other subjects did not experience the phenomenon. As a result, we diverted our research into this new area.

Through the years, our work progressed steadily in this seemingly new direction, attracting the attention, interest, and participation of several hundred researchers, scientists, engineers, educators, physicians, psychologists, and many others. They are the ones, not I, who have brought the Hemi-Sync processes to the level where they are today. I am still not sure I was the sole cause.

The effects? Over 200,000 people now have a good night's sleep without drugs, as a baseline. Many thousands more have learned better understanding and control of their mental, emotional, and physical selves. We believe it is an emerging learning system that might be called "Lifespan," applicable from cradle to grave.

Thus the purpose of this volume is to acquaint you with the various practical applications of the Hemi-Sync process, so that you too will begin to consider how you can make use of it, not only in your personal life but in many other areas as well.

Introduction
Ronald Russell

The predecessor of this book, *Using the Whole Brain,* was published in 1993. On the whole, I think it achieved its purpose as expressed by Robert Monroe: to introduce the audio technology known as Hemispheric Synchronization (Hemi-Sync) to the public at large and to describe the many ways in which it was used. So far, so good. But things move along. Many of the hopes and wishes of the thirty-five contributors to that volume have been fulfilled; tests and trials have provided more validation, scientifically acceptable, of the claims made for this technology. The technology itself has been further improved and has been employed in new areas, such as achieving lucid dreaming, coping with autism, working with chemotherapy, and providing personal growth courses for teenagers. Courses and workshops are now available in 17 countries outside the United States and people from at least 50 countries have attended courses at The Monroe Institute.

So it seemed as if the time were right for an update. Or nearly so. Some four years ago an appeal went out for contributions to a new edition. Just six replies were received. Clearly that wasn't the right time. Then, towards the end of a talk I was giving at the Institute's Professional Seminar in the spring of 2002, I heard myself say something about the need for a replacement for *Using the Whole Brain.* "What was this idiot talking about?" I wondered. "Whose crazy idea was this?" Well . . . 24 hours later at least 30 contributions had been promised, and the welcome offer of an assistant editor had been gratefully received. So, thanks to computer technology, a book that was to be published in the United States, dealing with a process developed and mainly employed in that country, was put together and edited in Scotland and Mexico with contributions from countries as far apart as Poland and New Zealand.

The years between the publication of these two volumes have seen many changes. First and most important was the death of Robert Monroe on March 17, 1995. His importance as a pioneer in the exploration of consciousness is now widely recognized, as is evidenced by the ever-increasing sales worldwide of his three groundbreaking books and his influence on consciousness literature (see Steve Graf's "Bob Monroe and TMI's Impact on Consciousness Literature" in the Scientific and Technical section of this book). There is a recently published perceptive survey of Monroe's work in *Dark Night, Early Dawn* by Christopher Bache, Professor of Religious Studies at Youngstown State University (a work described by Richard Tarnas as "the most important book I have read in recent years"). Bache describes Monroe's work as presenting "a profound challenge to the materialist vision that rules the modern mind." This work, as continued by Monroe's successors at The Monroe Institute through the courses it provides and the promulgation of its Hemi-Sync products, enables others to participate in that challenge.

Monroe wrote of Hemi-Sync: "We believe it is an emerging learning system . . . applicable from cradle to grave." This belief is now a reality. The **Opening the Way** series of Hemi-Sync recordings offered by TMI provides a supportive guide for pregnancy and birth, and the work of Dr. Suzanne Morris, Jacqueline Mast, and others, detailed in the following pages, demonstrates how Hemi-Sync can help with the problems and difficulties of very young children. At the other end of the spectrum, the *Lifeline* course and the **Going Home** series, devised by Monroe himself with advice from Dr. Elisabeth Kübler-Ross and Emeritus Professor Charles Tart, provide help and support for the dying, their families, and caregivers, and together with the *Exploration 27* course, open up the infinite possibilities of what lies beyond the grave.

Robert Monroe was succeeded as president of the Institute by his daughter Laurie. Under her energetic guidance, Robert and Nancy Monroe's former home on Roberts Mountain has become an extension of the Institute. The house itself has been renovated and an annex built to provide a comfortable setting for sixteen participants taking the more advanced courses available at TMI. A second research laboratory has been constructed adjacent to the log cabin where Monroe worked and wrote *Ultimate Journey*. Several new exercises on CD and tape are now available, including a number of enchanting Metamusic compositions. New residential courses have been created, as well as a Remote Viewing Practicum. The Remote Viewing course is designed by Skip Atwater, the Institute's Director of Research, who is one of the trainers. Skip was the operations and training officer of the U.S. Army's Stargate Remote Viewing program. Joe McMoneagle, Remote Viewer 001 in that program and holder of the Legion of Merit for his contribution to intelligence operations, worked with Monroe in the 1980s, finding that Hemi-Sync helped to refine his remote viewing ability and to control his spontaneous out-of-body experiences. Joe sometimes gives a talk to participants during the Remote Viewing course.

Research into Hemi-Sync itself and into its various applications has intensified, and findings have been published in a number of professional journals, ranging from *Anesthesia* to the *Journal of Scientific Exploration*. At the time of writing, studies and trials are in progress in various universities, hospitals, and research organizations, including Northern Arizona State University; Western Washington University; University of Virginia School of Nursing; the Rhine Research Center; Duke University Medical Center; Sussex University and Queen Mary's Hospital, Sidcup, in the United Kingdom; the University of Montreal; and the Institute of Transpersonal Psychology. Most recently, the United Nations has agreed to support a Hemi-Sync pilot study by Ursula Furstenwald, Director of OASIS, an organization assisting torture victims suffering from post-traumatic stress disorder. Serious sleep disturbances are one of a constellation of symptoms exhibited by survivors of torture, and Hemi-Sync will be employed as an adjunct to focused group therapy in an attempt to relieve insomnia. The study will be based in Copenhagen, Denmark.

To begin with, there was little expectation that the Hemi-Sync technology would attract attention outside the United States. Yet today there are trainers and workshop presenters in some 20 countries, and individuals from 50 countries have traveled to attend courses in Virginia. The texts of the various exercises have been translated into French and Spanish, thus opening up possibilities in Central and South America, as well as Europe. In some countries, notably Poland, Slovakia, and Germany, enthusiastic presenters have translated the texts themselves.

The Monroe Institute is devoted to the following premise:

> Focused consciousness contains definitive solutions to the questions of human experience. Greater understanding of such consciousness can be achieved through coordinated research efforts using an interdisciplinary approach.

Monroe was led into investigating consciousness through his own experiments with sleep learning, and later through his out-of-body experiences. Since those days, the subject of consciousness has moved into the center of academic inquiry. On one side there are the materialists who maintain that consciousness is solely a function of the brain. Consequently if consciousness depends on the existence of the brain, when the brain ceases to function consciousness must also cease to function. On the other side are those who claim that consciousness is primary—that the brain mediates it but does not create it, because consciousness permeates the universe—in other words, it is all that there is. "Everything we experience is a construct within consciousness," says Peter Russell. "It is eternal, everlasting."

Monroe himself never engaged in academic debate. He had no need to. The audio technology he devised—his Hemi-Sync—spoke for him. It enabled individuals to conduct their own explorations into consciousness and, if they chose, to investigate realities other than this physical world and to move into areas beyond the boundaries of physical existence. Those who have made these explorations need no further convincing about the nature of consciousness.

With very few exceptions, the contributors to this book concentrate on the practical applications of Hemi-Sync—its value in assisting personal growth and development, its use in medicine, in psychiatry and psychotherapy, with autistic children, in nursing homes, in sleep training, in education, and so on. Because it is unobtrusive, inexpensive, and readily available—but principally because it is so effective—Hemi-Sync appeals to professionals in many disciplines. It is proved to perform a remarkable number of practical functions relevant in everyday life. We now know much more accurately how it works, and examples of the research that demonstrates this can be found in the following chapters.

This book and its predecessor originated from discussions at the Institute's Professional Seminars, where members of its Professional Division assemble to listen to and discuss presentations on the findings of recent research and the many ways in which Hemi-Sync is proving to be of value. Keynote speakers at past Professional Seminars have included Dr. Elisabeth Kübler-Ross, the astronaut Edgar Mitchell, Peter Russell, Beverly Rubik of the Institute of Frontier Science, and Marilyn Schlitz, Director of Research at the Institute of Noetic Sciences. On a personal note, it was the existence of the Professional Division, coupled with the status of the Institute as a nonprofit organization, that persuaded me to overcome my doubts (as a cautious Brit) and sign on to my first Gateway course in 1986.

As The Monroe Institute faces the future with confidence, it is open to working with other organizations whose vision is in alignment with "making a difference." Such an organization is the Institute of Noetic Sciences. IONS, as it is generally known, has a worldwide membership of approximately 50,000. The Monroe Institute and IONS recently became strategic partners and are offering the **Gateway Voyage** at IONS campus in Petuluma, CA. Both organizations are dedicated "to explore consciousness for a world awakening through frontier science, personal enquiry, and learning communities."

Finally, let me say how grateful I am to all those who contributed to this book, many at very short notice, to Jeanne Basteris and Jill Russell for their great help with editing, and also to those for whose contributions we simply could not find space. The variety of interests, occupations, and experiences demonstrates more than any single statement that Hemi-Sync is indeed, to use Robert Monroe's own words, "something of value."

Focus Levels

In some of the following chapters references are made to various Focus levels. This is a convenient way, developed by Robert Monroe, of referring to certain states or phases of consciousness.

C1 (Consciousness 1): Everyday "normal" waking consciousness.

Focus 3: A state where the brain and mind are more coherent, synchronized and balanced than in everyday consciousness.

Focus 10: "Mind awake/body asleep." Deep physical relaxation combined with mental alertness.

Focus 12: A state of expanded awareness in which you become more conscious of inner resources and guidance.

Focus 15: Time as a construct of consciousness no longer exists.

Focus 21: A state beyond the restrictions of space/time in which you may explore more deeply and move freely into other energy systems.

Focus 22–27: For a guide to these areas, see pp. 295–298.

PERSONAL GROWTH AND DEVELOPMENT

Curiosity, said Robert Monroe, is the best approach to a course at The Monroe Institute. Come without any special expectations—certainly don't come expecting to have an out-of-body experience. Keep an open mind and see what happens.

What happens to many people is they find that somehow the experience itself brings about what amounts to a rapid—sometimes dramatic—acceleration in their personal growth and development. An attack of flu prompted Therese Bullard to attend to her mother Barbara's insistence that she try the tapes to see how they might help. Felicia Potter was one of the first to attend the Teenage Gateway program. Difficulty sleeping drove Tim Ambrose to take a friend's advice to listen to *Sound Sleeper*, and his subsequent experience with Hemi-Sync was largely responsible for his decision to create a Center for Healing Arts in Hawaii. Suzane Proulx and Gail Blanchette, in their different ways, discovered new perspectives that they eloquently describe in their contributions to this chapter. Anne Carpenter gives a vivid and moving account of the help she obtained in coping with autism from many of the Hemi-Sync exercises. In contrast, we have a personal account of the effects of the Gateway experience on a group of prisoners—the only group in that prison with black, white, and Hispanic participants.

These six contributions illustrate the effects of this audio technology in helping individuals to fulfill their potential by encouraging them to investigate new and often exciting ways in which they can grow and develop, no matter their age or pattern of life.

Mind, Body, Spirit, and Hemi-Sync
Theresa Bullard

Theresa Bullard has a master's degree in physics and is currently working on completing her Ph.D. at the University of Washington Department of Physics. Her experience with Hemi-Sync dates back to her teenage years, when her mother, Barbara Bullard, first became involved with The Monroe Institute. Theresa's extended experience with the Monroe products and their ability to enhance states of consciousness has helped to shape some of her career interests. She hopes to combine her experiential passion for exploring consciousness with her background and training in physics to conduct research in the area of science and consciousness.

Looking back on all the various experiences that I have had with The Monroe Institute and its technologies, it is hard to zero in on just one to share. In fact, it seems that the diversity itself is one of the greatest assets that TMI has. My initial uses of Hemi-Sync and Metamusic were rather pragmatic; I used them for promoting better sleep, visualization for enhancing athletic performance, boosting the immune system and bodily functions during the cold and flu seasons, using the *Surgical Support* series for a knee surgery, facilitating academic studies, conducting a psychology experiment with *Remembrance*, and more. Additionally, I have further enhanced my brain and body's affinity to the Hemi-Sync frequencies by attending one of the weeklong, intensive Gateway retreats, as well as experiencing a PREP session in the lab.

My introduction to The Monroe Institute and Hemi-Sync came in 1989, when my mother returned home from her first Professional Division Seminar at the Institute. She was so excited and impressed by the audio technology and its many potential applications that she told us all about it and started encouraging us to use the tapes for just about anything. At first I simply humored my mother, as teenagers often do, and used the tapes here and there without paying much attention to the effects. It took the desperation of feeling very ill from the flu to get me to finally use the tapes and recognize that they really worked! From then on, I used the tapes without question anytime I felt flu or a cold coming on. The tapes I typically used when I felt sick were *Lung Repair and Maintenance* for colds, and *Regenerate* and *Circulation* for the flu and general health. I found that, when I used these tapes, a cold that would typically take me two weeks to fully recover from would be gone in half the time, and any flu-like symptoms would also be greatly alleviated. As my mother explains it, the Hemi-Sync frequencies facilitate the body's process of achieving what is called a "trophotropic" state of healing. This state is relaxed and balanced through the Hemi-Sync, allowing the body's natural defenses and immune system to utilize a much higher percentage of its energy reserves to eliminate any harmful pathogens.

Another use that I found for Hemi-Sync was to help enhance my athletic performance through visualization exercises with the tapes, specifically with *See-Be*. As high jumper on the varsity track team in high school, and a varsity volleyball player in both high school and college, I was always striving to perform better. I found that the use of visualization was extremely effective for improving my technique and form. This fact is well known now and practiced by many athletes around the world. But with the addition of Hemi-Sync and its access functions to imprint and recall the memory of the proper technique, I found that my performance improved much more quickly than it did with regular visualization done without this support. *Synchronizing* was one tape I used for improving my speed, timing, and coordination for athletic performance.

I was even able to address the common, and unfortunate, occurrence of athletic injury using Hemi-Sync. No, Hemi-Sync did not prevent me from being injured—and believe me, I had more than my fair share of injuries—but it did help me recover from my injuries much faster and more completely. One of the worst injuries I ever had was when I tore all the ligaments in my right ankle. To make matters worse, I got an infection from all the swelling, which was extremely painful. I was in a walking cast for a month, and it was not until the week before I was to have the cast removed that I felt I could start walking on it. When the cast was removed, my ankle was extremely bruised and still very swollen. The doctor said we might need to do surgery if it did not start to heal better. It was at this point that I decided to use the Hemi-Sync tapes to see if they could help for an injury. After one week of using the tapes, the swelling in my ankle had greatly reduced, and the bruising had started to heal. These results were the first real visible and tangible evidence that I had for the healing power of Hemi-Sync.

My experience with using the Hemi-Sync tapes for athletic purposes was extremely positive and beneficial, and I would highly recommend they be added as an essential component of any athlete's sports bag, right next to the first-aid kit! The tapes I used most often for injuries were *Regenerate*, to facilitate healing, and *Circulation*, to reduce swelling.

During my student years, I have had many occasions to use Hemi-Sync, especially Metamusic, for my studies. When it comes to studying for tests, I have found using the exercise *Retain-Recall-Release* to be beneficial by helping me to remember the material more readily. I have also noticed that I can actually read faster and study longer without getting tired when I have the Metamusic selections *Remembrance* or *Einstein's Dream* playing in the background. *Remembrance* is also great for times when I am writing, whether it be writing a technical paper, a creative piece, or an article. I am listening to it right now! The words seem to flow much more easily, and I am able to keep my focus on the task at hand, yet still draw from my creative and expressive faculties.

When I was in high school, I conducted a psychology experiment to test the effects of *Remembrance* on short-term memory. The results from this experiment were illuminating in some very important areas, but not in the ones we were expecting. It turned out that we did not see any difference in memory-recall between listening to *Remembrance* with and without the embedded Hemi-Sync frequencies. We later discovered that the tape I had used for the version of *Remembrance* with the embedded frequencies had been a tape dubbed from the original. In the process of dubbing the tape, the Hemi-Sync frequencies were lost, due to their low volume level on the original. We also learned how important it is to make sure the Dolby Noise Reduction option is turned off on any stereo that is playing these tapes or CDs. Otherwise, the frequencies get treated as background noise and are filtered out by the Dolby system. The interesting result that we did get from this experiment, however, was that there was a significant increase in memory recall when the students listened to the *Remembrance* music versus when they had no music playing. If I had had the occasion to conduct a follow-up experiment like this, I would have added in two more portions, one being a piece of music that had lyrics and was similar to the popular Top 40 music, and another being some piece of music with no lyrics, like jazz or classical. And, of course I would have made sure that we used an original copy of the Metamusic version of *Remembrance* to test the effects of the embedded frequencies.

Often when I used the Hemi-Sync tapes, I would fall asleep. This made the tapes an obvious choice for the times when I was having trouble falling asleep due to a chattering mind. When I was in high school and college, it would often take me more than an hour to fall asleep. With the aid of the tapes, however, I would be asleep in 20 minutes or less. I found that *Restorative Sleep* is a nice tape to use, because it doesn't wake you up at the end, and it is designed for creating a restful sleep state. Another tape I often used for taking "power naps" was *Catnapper*. After waking up from using *Catnapper*, I would feel like I had taken a three-hour nap in just 45 minutes. This was a really important tape for me during college when I would stay up late studying and then have to get up early for classes. A more recent favorite of mine for sleeping is *Super Sleep*, which I became fond of after attending TMI residential programs. I enjoy the effect of gentle ocean waves lulling me to sleep each night. And of course, I have also found that many Metamusic selections, like *Inner Journey* and *Sleeping Through the Rain*, are wonderful for falling asleep. The added effect of the soft music and the absence of the verbal guidance make Metamusic ideal background music, to get uninterrupted sleep all night long. Over time, I have found that I no longer have any problems falling asleep, even without the Hemi-Sync or Metamusic. I attribute this to the long-term effect that these exercises have had in quieting my mind and training my body to quickly achieve a relaxed state with ease.

Another valuable use I have found for Metamusic is to play it while I am having any kind of body work or healing. I have listened to various compositions, such as *Remembrance, Inner Journey,* and *Higher,* while receiving massages, acupuncture, chiropractic treatments, Reiki, etc. In comparing my experiences and my body's response to the treatments when I listen to Metamusic versus when I don't, I have found that the Metamusic seems to enhance the session. Additionally, the practitioner usually enjoys listening to the Metamusic and benefits from it as well.

Two of my most dramatic healing uses of Hemi-Sync occurred while I was recovering from painful injuries. The ankle injury I described previously was one of these, and the second was when I recently tore the ligaments in my left knee. This knee injury was by far the worst I have ever suffered. I had torn the lateral, medial, and anterior ligaments, as well as the meniscus, all accompanied by some bone bruising. It required a reconstructive surgery, under general anesthesia, in order to replace the ACL and help the knee to heal. As this was the only surgery I had ever been through, I was quite nervous. When I heard that TMI had recently released its **Surgical Support** series, I knew without a doubt that I was going to use it. During the nights preceding the surgery I listened to the *Pre-Op* tape. I found that this helped me relax, which greatly reduced any anxiety I had. I listened to it again while in the pre-op room at the hospital, and when I asked the anesthesiologists to play and monitor the *Intra-Op* and *Recovery* tapes for me during and after the surgery, they were more than accommodating. I recall that when they were taking me into the operating room they commented on how relaxed I already seemed from listening to the tape.

The next thing I remember was being awakened by the *Recovery* tape while they were rolling me out of the operating room. I was amazed at how the tape precisely timed my awakening. The anesthesiologist told me afterwards that they didn't even need to give me the full dose of the anesthetic. That was great! In the recovery room, I quickly regained my awareness and focus, and I remembered most of what the doctor said to me about how the operation went. This surgery required an overnight stay in the hospital so that they could monitor me and make sure I had help whenever I needed it. They warned me that typically people don't sleep well after having surgery, but I had absolutely no trouble sleeping while listening to the ocean waves of *Surf*. It was wonderful. I just played the tape continuously through the night and into the next morning, and felt great. I experienced almost no pain aside from the occasional muscle spasm, which was, I admit, pretty awful. My recovery during the following nine months went about as smoothly and as quickly as anybody recovers from that type of procedure. One of the student interns had called me up a few days after my surgery to see how I was doing and what my pain levels were. I told her that I was doing just fine and was not experiencing any major problems. She was happy to hear that. Then she mentioned that the guy she had called before me, who underwent the same operation on the same day with the same surgeon, was in a lot of pain. I have no doubt that the ease of my surgery and the quick recovery were in large part due to the **Surgical Support** series, and I am so thankful that I used it.

Since the time I first started using the Hemi-Sync tapes as a teenager, my involvement with TMI has increased. In July 2001 I attended the Gateway Voyage residential program, and I was so moved by it that I joined both the Dolphin Energy Club and the Professional Division. I returned the following March to attend the 2002 Professional Division Seminar. During my attendance at these residential programs, I experienced and explored new reaches of my own consciousness, as well as many more of the facets and applications of Hemi-Sync technology. The Professional Seminar was especially appealing to my scientific side, as it stimulated many interesting conversations among the professional members in attendance. From these conversations, a number of ideas came to mind for applying the TMI technologies in new ways.

I am confident that TMI will continue its long tradition of excellence and exploration. In addition to the many benefits I have gained, the culmination of all these experiences with TMI has greatly influenced my interest in pursuing a career in the field of science and consciousness—a career that is based on both intellectual studies and scientific research, as well as experiential explorations.

A Place for Me to Grow
Felicia Potter

Felicia Potter is studying at Sarah Lawrence College, New York. She was a participant in one of the earliest Gateway Voyage programs for teenagers.

After my last trip down to Faber, Virginia, and the Blue Ridge Mountains, it seems that life has been unfolding dramatically. I'm in my second year at Sarah Lawrence College, where I'm studying theater and my newfound interest, Spanish. My schedule is always full of the good things and, from time to time, the not-so-good things. It can be easy to get wrapped up in the everyday business of life, so sometimes it's really nice to remember the moments in my life that have helped me see more clearly. I look on my experiences at The Monroe Institute as being such times.

Thinking back on the first day of my Teen Gateway Voyage program, I'm reminded of how nervous I was, and it makes me laugh. I thought it would be a long week, not knowing what to expect. As I walked around for a little tour after I had settled into my room, I was pleasantly shocked by the tranquillity and homelike quality of the grounds. The other kids, who had arrived earlier that day and had spent a little time absorbing the surroundings, seemed so calm to me despite their excitement at the prospects for the coming week. I was soon to learn that the Institute lends itself to helping people find this tranquillity. It was refreshing to see people my age in this light, having come straight from the hallways of my high school.

I remember the moment later that evening when our trainers, Penny Holmes and John Kortum, collected our watches and timepieces. I was terrified by the idea of not being able to know what time it was. Yet this became an amazing aspect of the program. I had never thought of it before, but I realized that week how much we can be conditioned by the notion of time. Without knowing the exact hour, I was forced to readjust my connection to the experience of the present moment. I became aware of how much I depended on the clock to orient me within the passing moments. I was actually quite upset when we had to take our watches back at the end of the week.

The experience of not knowing the exact time set us up for a great week of exploration and relearning ourselves. I found during my first encounter with the Institute that without certain aspects of my everyday life (e.g., television, clocks, old friends, etc.) I was free to just be me, without prior judgments based on how I relate to such things every day in my life. I started to realize through the Gateway Voyage that experience is very much dependent on perspective, and that there are no limits to the number of experiences and perspectives one can have.

The Gateway program was really amazing for me because I was finally able to interact with my peers in a virtually judgment-free atmosphere. We were liberated from the conditions of being teenagers in high school. This new environment allowed us to explore a different kind of group dynamic. We were able to strengthen our own states of being, which in turn strengthened the group as a whole because of the shared experience of exploring different states of consciousness.

My second program at The Monroe Institute, almost two years later, was MC^2, Manifestation and Creation Squared. It was different from my Teen Gateway Voyage, yet shared some similar features. Everyone was much older than I, seeing that I was 18 years old at the time. I was a little apprehensive going into an older group, but once the tapes started rolling and the experiences were discussed, the MC^2 group ended up functioning very much like the Gateway group, in that it became a safe place to share information and grow individually.

Knowing The Monroe Institute was a place for me to grow, I felt more prepared going into MC^2 to begin an exploration of manifestation. During my week at MC² we listened to a tape that was geared toward letting go of excess baggage, such as guilt. Being given the opportunity to confront some judgments I had been placing on myself, and to forgive myself, cleared the way for more room to grow, and I was able to move on in a much more productive manner. I was able to think about what creation is, and how to create some things I desired in my own life. Being a high school senior, I was applying to colleges and for the first time seriously thinking about my future and how to manifest my desires.

I hope never to forget a moment I had at MC² while rolling dice as a manifestation exercise. I was trying to roll the number nine, and after trying and trying I decided it was useless. Then I decided I'd throw the dice again. The dice were in the air and somehow everything became clear. Words really can't describe the sensation, or rather the knowledge, I had at that moment, but I felt myself as a force of creation and nothing more. It was a simple moment of trusting my intention and letting go of the outcome. I merely observed the dice as they fell, placing no judgment on them. And when they landed, I had rolled nine. I was extremely pleased with the experience. And though I was only rolling dice, the feeling was not that of being lucky, but more like being sure and being able to trust my intention.

Another experience during MC² was the prayer circle. The group would sit in a circle around one of its members to pray, or to send energy to that person or to a part of their life that was in need. While I was in the middle I asked that people focus on helping me grow and fulfill my potentials. It was an amazing and gratifying experience. It is truly special when a group of people put their energy together. To be at the center of the collective focus such as this is an immensely positive affirmation of one's own existence and potentials. In just the memory of the circle I feel a sense of power still coming from it.

I believe that something I began to manifest that day was the growth of a will and the desire to fulfill my potentials. After the circle I felt more at peace with myself, and having had such an affirmation from the outer world I was more confident that I could change things in my life without fearing the death that comes with the growth of new life. Gradually I've become more receptive to opportunities, and I hope to continue to expand the ability to take life by the moment and fulfill my potentials.

Most importantly, I think I'll always remember the people I have met during the Gateway Voyage and MC². These are people who have helped me value my time on Earth. They have come together in these special moments to celebrate themselves and each other. I love the memory of late-night labyrinth walks, incense in hand, with my Gateway companions—and the fire alarms that would sound for no apparent reason! I love that my friends in MC² became again that week the children that they are. I love the growth that is fostered when humans are allowed to explore—without judgment—their own being, in an environment that reflects the beautiful transformations that are taking place within.

It Changes You . . .
Timothy K. Ambrose, Ph.D.

Timothy Ambrose was educated at Dartmouth College and Rutgers University, obtaining his Ph.D. in 1999. Before then he had lived in France, Germany, Australia, Japan (where he opened a language school), and Zimbabwe (where he wrote a novel). He also traveled extensively elsewhere in the world. In his clinical training he specialized in HIV/AIDS in minority populations and in Borderline Personality Disorder. He has also worked for the New York City Department of Health. In 2001 Tim moved to Hawaii to build the Miranon Center for the Art of Healing.

My first experience of Hemi-Sync was in the summer of 2000. Before then I had no knowledge of consciousness exploration, and all I'd come across on OBEs or past lives were Shirley MacLaine's *Out on a Limb* and Barbra Streisand's *On a Clear Day*. Then one day I found myself floating out of my body above Harald Holler's meditation center, over the coast of Costa Rica, up into space and back in time, recognizing my energy back to the origin of time. A few days later on a plane returning to New York, I was reading *Mysteries of the Big Island Revealed* (Harald and I had decided to move to Hawaii to build a center there) when I saw in front of me, as if in another dimension, my many close friends who had died. They expressed their pride and joy in my happiness. As they moved away, one of them, John, turned back and told me he and the others were often with me and had gathered specially at that time as if to celebrate my decision.

To begin with I tried Hemi-Sync on myself. As I was a poor sleeper, Harald suggested *Sound Sleeper* and *Super Sleep*. I began sleeping well for the first time in years. Then after attending courses at The Monroe Institute I began to use Hemi-Sync with my patients.

The **Surgical Support** series has proved very helpful, as has the *Pain Control* exercise. I used both with a friend with AIDS who had undergone seven surgeries in 15 months for recurring polyps in the colon. After the first surgery he was completely debilitated for weeks and in excruciating pain which only morphine could help. Hearing he was due for another surgery, we sent him these tapes. His doctor would not permit him to use headphones during the operation but said he might have them in recovery. He did manage to use the *Pre-Op* tape and the post operation tapes and reported that the surgery went well and he had much less pain than before. Using *Pain Control* and *Energy Walk* meant that he needed fewer and less potent painkillers.

Last year my father underwent reparative surgery for torn tendons in his shoulder. He took the **Surgical Support** series into the hospital, explained it to his doctors, used *Pre-Op* and *Intra-Op* as instructed, and was listening to the *Recovery* tape when he awoke. He required no painkillers and felt ready to leave within 15 minutes. His doctors declared they'd never seen anything like it! My father worked with the tapes during the following week and needed a painkiller only once.

A few weeks later, my father complained that the pain in his shoulder had returned. We decided to request a Dolphin Energy Club remote healing. When I called him later he told me his shoulder had started feeling better. "They did the first meditation last Thursday," I said. "Huh!" he exclaimed. "That's when it started feeling better."

For many years I have been involved in various areas of HIV/AIDS research, and since moving to Hawaii I have begun exploring alternative healing methods and possible treatments. I have also begun to rethink my understanding of HIV and the changes it has wrought on humanity and most, if not all, of humanity's systems. On the positive side, advances in medical science have increased exponentially through immune system research. Ironically, HIV is also in large part responsible for the increasing acceptance of gays in mainstream culture. Nevertheless, AIDS continues to ravage populations throughout the world and the epidemic is by no means over in the United States either. While new drugs have helped prolong the lives of those with access to good medical care in the developed world, elsewhere the epidemic grows unchecked. But as the threat posed by HIV became less imminent for those with access to medication, most of the developed world became more complacent about the problem. HIV is considered by some to be a neurological disease. One of the first effects following infection is a breakdown in communication between the brain and the immune system, so that normal immune responses to emotional stimuli are suppressed. Could Hemi-Sync help individuals restore that communication?

We have given the *Positive Immunity* Program to a few friends who have AIDS and whose health is unsteady. They all appreciate and like the different exercises. I shall continue following them, checking to see if they are using the program. I see patients through the Big Island AIDS project in Hawaii and have discussed the possibility of doing trials with this program. I hope this project may yield useful information.

I am intrigued by the possibilities for different healing applications of Hemi-Sync and have been hypothesizing about what the active mechanism might be. At a recent seminar, Jill Russell spoke of her "disappearing" osteoporosis diagnosis after many weeks of using a CD recording of cat's purring embedded with Hemi-Sync. What might be responsible for this? One theory I'm considering is that it may have to do with vibrational frequencies—or possibly genetic or even spiritual blueprinting.

Metal that has been bent out of shape becomes first rigid and then brittle. If you raise the vibrational frequency of the metal by heating it up, it takes the metal to a more fluid state, closer to its lower energy form—a process called annealing. While this may be a simplistic analogy, what if Hemi-Sync operates in a similar way?

I'd like to tell the story of Jim. He's a 56-year-old artist, living in Hawaii on as little as he can. Some would call him a beach bum, but in reality he's a highly intelligent man with a very colorful history, roots in Texas, and paintings hanging in expensive homes, hotels, and museums. In 1987, however, while walking along the side of the highway, he was struck by a car traveling at about 60 miles an hour. The accident left Jim without any short-term memory. Without this faculty, it is very difficult to get information into long-term memory.

When we first met Jim, his eyes displayed his intelligence but his conversation often bordered on the unintelligible. Jim reads voluminously. He collects and memorizes meaningful quotations from any imaginable source. His conversation consisted mostly of a string of quotations. He would often rush them out one after another, as "Don't complain, don't explain—Henry Ford II," or "Life is either a daring adventure or nothing—Helen Keller." I paid close attention to the content of what Jim was saying and found it unerringly relevant. I began to understand Jim's somewhat passive way of communicating. For instance, if he sensed that I had had enough of the conversation, he would say something like, "A good speaker knows when to stop." Anxiety seemed to exacerbate this tendency sometimes to the point where I couldn't understand him. As he saw I was willing to listen, he made a little more effort, but conversations were still painstaking.

Harald and I discussed Jim's condition and told him about Hemi-Sync. We gave him a CD player with headphones and started him with *Remembrance, Einstein's Dream,* and another Metamusic composition. Jim was thrilled. We checked in with him several times a week and noticed that within the first month he was already exhibiting changes. He began taking more interest in his physical appearance, becoming less unkempt.

Jim used Hemi-Sync frequently and took great pleasure in it. One day he came up to me on the beach and said, "You know, the music is really great for reading. I've been listening to it a lot." I began to observe subtle changes in Jim. He was reading long novels and discussing them with me. During one conversation, he asked for a guided meditation to help him reach other states of awareness. We gave him *Moment of Revelation*, Metamusic for relaxation, and a copy of Bob Monroe's first book.

Over the next six to nine months, Jim went through a transformation. His ability to engage in meaningful, interesting, and for the most part lucid conversations improved significantly. We learned a great deal about his colorful history, his heritage, his views on things, and his keen insight. He has a dry and biting sense of humor that goes unnoticed by those who don't "see" him. His collection of quotations continued to grow, and they are often very timely and even helpful.

As well as the improvements in his memory and conversational ability, Jim made significant improvements in his life. He began to exercise more regularly. He asked one day about our diet and how we stay lean, and I told him. He has subsequently lost much weight, and the leg that was seriously injured in the car accident doesn't appear to be giving him as much trouble.

Most striking to me is how Jim managed a very challenging situation. He was threatened with eviction and was being harassed by someone who did not have the authority to evict him. As the harassment escalated, Jim was very concerned about his safety.

About this time, I had to go to the mainland for a conference, and it was several weeks before I was able to get to the beach. When I did meet Jim, he happily recounted what had happened. After learning what his rights were, he went directly to the official in charge. He explained he had been offered another place to live but that it would take time for him to arrange to move. He told the official he was being harassed without having received a formal eviction notice. Jim pointed out that because the property belonged to a friend, he knew there would be no such notice. The matter was resolved, and he was given as much time as he needed to move.

Jim's life continues to improve. He has finally moved into a much better place with plenty of space for him to paint. While he still believes his short-term memory is gone, what he doesn't yet recognize is that his ability to encode information has significantly improved. He told me that if he repeats something several times it's there to stay. He believes it is all contingent on the time interval. In a sense he is correct, but what he cannot gauge is how much more efficiently he encodes new information. The habits Jim developed for survival—listening and reading for content, learning to communicate through others' words, and learning to memorize through repetition—have provided a solid foundation. Hemi-Sync appears to have helped him bridge the interval between short-term and long-term memory by cutting down his processing time. Despite what he thinks, I've been observing him for almost two years and the difference is striking. The quotations are no longer his means of expression, but wonderful and pointed comments to pepper his conversations.

One day we had been sitting on the beach talking about Hemi-Sync. As we were leaving, Jim stopped and looked at me. "It changes you, doesn't it?" he asked. I considered his question. "Yes, Jim, I think it does," I replied.

In Jim's case, I believe the changes I have observed are more than behavioral. I believe he may be building new neuronal pathways, and Hemi-Sync may be the responsible agent. When I talk to patients about their emotions, I often use the analogy of a highway system. People who are depressed have multilane highways with lots of on-ramps and few exits. Many thoughts will nudge an individual into the traffic stream of their own negativity. I talk to them about building new roads towards more desirable directions, so that their negative thinking/feeling highways will eventually fall into disuse. The brain is also like a highway system, with different neuronal pathways and connections. The same physical changes occur in the brain when depression is lifted, whether it be through antidepressant medication or psychotherapy.

If Hemi-Sync is able to stimulate other levels of consciousness, it stands to reason that it alters our behavioral experience and thereby begins the process of altering our view of the world. Challenges to ingrained systems, conscious or unconscious, are often the catalysts of change. When those challenges come in a gentle, loving, open way, they are more easily accepted. Monroe's approach of teaching individuals to integrate these tools into everyday life without supplanting their own practices provides a stimulus for change.

To conclude, I'd like to say something about the center that Harald and I are building in Hawaii, and its purpose. Without going into detail, I want to share the vision that is driving me to build this center. My use of Hemi-Sync and my meeting with Harald have been instrumental in this.

I have a vision of a world that is a better place. A world in which all beings are treated with respect, in which famine doesn't exist, where cooperation is valued, where competition exists only to push individuals to achieve their higher purpose. In this world, we recognize the beauty of life and the richness of our environment. We create energy systems that are self-sustaining, using the abundant renewable natural resources to power the machines in our lives. Life is valued above all else. Our time on this planet is in the service of the evolution of the soul, the evolution of consciousness.

The Miranon Center for the Art of Healing is a place for such visions to be explored and developed. It is a place that will provide the environment and tools for people to connect to their higher selves while also connecting with others. Connection with other living beings is the ultimate value that drives our mission. The Center will be a gathering place for spiritual leaders, teachers, and healers of all sorts. It will be a healing think tank and training center for different aspects of well-being. We chose the term Healing Arts because healing comes in many forms and is not limited to the traditional or non-traditional methods. Joy, fun, pleasure, and play are all essential components of this mission.

We all come from the same unity, and to the same unity we all return. It is time for the healing to begin, for humanity to accept this challenge if we are to change our path. Although many may find such notions idealistic and feel threatened and fearful as human connection begins to supplant materialism, we must embrace all humanity and not persecute those who have followed a path so clearly defined by society. This is not a movement of persecution and separation, but one of connection, communication, and recognition that our commonalities will always outweigh our differences. Our mission is to enable and empower those who have followed the material dreams of society to use their abilities for the benefit of their fellow man. We do not seek to level humanity but to raise all of humanity to a higher level. It is through our differences that we learn and grow, but it is through our commonalities that we steer to reconnection with the source, to the state of Love. We can praise individual gifts with the understanding that such gifts are intended to be shared with all, and that in so doing we enable connection.

Hemi-Sync has helped me to recognize and strengthen my connection to the source. I still have a great deal to learn. As a scientist, I am curious and intrigued and will continue theorizing and seeking to explain how it works. As a clinician, I choose not to wait for the explanation. Hemi-Sync is not a panacea, but I believe it can help.

A New Perspective
Suzane Proulx

Suzane Proulx lives and works in Quebec, Canada. She has master's degrees in career counseling from Laval University, Quebec; in communications psychology from the University of California at Berkeley; and in education from Sherbrooke University, Quebec. Since 1983, Suzane has been working in human resources management, training, performance appraisal, and strategic coaching. In 1985, she created her own company, SUMAE, Inc., focusing on business management consulting, corporate coaching, career transition, and training. In 1986 she published her first book, on adult career transition and professional changes. She has subsequently written four more books, all related to business management.

I first heard about The Monroe Institute through a friend who owned a bookstore. Being in contact with Hemi-Sync and using the tapes since 1990 has helped me to put into perspective the changes I was living through at that time. The technology aided my understanding of what was happening. It helped me to reach a deeper level of concentration, which enabled me to connect more strongly with my powers of intuition. People used to tell me that I was already very intuitive, but by achieving that deeper level of concentration I discovered a new way to "discuss" things with my intuition. It opened up a two-way communication, a process that I enjoy very much.

The more I used Hemi-Sync, the faster I could go into an area of my mind where I found great peace. I really needed that peace of mind to keep me going and do what I was expected to do. During that time,

I was very confused by all the events happening in my personal life, and this situation seemed to trigger a major transition in my life, something that I did not recognize right away.

My work was always a shelter for me, an activity through which I was able to regain control of my life for at least those eight hours. However, during that transition period, it seemed that nothing worked out as I was expecting, until the Hemi-Sync process helped me to achieve a different perspective.

The tapes I used the most were *Moment of Revelation* and the *Discovery* album from the Gateway Experience. Gradually, a new way of thinking about and observing my life emerged. I was able to better understand *why* I was living *what* I was living at the time. The deep inner pain, which seemed to have penetrated right into my soul, started to heal by itself. I was a witness to my own spiritual healing process, because I was connected, at oneness with my soul. I was able to understand from a point of view within myself the reasons why I was experiencing that major (and very painful) personal transition.

Through the regular use of Hemi-Sync tapes, I initiated an inner journey that generated a major change in my professional life also. A new path was confirmed for me. I just followed the guidance coming from my intuition. "Keep it simple," it once told me. The new direction in my professional activities has since led me to study for my Ph.D. in management. Of course I have also maintained my career as a corporate-level trainer. I am very happy with these endeavors.

In my professional coaching work I use my intuitive abilities to communicate a project management system that I developed many years ago. It has been quite successful in the Montreal area. The system employs inner communication, something that the Hemi-Sync process helped me to cultivate. Hemi-Sync gave me the confidence to use intuition more. I incorporate that concept into my training sessions. I have recently been working with guidance counselors, and with more managers, teaching them to use my technique. I recommend Hemi-Sync to them as a way to open themselves to their own intuitive capabilities.

There is always a reason and meaning for any transition. This I found out through the use of Hemi-Sync, slowly but surely, along with the help of my closest friend, my intuition!

A Catalyst for Profound Personal Growth
Gail M. Blanchette

Gail Blanchette is a self-employed business coach and trainer in Winnipeg, Canada. Her company, Business Basics & More, Inc., was established in 1997. Her main clientele consists of small business owners and people wanting to establish small companies. In her self-published book, *Harsh Lessons and Unexpected Gifts,* she expresses her belief that the future does not have to be shaped by the past. She shares that ideal with those who are struggling in their lives, businesses, and relationships. Gail is also a distributor for Monroe Products, which she promotes through her consulting work.

The story I would like to share about Hemi-Sync is very personal in nature. I grew up in a family that was plagued by addictions, violence, and acutely dysfunctional behavior. My childhood and young adult years were a living nightmare that left many deep scars on my life. Many times my ability to cope was pushed well beyond the normal boundaries of human emotional endurance. Somehow I managed to persevere and survive.

It was not until I was in my mid- to late 20s that I began to recognize that my life was not and had not been "normal and healthy" in any psychological context. As my awareness of this reality grew, I began to search for answers to many deeply disturbing questions. My life was extremely unhappy, and I had a young son to raise. I certainly did not want to repeat the mistakes my parents had made. In my quest for answers I began to read voraciously. I must have read hundreds of books by every self-help or personal growth author I could find. I attended numerous seminars and workshops. I studied psychology, sociology, and other topic areas, trying to understand the dynamics of my childhood traumas and how to change my life. Nothing seemed to help. I kept falling back into old traps and dysfunctional behavior patterns.

In my late 30s I found a clinical psychologist who specialized in the types of traumas I had experienced, and this was when my serious self-discovery work began. It was a slow and sometimes very frustrating process. The biggest challenges were that I had lost my ability to cry and I could not speak or write about many of my thoughts and feelings. It was as if a part of me were frozen solid, like an iceberg. No amount of prompting or support could encourage me to let go or speak up. My therapy sessions continued on and off for the better part of ten years. Much progress was made during that time but the past continued to haunt me in many ways, coloring every aspect of my daily life.

That was when I discovered Hemi-Sync. A friend of mine who had used the technology in her meditative practice suggested I try it, and she lent me some of her tapes. Intrigued but skeptical, I listened to the tapes. I was curious about the audio guidance techniques and whether or not Hemi-Sync could assist me in my healing process. The sounds had a very calming effect and were quite pleasant, but I was still not convinced of its value or how it might improve or change my life.

In the fall of 1997 I decided to attend the Gateway Voyage program at The Monroe Institute. It was a life-altering decision that would have far-reaching consequences in my psychological healing process. Within hours of beginning the program, I began to experience feelings and responses that were foreign to me. I marveled at how safe and secure I felt in the Institute environment, as that certainly was not a typical reaction from me. By the end of the second day I actually cried for the first time in many years, without shutting down and disassociating from my body. Slowly I began to trust that I could allow myself to feel some of the emotions and painful experiences that were so deeply embedded in me without being overwhelmed.

By the end of the program, I felt that a crushing weight had been removed from my body and I could actually breathe again. There was a new sense of emotional freedom and well-being I had never experienced before. Despite how great I thought that feeling was, it was nothing compared to the psychological progress I would make during the following year of therapy.

My psychologist was thrilled with the "quantum leap" of advancement I made. It was as if I had been given some kind of key that unlocked the closed doors of the past. I was able to make connections between events, experiences, and negative emotions, processing them in a much healthier and more expedient way. More importantly, I could understand how the past had so dramatically affected my present everyday life and what I could do to change it.

However, I hit an emotional roadblock once again. There seemed to be a residual piece of "something" I just could not clear. Despite my continued use of Hemi-Sync at home, I was not at peace or feeling comfortable with my life. I still experienced terrifying nightmares and overwhelming negative emotions. Frustrated with this plateau in my self-discovery, I returned to the Institute in 1999 to attend the Heartline program.

Heartline was quite different from the Gateway Voyage. Again, within hours of starting the program, a whole new range of feelings and emotions began to surface, much to my surprise. After many years of receiving counseling and extensive personal self-development work, I had not thought there was anything left in my being that I did not know about. Boy, was I in for an enlightening experience!

From my perspective, Heartline is the ultimate healing process for my inner child. I had several profound experiences that clearly pointed out to me how I had literally disowned parts of myself at several stages in my life. I had rejected the severely traumatized and raped three-year-old. I had also disowned the awkward and demoralized 16-year-old who had no friends. More importantly, as an adult, I did not understand how to reconnect with those parts because I was not even aware they existed. During the program, I found the missing parts of myself. That positive experience and realization were life-altering and profoundly healing for me. These were clearly the pieces of myself that I had been subconsciously searching for.

To summarize, Hemi-Sync, as it relates to my life and experiences, is no more and no less than a vibrational audio technology that has helped me shift my consciousness level and reconnect to important aspects of my early life experiences. When I was a small child I didn't know the words to describe some of my traumas. Hemi-Sync became a very effective tool for clearing the negative memories that could not be verbalized. It also seemed highly effective in unlocking my frozen emotions as an adult, and I am not alone in that realization.

The best part of discovering the amazing effects of Hemi-Sync is the opportunity to share it with others. I use the tapes and CDs in my professional work. I have approximately three hundred clients who have purchased the materials through my business. These individuals have told me numerous heartfelt stories about how this audio technology has changed and improved their lives in so many ways. Their experiences include improved learning abilities, health and wellness issues, personal growth, and new levels of calmness and serenity. Many of their experiences parallel my own, and I delight in seeing the excitement and joy within their personal self-discovery journeys.

My own measurement of my progress is that I have recently written and self-published a book about my life and how I learned to grow and change. I have also made some significant and healthy changes in my life. I have a sense of freedom and serenity that I enjoy every day. Hemi-Sync was a very instrumental piece of my personal growth and healing process and continues to be an important part of my life now. I am most grateful for the visionary work of Robert Monroe as well as his family, colleagues, and the Institute staff that carry on his work today.

Challenging Autism with Hemi-Sync
Anne Carpenter

Anne Carpenter was born in February 1957 with congenital rubella—a result of her mother's illness during pregnancy. Cataracts were removed and a defective heart valve was repaired at an early age, though right-ear nerve deafness persisted. She walked late, only began to talk at five, and related to others with difficulty. Life was a difficult puzzle. A number of unusual behavior patterns manifested. She began spinning in circles, flapping her hands, and making involuntary noises. Despite these obstacles, Anne attended public school for most of her education, supplemented by a class for blind and partially sighted children and a special school in Pennsylvania. Her mental and social skills improved with maturity, and she went on to achieve a master's degree in library science. Now, although many of the old habits are gone, she still must live with autism.

The first part of the following article is reprinted from *TMI Focus*, vol. XIX, no. 1, Winter 1997.

Although many of my earlier problems with autism are gone, it now expresses itself in a different way. I am often anxious and compulsive (e.g., feeling a need to check the stove or doorknob several times to "make sure" everything is all right). My sleep cycle is irregular, and I often go to bed too late because I just don't feel tired. This leads to oversleeping the next day. My part-time job at the Autism Society of Michigan (ASM) requires that I get up early to be at work on time, so I wind up very tired and groggy as a result. Sometimes I become hyperactive and discharge excess energy and anxiety by jumping around and making noises when I'm alone at home.

Three years ago, when I was speaking at a workshop at the ASM office, a woman played a tape with beautiful music. When I asked what it was, she showed me the Hemi-Sync tape *Inner Journey*. My sleep over the next few nights was better than it had been in a long time. I was given a copy of that tape, as well as *Sleeping through the Rain*. Falling asleep became much easier, and my anxiety level lessened. My fascination with the Hemi-Sync process grew, and two years ago I got a Monroe Institute Sustaining Membership as one of my birthday gifts. Of course it has been renewed.

Since then I've used Hemi-Sync frequently, and I regularly fall asleep when listening to the tapes. When the tape is over, I feel a clarity of mind and realize that my sleep was exceptionally refreshing. When using Hemi-Sync, I feel calmer—yet highly aware of everything. My hearing seems super-sensitive. It's easier to solve problems and come up with creative solutions. My attitude becomes more optimistic, as though things will really work out for the best.

Another outstanding effect I've noticed is "kabooms," or explosions of insight about how the brain might work or how things might be. The human brain has been a fascination of mine since a neurological examination at the age of twelve.

Kabooms are most likely to occur late at night when I usually listen to Hemi-Sync or the *Time Out for Sleep* CD. As a matter of fact, they might happen even on nights when I'm not using any of the tapes. It's as though my brain has a timer that starts on a regular schedule. Lately I've been using *The Miraculous Principle* (the Spring 1996 quarterly tape). That triggered a series of kabooms and left me more energized for helping to conduct a workshop in April. Kabooms are more frequent since I've been using the *Brain Repair and Maintenance* function command "Plus Flow Better" to myself throughout the day. This may also be related to working with the *Discovery* album from the **Gateway Experience**. Sustaining the kabooms for longer periods of time allows me to suspend autistic behavior such as picking at my fingers and making involuntary mouth noises.

Hemi-Sync is very beneficial, but there are instances when it is not as effective. Taking in caffeine, being very tired, and having PMS markedly interfere with its influence. And when Hemi-Sync use is infrequent or irregular, my response diminishes over time.

Application of the Hemi-Sync process may not cure my autism, but a cure is irrelevant to me. We have not even scratched the surface of the brain's potential, and it's possible that potential may be unlimited and infinite. Wouldn't that be wonderful? Rather than being disappointed at the lack of a cure for autism, let's focus on tapping into more of the brain's capacities. Maybe then autism and other mental disorders won't be such a problem. In a dissociative state, my autistic symptoms diminish. An imbalance between focused attention and disassociation may be a major obstacle to accessing our full abilities as human beings, as well as a factor in the repetition of destructive behavior patterns.

Update 1997–2002: The Big Kahuna

After many fits and starts, the feelings of aha! or the Kahunas as I now think of them (those feelings that I earlier described as kabooms) are now starting to become one big Kahuna, and I have been able to sustain this powerful mental state for longer and longer periods of time. While in this wonderful state of mind, I realize that my whole life is one big movement and regulatory disturbance, since everything I do is movement: motor movement, perception, emotion, behavior, and yes—even thought. This is a theory of autism that was proposed some years ago but then lost favor. However, when seen in this light, it seems that this is probably the foundation of autism. This includes everything I do at every moment, in every nanosecond, and I have realized that some things that I didn't think were related actually are. For example, when I get up in the morning I feel rested and refreshed on some days, but on other days I still feel tired and groggy. I now think that it may take me more time to warm up and get started. Another example is anxiety. When I feel anxious, this big clot of anxiety stays for a while, but when I do something else it just goes away by itself as though it were a seizure. But at other times when I am anxious about something, I figure out a way to solve the problem and the anxiety goes away.

This wonderful Kahuna can best be described as a feeling of being relaxed yet highly aware of everything. All of life seems so interesting and wonderful. While in this state of higher awareness, I feel a continual mild euphoria—the anxiety melts away, I feel calmer, and I savor and appreciate the details of the present moment. I feel suffused with this, and my mind is sharper when in the Kahuna. I feel better able to think through problems and to solve them in a calmer, less frantic way, and I am able to think of solutions more quickly. This is part of a general slowing-down, or quieting of the mind. This is when I feel as though I can move through life like a warm knife cuts through butter—a smooth, easy, flowing motion. In addition, being in the Kahuna can best be described as a feeling of knowing, a general feeling that I am on the right track, that I am *positive* that "this is it." This sense of "knowing" suffuses every neuron and affects every thought and action.

The affirmations in the tapes in the **Network of Light** series (particularly in the *Nervous System* tape) that I receive as a member of TMI have had some powerful effects. Using the affirmations in the *Nervous System* tape intensifies the effect of the Kahuna, making it even more powerful. Because Hemi-Sync is a process of entrainment, once I know what it feels like to be in the Kahuna I can go back to it or stay in that frame of mind. So when I get off track, I can figure out what needs to be done. This is important, since I will always have this difficulty with movement and regulation because autism is a *lifelong* disorder. The Hemi-Sync technology should in no way be seen as a cure for autism. Rather, it should be seen as a tool to help the person tap into his or her brain's vast, untapped, unlimited potential.

While in the Kahuna, some interesting things seem to happen, including synchronicities. For example, I was thinking about a dear friend of mine who was my babysitter and who was to be ordained as a church deacon at the end of September 2002. At once, I received an e-mail from her. Then my mother showed me an invitation that she had just got for my friend's ordination.

In addition, I have become more spiritual and have had some powerful insights about what God might be. I have also noticed that machines seem to be affected in some way; the energy is so powerful that I get error messages on my computer when checking e-mail (though maybe it's not me but the software itself), and on some occasions my TV sound would go on and off. One time when I was using Hemi-Sync materials frequently, the copier at work went on the blink when I was in the Kahuna.

As the Kahuna became more powerful, I noticed other, more subtle changes in myself, in addition to being calmer. While in this frame of mind, I realize even more that we are truly more than our physical bodies and that we *can* tap into forces that are greater than ourselves.

Hemi-Sync behind Bars
Ronald Russell

For some years the Institute's Director of Programs, Dr. Darlene Miller, has organized a prison outreach program. Corcoran was one of the prisons where the authorities agreed that the program could take place. After initial instruction in the use of Hemi-Sync, a group of prisoners, already meeting as a spiritual study group, took over running the program themselves.

The prison chapel had a number of small rooms, and it proved possible to operate the program by using one CD unit with connections to each room. By utilizing double jacks, two people could listen in each room so that each became a kind of CHEC unit. Individuals were also permitted to use Hemi-Sync in their cells when the group was not in session. To begin with, the first two albums of the *Gateway Experience* were employed, as well as a number of *H-PLUS* exercises.

The program produced many significant results. Exploration of levels of consciousness never before experienced allowed the participants to examine many inner conflicts that were responsible for shaping their lives negatively. Painful events in childhood were revisited, and images of being unlovable, feeling worthless, being guilty, and failing at relationships were summoned up. The Gateway exercises help to dissolve old conditionings and patterns along with their associated feelings and thoughts. Two men found they now were able to kick their smoking and alcohol habits, and several discovered that they acquired

31

effective control of negative emotions. In particular, one participant, well known to the guards, changed in attitude so remarkably that they wondered what had happened to him. Their interest was aroused when they were told that he was a participant in the prisoners' sound technology program, and some of them bought Hemi-Sync CDs and tapes for their own use.

In discussion the participants found that their true power came from the recognition and acceptance of their own imperfection and the imperfection of the world around them. They found themselves able to accept and welcome their own shadow material and to understand the truth of Lao-Tzu's dictum: "Darkness within darkness—the gateway to all understanding." With Hemi-Sync and their regular meditations they could see further into darkness, further into their sealed-off pain, because that was where the light would be found.

The program continued through the next two Gateway albums and then the final album, *Odyssey*. The whole program was found to be a transforming, inspirational tool enabling each participant to directly and immediately experience the goal of all transformation—his own inner Self. They discovered that when the mind was silent, when it had given up trying to understand, when its false imaginings and projections had been exposed, a tremendous knowing became manifest. Now they could see the very causes of conflict, fear, and doubt that lay within them. In earlier years each of them had been seeking some form of liberation and believed they could acquire this by setting out to add happiness, prosperity, love, and success to their lives. But whatever they added through drugs, crime, or violence, still they were not whole. Listening to *Odyssey* revealed, to their amazement, how many self-limiting thoughts they all had, reducing some of the participants to tears.

The group is continuing with its exploration, now with added numbers as others, hearing of what was happening, have joined in. It is the only group in the prison that has participation from all races—black, white, and Hispanic. Before Hemi-Sync was introduced into the prison, this would have been unbelievable.

YOUNG CHILDREN

Dr. Suzanne Morris pioneered the use of Hemi-Sync, in particular Metamusic, in remedial work with infants and young children. Her work is internationally recognized, and her New Visions Center, situated in the foothills of Virginia's Blue Ridge Mountains, is a focus of best practice. In her first paper in this chapter, Dr. Morris discusses the nature of Metamusic and from her long experience suggests how to select which compositions to use and how best to proceed. In her second paper she looks more closely at children with developmental difficulties, especially those with feeding problems, and shows how Metamusic combines with treatment to enhance the learning environment, thereby enabling these children to increase their skills.

Metamusic is also employed in Argentina by Nora Rosen and Berenice Luque, who report on its effectiveness in a number of case studies of children with autism. In the fourth paper, Jacqueline Mast, an experienced pediatric physical therapist, explains the philosophy of her practice and demonstrates in five case studies how Hemi-Sync tunes her own intuitive abilities and enriches her work with infants with major developmental problems.

Guidelines for Using Metamusic to Support Learning in Young Children
Suzanne Evans Morris, Ph.D.

Dr. Suzanne Morris is a speech-language pathologist and certified music practitioner who has been using Hemi-Sync with companion animals since 1981. She is the director of New Visions, which sponsors innovative workshops for the teaching of feeding-related skills, and for providers of family-oriented clinical services. Her work includes direct clinical services, continuing education workshops, development of clinical materials, and clinical research. She contributes three papers to this volume.

Metamusic offers a series of possibilities for supporting the physical, mental, and emotional growth of infants and children. Parents, educators, and therapists frequently ask questions related to appropriate selection of specific Metamusic tapes or CDs: Which tape should I use? How do I know if the tape works for my child? When should I use the tape? How often should I play Metamusic? What kind of equipment do I need? This paper addresses these questions and provides a guideline for selecting and monitoring the use of Metamusic recordings to support the learning of young children. A special emphasis will be placed on the use of Metamusic in therapeutic environments.

Metamusic

Robert Monroe's initial Hemi-Sync tapes were geared toward adults and adolescents whose auditory comprehension allowed them

35

to follow verbal instructions. However, in the early 1980s, Monroe began to incorporate many of the Hemi-Sync patterns developed for the guided tapes into a music background, which he called Metamusic. Metamusic recordings opened the door for children to benefit from Hemi-Sync sound patterns, since the verbal content of the original tapes was inappropriate. It allowed listeners of all ages to enjoy Hemi-Sync as an open, non-directed background for other activities such as reading, studying, sleep, and self-generated imagery.

Three distinctive Hemi-Sync sound patterns may be blended with the music component of Metamusic. Since there is a correlation between the predominant frequency of brain-wave patterns and states of conscious awareness, different subjective states will be observed as listeners are introduced to different binaural beat combinations.

Relaxed-focus tapes are based on Hemi-Sync sound patterns that facilitate lower-frequency brain-wave patterns in a predominantly theta (4-7 Hz) range. This hypnagogic state has been associated with greater openness for learning. Most listeners experience the unique combination of increased physical relaxation with a high level of mental alertness and a wide or open focus of attention.

Concentration tapes incorporate higher-frequency Hemi-Sync patterns in the alpha (8–12 Hz) and beta (13–26 Hz) ranges. Subjective reports include high-level alertness combined with the increased narrow focus of attention used in task-oriented activities.

Sleep tapes create the pattern of binaural beats that gradually move the listener into the very slow delta state (1–3 Hz) associated with deep sleep.

Selecting Metamusic

Identify the child's typical sensorimotor, emotional, and learning behaviors that could be influenced by Metamusic. Observations may include focus of attention, activity level, response to touch, response to passive and active movement, muscle tone, motor coordination, breathing, acceptance of unfamiliar activities, and imitation abilities. Don't introduce Metamusic until you are familiar with the child's typical responses in the environment in which you are planning to use

Metamusic. For example, if you wish to use it as a background for studying, how does the child typically respond to the studying/learning session without the support of binaural beats? This gives you a baseline with which to compare the child's response when a Metamusic recording is included.

Select a category of Metamusic (or relaxed focus, concentration, sleep) that supports your general goal directions for the child. The relaxed-focus recordings such as *Inner Journey, Cloudscapes,* and *Masterworks* provide an excellent background for most children with sensorimotor difficulties. Because they stimulate an open focus of attention, they work well in an interactive environment with a therapist or teacher. They also support sustained physical and mental relaxation when the child is alone. Relaxed-focus tapes are usually selected for children with high muscle tone or sensory processing and integration problems (including those of autism and pervasive developmental disorders). The concentration recordings such as *Remembrance, Baroque Gardens,* and *Einstein's Dream* are designed for a narrower focus of attention and a higher level of alertness. They are appropriate for many children who have poor attention skills and hyperactivity. The higher-frequency binaural beats in the tapes stimulate brain-wave patterns in the high alpha and low beta ranges that are often missing in children with attention deficit disorders. These tapes may also be more effective for children who consistently become sleepy when the relaxed-focus tapes are used. Sleep tapes or CDs, such as *Sleeping through the Rain*, are used primarily to promote a restful sleep or unstructured relaxation.

After selecting a category, choose the composition that you like. When a recording is used at home, in the classroom, or in therapy over open speakers, it is very important for everyone listening to like the music. Remember that the specific composition that contains Hemi-Sync is just as important as the binaural beat signals. If you select music that is unpleasant for you, you automatically communicate your discomfort to the child. Hemi-Sync doesn't make the brain respond in a specific way just because of the sounds. It invites the brain to participate. If an adult or child responds negatively to the sound of the music, the brain won't participate, and Hemi-Sync won't work.

Identify the child's verbal or nonverbal patterns of communication. How does the child express likes, dislikes, or preferences in other situations (e.g., turning away, increasing the level of hyperactivity, reducing eye contact, arching, crying or fussing, looking toward the object, reaching, smiling)?

Choose quiet times to introduce Metamusic when Hemi-Sync can support the general activity you have selected. The tapes/CDs are especially effective at mealtimes, while reading the child a story or looking at a book, while studying, or at other similar times when quiet focus of attention is an advantage.

Watch very carefully for any cues that the Metamusic you have selected is not acceptable. Even very young or delayed children will tell you through nonverbal cues whether the music and Hemi-Sync are fine for them. If you sense that it's not acceptable, don't use it. Children may turn off the music, become irritable, cry, or tune out. If you suspect that the sound is aversive, turn it off for that session. Explore several different tapes during other therapy sessions. Observe the child's response again. This will help you know whether the child's negative response is to a particular piece of music, a category of Metamusic, or to the binaural beats of Hemi-Sync. Hemi-Sync should never be used with a child who does not like it.

Observe the child's reaction for cues that he enjoys Metamusic and likes to have the music on. A child may become more relaxed or may smile or participate more fully in the activity. Some children look toward the tape player, or ask for more music if the tape is turned off. The child may not react differently when Metamusic is used initially. However, if the child's reaction is neutral and Metamusic helps you yourself to focus or relax, continue to use it.

Initially keep a journal describing the child's behavior and responses when you are using Metamusic. You may wish to select a specific area or behavior to measure. If you have taken the same measurements for a number of sessions before you introduce the music, you will have established a baseline for comparison. The journal and any measurements you make will allow you to decide how valuable the Metamusic background has been for the child. It is also useful to keep a journal describing your own reactions. This will help you decide whether Metamusic enhances your own learning, creativity, and interaction in therapy.

Although generalizations can be helpful in selecting Metamusic, be aware of unique individual responses to specific recordings. While the Metamusic concentration recordings help most individuals become more alert and focused, they can put some children to sleep. Many hyperactive children prefer the concentration tapes, while others are able to concentrate quietly with the relaxed-focus tapes. A few hyperactive children have listened to a sleep tape during the day. Others fall asleep immediately with a sleep CD at night and are alert and irritable if the same recording is played during the daytime.

The speed of behavioral change shows many individual variations. Some children and adults change dramatically. A few children with severe sensory defensiveness respond very rapidly, often showing observable shifts in the sensory threshold and comfort level within ten to 15 minutes. Others like and accept the music and show slower or subtler changes in behavior or learning. Be aware of small changes that occur, and resist the temptation to eliminate Metamusic because large shifts do not take place quickly. For example, a child may engage in a familiar activity such as working a puzzle in the same way with or without the music, but when the music is on, the child shares the activity with the mother and even leans against her. When the child works the puzzle without Metamusic, he moves slightly away and prefers to play alone. If changes in working the puzzle were the sole measure of effectiveness, the more subtle interpersonal change might go unobserved.

There is no set schedule for using Metamusic. Some children profit from using Metamusic throughout the day; others benefit more from brief (30- to 45-minute) periods once a day. Monroe likened Hemi-Sync to the training wheels on a bicycle. Hemi-Sync tapes are essentially training wheels for the mind that assist the brain with a new way of organizing and integrating sensorimotor experiences. Once this has been learned, the training wheels are no longer necessary. A long-term learning or carryover effect is thereby created. Therefore, it is not necessary to use Metamusic throughout the day for it to be effective. Many children who listen to Metamusic only during an hour-long weekly therapy session have made long-lasting physical and behavioral changes. If Metamusic is used throughout the day, it is important to use breaks during which no music is played. This creates a contrast for the child and provides an opportunity to continue the behaviors facilitated by the music.

Equipment

Metamusic must be played on a stereo tape or CD playback unit. The Hemi-Sync effect is created by slightly different frequencies on the two channels of a stereo recording. This will not occur if the tapes are played on a monaural tape player. A tape player with a continuous auto-reverse feature or a CD player with programmable repeats is preferred. This type of player eliminates the distractions that occur when a tape reaches the end and must be turned over in the middle of an activity, and allows a tape or CD to be played all night.

Although the binaural beat effect is stronger when headphones are used, this is often undesirable or impossible with infants or young children. A simple stereo "boom box" works well for individual or small group therapy using an open-speaker presentation. The boom box can be placed in front of or behind the child. It is very important that the child be between the speakers. Do not place the speakers to the side of the child or have them in a different room of the house. A boom box or other stereo unit with detachable speakers is required to give the widest possible stereo sound separation if a tape is played for larger groups or in a classroom.

Headphones may work better with certain children or in special environments. They allow the child to listen to music at a low volume in an environment where an open-speaker system is unavailable or undesirable. Music through headphones makes it possible for a child to listen to quiet music while traveling by car, in a classroom, or while taking a school examination when music is not appropriate for others in the same room. Since the binaural beat effect of Metamusic is more intense with headphones, listening through headphones may be important for children who have difficulty with focus of attention. Many children and teens enjoy having their own portable tape unit with headphones in imitation of an older sibling or a friend.

Location

Metamusic can be played softly in the background during individual therapy sessions, at home, and in the classroom to assist with relaxation and learning. When Metamusic is used in individual therapy or learning sessions, the child's responses to the music and to learning can be carefully observed. If the music is played in the background for therapy activities that are familiar, differences in the child's responses can be observed more easily. The therapist can identify individual areas of change in response to binaural beats and can help parents and teachers design a Metamusic program for other environments. Therapists can help the teacher identify individual children in the classroom who might benefit from the group use of this type of music.

When Metamusic is introduced into the home setting, the therapist (or teacher) should develop a plan with the family. This would include an agreement on the tapes to be used, the times or activities during which they will be used, and the frequency of use. It is very helpful for the therapist to keep a library of tapes or CDs that can be loaned to a family for several weeks. This enables them to listen with the child and decide which recordings work well at home. When the family has identified recordings that everyone likes, these can be purchased. Metamusic can be used at mealtime, bedtime, or in specific play or learning activities in which the child can benefit from physical relaxation, mental alertness, or social interaction. Music can be used during an activity or prior to it. For example, the child might spend a quiet time with soft music playing for 30 minutes before the dinner meal; or the music might be used during the meal itself.

The teacher can have relaxed-focus Metamusic playing in the background as children enter the classroom. This sends out a nonverbal message that the students can become more quiet and ready for the school day. Different compositions can be used for different classroom activities. For example, in a preschool program one recording might be played during lunch while another would be used during rest time or table activities. In an elementary school classroom, a concentration tape might be played during reading, while a tape that created a more relaxed focus might accompany creative language activities. Children will gradually associate the music with the activity and will learn to carry over the behaviors experienced when the music is not playing.

If Metamusic is to be used in the classroom with children with neurological or emotional dysfunction, it is particularly important to observe each child's reaction individually before playing the music to the whole class. A small number of these children may show a more disorganized or aversive response to the Hemi-Sync signals. If there are children in the classroom who are clearly irritated by Metamusic tapes, do not use them while these children are in the room. The tapes, however, might be used with other children while a sensitive child is involved in a pullout activity. Speakers can be directed so that they are not facing children who respond negatively to the binaural beats in a Metamusic tape.

Metamusic and the Child with Feeding Problems
Suzanne Evans Morris, Ph.D.

The success of programs for children with special needs depends upon the learning environment created by the therapist, educator, and parent. An auditory environment incorporating Metamusic opens the door to learning for many of these children. This paper describes the author's clinical experience using Metamusic in the rehabilitation of children with oral feeding disorders related to cerebral palsy and other sensorimotor disabilities.

The Challenge

Children with oral feeding disorders create a subgroup of infants and young children with developmental disabilities due to cerebral palsy and other sensorimotor disorders. Many of these youngsters present a complex picture of poor coordination of sucking, swallowing, and breathing. Others experience severe defensive reactions to the sensory input of food, with major difficulties in transitioning from breast or formula feedings to solid foods. Negative experiences related to gastrointestinal discomfort, force feedings, and silent aspiration may further complicate the picture, resulting in feeding resistance. Many children receive most of their nutrition through feeding tubes as they make the slow transition to oral feedings. Others move slowly through the developmental progressions of feeding.

As a group, these children provide a major challenge to parents and therapists. We live in a culture that highly values the ability to eat. A mother's feelings of nurturing and parental adequacy often are connected to her child's eating. Family stress increases when the child is unable to eat orally or has major feeding difficulties. Parents feel pressure when they need to get a calorically and nutritionally adequate diet into a child who eats slowly or is a picky eater because of sensory processing problems. This increases the anxiety level of both parents and children.

Therapy addresses the child's underlying problems with postural tone and movement of the body that influence coordination of the oral-motor and respiratory systems. Issues with oral defensiveness are addressed as part of a larger problem of sensory processing and integration. Approaches to reduce anxiety and increase self-confidence and trust enable both parent and child to learn the skills needed for the child to become a competent and efficient feeder. Although specific strategies or techniques are introduced to facilitate this process, the underlying journey is one of empowering the child as a learner and self-healer.

Metamusic and the Child with Developmental Disabilities

Formal Observation

Between 1981 and 1985 I completed a pilot study of 20 developmentally disabled children. The children in this group were enrolled in a therapy program to remediate their oral feeding problems. An initial baseline period of four to six sessions observed the child's response to therapy without music. This was followed by a second period of two to four therapy sessions with a music background that did not contain Hemi-Sync sounds. These two segments of the program created a clinical observation profile for each child in a non-Hemi-Sync environment. A third period of observation introduced Hemi-Sync signals in the theta range (i.e., relaxed-focus tapes) into the same music that was used in the second phase of the study. Informal written and videotaped data were recorded to document the child's progress in therapy under each condition. Many children received therapy with a Metamusic background for one to two years.

Two of the children (10 percent) responded negatively to the music containing Hemi-Sync, and its use was discontinued. Three children (15 percent) showed minimal or inconsistent changes in the Metamusic environment. Fifteen (75 percent of the total) of the remaining children who continued to receive the music containing Hemi-Sync showed positive changes in the behaviors being worked on in treatment. Changes that were observed included improved focus of attention, reduction in tactile defensiveness and overall improvement in sensory organization, increased physical relaxation, improved motor coordination, and reduction in fearfulness. All of the children exhibited a greater openness and enthusiasm for learning. Changes were not evident until Hemi-Sync was introduced. In several instances behavioral changes were noted with the calming music background; however, the degree of change and permanence of change were more pronounced when Hemi-Sync was combined with the music.

In 1988 Karen Varney completed a study of six boys between the ages of 15 and 29 months who were enrolled in a home-based early intervention program. Diagnoses included Down syndrome, neurological disorder, and developmental delay. Varney used a modified single-subject design to compare the responses of three children, who listened to Metamusic (relaxed-focus tapes) during weekly one-hour intervention sessions for a period of four to five weeks, with the responses of three matched children who listened to the same music without the Hemi-Sync signals. Five of the six children in the study demonstrated improvements during intervention. The three children who listened to Metamusic with Hemi-Sync during intervention demonstrated greater improvement than the children who listened to the same music without Hemi-Sync. She concluded that playing Metamusic with Hemi-Sync during intervention appeared to improve the imitation of gestures, facial expressions, two-word phrases, and spontaneous use of two-word phrases. Significant increases in attending behaviors and child-initiated interactions also were observed.

During intervention with Metamusic with Hemi-Sync, changes in behavior occurred more quickly than would be expected. All three of the children who listened to the Metamusic with Hemi-Sync demonstrated steeper slopes of change during intervention. For example, one child increased recorded behaviors from 0 percent to 100 percent between the first and second intervention sessions. The other two children made increases of 42 to 45 percent between two or more intervention sessions. These changes also occurred earlier in the intervention program than did the changes observed in the three children listening to the music alone. Seizures did not increase for the child with a neurological disorder and a history of a seizure disorder during the period in which the Hemi-Sync signals were included in the intervention. This is also in agreement with my own findings in 1983 and 1985. Varney concludes that the study

> offer(s) evidence supporting the use of Metamusic with Hemi-Sync as an effective adjunct to a communication program which is appropriate to the needs of young children with developmental disabilities. . . . Although the usefulness and effectiveness of Metamusic with Hemi-Sync require additional empirical evidence, interventionists may find that playing Metamusic with Hemi-Sync during intervention with young children with developmental disabilities will improve attention behaviors, social interactions, and communication.

A study by G. Guilfoyle and D. Carbone ("The Facilitation of Attention Utilizing Therapeutic Sounds," *Hemi-Sync Journal*, Vol. XV, No. 2, Spring 1997) reported the results of a preliminary study of 20 developmentally disabled adults with mental retardation. Subjects were matched on the basis of IQ and were divided into experimental and control groups. Each group listened to music on stereo speakers while watching nature videos without sound tracks. Hemi-Sync signals in the alpha-beta range for focused attention/concentration were present in the music played to the experimental group. The control group listened to the identical music without Hemi-Sync. Subjects were tested (pretest and post-test) for short-term auditory memory and sustained focus of attention before and after the video and music. In addition to the formal testing, each subject was rated on six scaled measurements of attentiveness and associated behaviors. Each subject attended 15 half-hour training sessions. Differences between the pre-test and post-test scores were compared for the experimental and control groups.

The group listening to the music containing Hemi-Sync signals showed statistically higher scores on the digit symbol test and significantly higher ratings on resistance to distraction, attention to speech, level of alertness, and level of irritability. The control group, listening to music only, did not show similar changes.

Anecdotal Observation

Since 1988 a larger group of therapists and educators has been using Metamusic tapes in remedial programs. Although formal research is not available to document these observations, the consistency with which the same observations are made by different professionals, in different settings, and with different children, gives some validity to the observations.

Children with sensory processing disorders frequently show increased abilities to modulate or regulate their responses to sensory input. They are calmer and more focused in their attention. Their negative reactions to touch, texture, and other natural sensory stimuli diminish, and they are more comfortable with physical touch and a wider variety of food. Many children with severe sensory processing issues have a diagnosis of autism or pervasive developmental disorder. Greater eye contact, reduced stereotypic behaviors, and increased attention to language and social environments are often seen in this group of youngsters.

Children with cerebral palsy and other disorders resulting in movement dysfunction often show a reduction in spasticity and hypertonicity, easier movement patterns, and greater coordination of sucking, swallowing, and breathing. Their overall feeding patterns are often smoother and more rhythmical.

Medically fragile children and those with a history of frequent hospitalization and invasive procedures are often highly resistant to feeding intervention. They have created internal barriers to protect themselves

47

from the discomfort that has been associated with suctioning, intubation, and nasogastric tubes. In a Metamusic environment, these children become more discriminating of adult intentions. They are more open to adults who introduce them to oral input in a caring and gentle manner, developing greater trust in pre-feeding and feeding approaches in a child-directed therapy program. They will generally retain the protection discrimination and resistance to adults whose intention is to invade the mouth and obtain compliance. Their high level of anxiety is reduced, and they show more mature coping strategies.

Children with attention deficit disorders (with and without hyperactivity) are often helped by Metamusic. They learn to sit quietly without fidgeting for longer periods and are better able to focus their attention.

Case Study: A Child with Autism

A two-year-old boy with autism showed severe sensory overload and disorganization of his response to sensory input. He had limited eye contact and engaged in stereotypic behaviors such as rocking and flapping his hands. He was fussy and irritable, or withdrawn into his internal world. He disliked touch to his upper body, hands, face, and mouth. When he reached a state of sensory overload, he released the stress through gagging and vomiting. Although he liked children's music tapes and quiet classical music, these types of music had no effect on his sensory behaviors. In some instances they appeared to increase his difficulty with his environment. He drank formula from a bottle and seemed more organized with the rhythmical sucking pattern that it required. He ate three small meals of pureed food per day; however, the random sensory input from the spoon, food tastes, and texture created maximum stress. He pushed back in the chair, clamped his mouth closed, pushed his mother's hand and the spoon away, and cried. He was able to cope with the situation by focusing his attention hypnotically on a child's music videotape to cut out interaction and other sensory input.

After an initial 30-minute session with a relaxed-focus Metamusic tape, he accepted touch to his hands and chest, initiated eye contact and smiling, and appeared to be calm and peaceful. Metamusic tapes were incorporated into a sensory-based treatment program for the next week. He was seen for five hours of intervention each day, with Metamusic used approximately half of the time. He continued to show increased interaction and eye contact, began to explore toys, imitated body movements and facial expression in a mirror, and was able to regulate his response to sensory input more efficiently. Gagging and vomiting ceased. During mealtimes he was more open to changes in his physical position in the chair and presentation of the food. Although he still needed his videotape at mealtimes, he was more interactive with his mother and began to come forward to initiate a bite from the spoon when a Metamusic tape was played 30 minutes prior to the meal. He no longer cried and pushed the food away.

During the next six months of home programming, his parents felt that he was less alert and tended to become sleepy when a relaxed-focus Metamusic tape was played. When a concentration Metamusic tape was substituted, he was more focused and no longer became sleepy. Within ten months he was taking a wide variety of foods and had progressed to chewing mashed and chopped foods.

Case Study: A Child with Cerebral Palsy

A three-year-old boy with cerebral palsy received most of his meals through a gastrostomy feeding tube because of severe disorganization of swallowing and breathing. He had recently shown an interest in eating, and his parents gave him small oral feedings each day. During these meals, his breathing was noisy and labored, and he showed frequent choking and coughing. He had great difficulty moving his body volitionally because of high muscle tone and strong tonic reflex movement patterns. He frequently arched into hyperextension of his body and head. He drooled profusely. The base of his tongue was pulled back into a slightly retracted pattern, intermittently occluding the airway. This pattern contributed to his difficulty with breathing coordination during eating and drinking. Although it was possible to use gentle manual traction under the chin to draw the base of the tongue forward, he consistently resisted this treatment strategy. His sleeping patterns were stressed. As he fell asleep, his body went into strong spasms that were accompanied by tongue retraction and severe obstruction of the airway. These episodes of obstructive sleep apnea were terrifying because of their sudden onset and his inability to breathe. His panic and increased tension resulted in stronger reflexive retraction of the tongue and long periods of apnea. He resisted going to sleep, and it often took three to four hours for him to calm down and sleep. When a sleep medication (such as chloral hydrate) was given, he was groggy and unalert the following morning. His parents preferred to help him learn to go to sleep while they were up. They gave lesser amounts of the medication in the late evening when they went to bed. Without this medication, the sleep-wake-apnea episodes continued throughout the night, and the whole family experienced sleep deprivation.

A relaxed-focus Metamusic tape was used initially during quiet, on-the-lap activities such as listening to a story. This enabled the therapist to feel any changes in muscle tone and movement coordination that were related to Hemi-Sync. During these sessions, his postural tone reduced, and he could interact with a storybook as his hand was guided to different pictures. He accepted the therapist's hand under his chin to facilitate a more forward position of the tongue. He was interested in the contrast between his noisy and quiet breathing patterns and began to maintain the quiet pattern independently for longer periods.

Oral feeding sessions were held with the child supported on his mother's lap. Physical assistance was given to keep the tongue out of the pharyngeal airway. Sucking and swallowing movements became more regular and rhythmical and were well coordinated with breathing. There was no coughing or choking. A modified barium swallow study several months later showed an efficient swallow with no aspiration. A relaxed-focus Metamusic tape was used at each meal and intermittently throughout the day. The child learned to use a more forward head position and keep the base of the tongue out of the airway. At the end of the five-day intensive treatment program, he used a quiet breathing pattern more than 75 percent of the time and was spontaneously swallowing his saliva. Drooling was minimal.

Evening therapy sessions were held at bedtime. A Metamusic sleep tape was introduced to help him relax and fall asleep with less physical and emotional stress. The therapist used the positive suggestions that he could sleep peacefully and breathe quietly. Intervention to inhibit his tonic reflex patterns and keep the tongue in a more forward position was used at the first sign of the spasm. Over a four-day period he was able to fall asleep within 30 minutes. He had one or two small spasms during the initial sleep period but was free from apnea episodes. An adult remained with him for physical and emotional support during this period, repeating the positive suggestions for easy sleep and helping him maintain a forward tongue position. Three weeks after the program began, his parents weaned him from the sleep medication and he slept through the night.

Summary

Metamusic containing the binaural beat patterns of Hemi-Sync opens the door to learning for many children with developmental disabilities. Children with oral feeding difficulties have increased their skills and comfort level more efficiently when Metamusic was included in the learning environment. The sound technology is inexpensive, noninvasive, and effective. Metamusic makes an important contribution to most rehabilitation programs.

Hemi-Sync and Autistic Children
Nora Rosen and Berenice Luque

Nora Rosen, Monroe Institute Gateway Outreach trainer in Argentina, collaborated with Berenice Luque, a mental health specialist in the city of Rosario, to bring the Hemi-Sync technology into the treatment programs of a group of autistic children under her care. The case studies below represent some early results from that initiative, reported a few months after the treatments began.

Berenice Luque is a speech and development therapist who works with children, adolescents, and adults who have communication and speech disorders and other dysfunctions. During therapy sessions she uses Hemi-Sync recordings played over speakers in the consulting area while the patients are working at various activities with her. The patients she works with do not have Hemi-Sync while at their special schools, only during her 45-minute therapy sessions with them, usually twice a week. Most of them also listen to Hemi-Sync at home.

Case Reports:

Ezequiel L. 12 years old.

Diagnosis: Generalized Development Disorder. Therapy began in June 1999, and Hemi-Sync was integrated in May 2002.

General Characteristics: Ezequiel is a flexible child, well disposed to learning and to direction from his therapist. He is happy and docile. His language skills are limited to single words and simple statements, accompanied by basic gestures. He has a contextual comprehension level. He attends a special school where he has shown notable advances in the course of his therapy.

Tape Used: *Remembrance* (for mental focus and concentration).

The daily regimen for listening was during 20 minutes each morning before going to school, and then for one hour in the afternoon while doing homework.

Hemi-Sync Exposure Results: His parents commented, "During the first 20 days, and lasting for a few seconds as the tape began to play, he would become nervous, but after that he would calm down as if he'd been sedated, and from that moment would be more committed to his homework. After the first 20 days he no longer became nervous at the sound of the tape. He concentrates more on whatever he is doing, is curious, asking questions about things that previously did not interest him. He is always ready to learn, tries to read schoolroom charts and posters, forms short words using letter cards, and can remember his grandfather's telephone number. He likes to sing or dance when he hears the music."

His teachers at the special school concur in their observations that he concentrates more on what he is doing, is more connected to the other students and to his teachers. As of August 2002, due to the advances he had made, he was promoted two levels and has begun attending class for full days instead of his previous half-day attendance.

While listening to the Hemi-Sync music, Ezequiel makes more eye contact, is more attentive and motivated, remembers more of what has been learned, pronounces the words he has trouble with in syllables, reads single words with less help, and solves jigsaw puzzles that he was unable to do before.

Claudio L. 15 years old. (Ezequiel's older brother)

Diagnosis: Autism. Therapy began in October 2001, and Hemi-Sync was initiated in May 2002.

General Characteristics: Claudio suffers from autistic complications and retardation. He is inflexible and adheres to routine, and he has obsessive fixations with certain objects. His language skills display brevity, using words that have no communicative meaning; he speaks with descending voice intensity, with closed and deficient articulation.

He attends a special school for autistic children and is receiving treatment from a psychologist. During the course of Hemi-Sync treatment, he has improved notably, in the same way as his brother.

Tape Used: *Remembrance*. Claudio follows the same listening regimen as his brother: 20 minutes in the morning before school and an hour in the afternoon while attending to homework.

Results: His parents said, "Just like his brother, for the first 20 days he went through the same nervous response to Hemi-Sync for a few seconds when the tape was first turned on, then settled down, quietly concentrating more on whatever he was doing. Now he does tasks like cutting out figures and pasting them onto paper. He paints without going outside the lines and can assemble simple jigsaw puzzles. At the special school he attends, his teachers say that he is more connected and relates better to the other students and to his teachers."

During the sessions with Hemi-Sync, Claudio smiles a lot more than normal, makes better eye contact, and uses intelligible words that have communicative meaning. He can sort vocabulary cards, play games respecting the rules, and accepts teacher interventions much more readily.

Ivan B. 8 years old.

Diagnosis: Autistic Disorder. Therapy began in April 1999, and Hemi-Sync was initiated in May 2002.

General Characteristics: Ivan has complications from autism but has a good cognitive level. He is inflexible and displays disruptive behavior. His language skills are composed of sentences that apply well to context, although he is repetitive with some of these. He also forms obsessive repetitive questions. His level of understanding is acceptable, although he does not comprehend discussions. He can follow dialogue but with limitation. The change in this boy during the course of Hemi-Sync treatment has been most favorable. He attends a special school and receives treatment from a psychologist.

Tape Used: *Einstein's Dream* (for brain tasking and focused attention). After a short period of using Hemi-Sync, it was discontinued due to the lack of audio equipment at home.

Results: His mother relates, "In spite of the fact that Ivan's treatment has not been continuous because I did not have a tape player of my own, I have observed that while he is at the special school he has progressed. He can now copy out his name. He likes to listen to the Hemi-Sync music and doesn't want it turned off. He is more attentive, responds more quickly, and makes more eye contact. I find him more tranquil, and above all more integrated with older and younger children. His language skills have become more expressive, he makes comparative judgments, something he did not do before, and he answers when he is questioned."

Bartolome G. 3 years old.

Diagnosis: Autistic Disorder. Therapy began in August 2000, and Hemi-Sync was integrated in May 2002.

General Characteristics: Bartolome is a hyperactive little boy, with attention and motivation difficulties. He is inflexible and sticks to certain routines. It is hard for him to adapt to change. His communication skills, as of 2002, were limited to two or three words with gestures. His comprehension is contextual; he smiles a lot and makes good eye contact. He seeks out the company of adults or children smaller than himself. He has advanced notably with the Hemi-Sync treatment. He receives treatment from a psychologist and attends nursery school three days a week.

Tape Used: *Einstein's Dream*, used daily.

Results: His mother says, "In the beginning he covered his ears, he would listen to just one side, or turn the player off completely. He threw things, shouted, waved his arms like he does when he is nervous, and this went on for 15 days. Finally he accepted hearing both sides of the tape, and now he listens without any fussing. He has begun to speak more single words, indicates by pointing with a finger, and pays more attention. He spends more time seated at play and does not leave the table while he is eating. Before he was very selective, only eating one type of cookie or treat."

While listening to Hemi-Sync, Bartolome is more connected, makes a lot of eye contact, asks with gestures, points to what he wants, and accepts intervention in his activities. In spite of continuing to be very hyperactive he appears more motivated and attentive.

Leandro C. 13 years old.

Diagnosis: Generalized Development Complications. Therapy began in December 1994, and Hemi-Sync was introduced in May 2002.

General Characteristics: Leandro is a boy with general motor skill difficulties. His language ability is slow and laborious with his comprehension severely reduced, causing him to fail to pay attention, remember things, or be motivated to any systematic learning or even shared games. He is inflexible. He has made significant advances in the course of Hemi-Sync treatment in spite of the fact that his attendance has been sporadic. He goes to a special school.

Tape Used: *Remembrance*, once a day and again at night before going to sleep.

Results: His parents comment, "He was always difficult to get into bed at night, and now 15 days after beginning to listen to Hemi-Sync, he asks to have the tape put on, listens to one side, and then gets up to ask that the tape be turned over. He listens while lying quietly with the light off, and usually falls asleep that way. Since he was very small, Leandro would get up from his bed about three times during the night, often falling down. His body was always tense and his breathing very loud. Now his body and breathing are normal and he no longer falls down, thank goodness. He makes comments to us regarding school and names his teachers. There are many changes in him, notably the relaxation that he is achieving. He shares and integrates better in games with other children. Before, he was anxious and impatient; now he is able to wait his turn.

"Leandro bathes himself now and has learned to put on his shoes alone. Before, if he got them on the right foot, it was only by accident. This is a great achievement in Leandro's life. We have an older son who is 26, and he recently lost his job. He became very irritable and was unable to get to sleep at night. One night when he went to bed early, he was listening to Leandro's tape. Much to his surprise, he automatically went off to sleep in less than ten minutes. His tension diminished, and he commented to us that he was amazed at the totally positive effect it had on his nerves and stress."

During his Hemi-Sync treatment Leandro is much more attentive, makes eye contact, and tries to correct his defective speech articulation, making it more intelligible. He remains seated and accepts the interventions of adults in his activities. There have also been improvements in his inflexibility, as well as his general motor skill coordination.

Tomas P. 4 years old.

Diagnosis: Autistic Spectrum. Therapy began in May 2001 with Hemi-Sync integration in August 2001 (*Surf*) and May 2002 (*Einstein's Dream*).

General Characteristics: Tomas is a hyperactive child with attention and motivation difficulties. He is inflexible and routine-oriented, and it's hard for him to accept limits. He shouts, becomes angry frequently, and sometimes becomes disconnected, speaking without communicative meaning. He is able to make statements that apply well to context but with some articulation and syntax difficulty. His level of comprehension is contextual. His progress during Hemi-Sync therapy has been very satisfactory. He also receives therapy with a psychologist. He recently began attending a nursery school; before this he was at a small school from which he had to be moved due to his failure to adapt and his subsequent poor conduct.

Tomas listened to the Hemi-Sync tapes in the morning and afternoon. According to his mother, "When he began to listen to *Surf*, he didn't like it, even if I lowered the volume. He would turn it off, saying, 'I say no!' We continued to play the tape for two weeks, but he would systematically turn it off. However, with *Einstein's Dream* there are no problems; he is more connected and attentive. His social relationships have improved, and he is more interactive and communicative. He concentrates on what he is doing, and now he can even manage to play video games without any problem. He accepts more food changes, whereas before he would only eat one type of treat or dessert food. Now he will try a different treat if he doesn't find his favorite. He adapted very well to the school change."

During the Hemi-Sync sessions, Tomas is more connected, answers questions using adequately structured syntax, comments on things he has experienced, and is more attentive and concentrated in his play. There are fewer moments of disconnection, and his hyperactivity has diminished notably.

Hernan C. 4 years old.

Diagnosis: Autistic Disorder. Therapy began in October 2001, and Hemi-Sync was initiated in May 2002.

General Characteristics: Hernan has severe autistic complications. He rarely makes eye contact, smiles very little, does not like to be touched, and responds to his name only sporadically. He does not speak or make signs, and if he wants something he looks for it or picks it up himself. He is inflexible and cannot support change. He always plays with the same thing and screams or throws things when he is angry. There have been few changes during the course of his therapy sessions with Berenice. He receives treatment from a psychologist and has music therapy. He does not attend any nursery or special school, for lack of economic resources.

Tape Used: *Einstein's Dream*, once or twice a day.

Hemi-Sync Results: His parents commented, "He makes more eye contact and responds better to his name. He is more interested in his grandparents, relatives, and people in general. He allows himself to be touched more than before. His treatment attendance has been intermittent due to health problems."

Jesica B. 10 years old.

Diagnosis: Generalized Development Disorder with Autistic traits. Therapy began in March 2002, and Hemi-Sync was initiated in May 2002.

General Characteristics: Jesica is a young girl with generalized motor skill complications. She drools and when she is angry will throw things and scream. If she doesn't like something she will throw it on the floor and step on it. The most serious problems in school were always related to her defiant conduct, hyperactivity, and lack of attention and motivation to learn. Her language skills are reduced to a few single words, gestures, and sounds. Her comprehension level is contextual. She attends a special school.

Tape Used: *Remembrance*, morning and afternoon.

Results: According to her mother, "When she first heard the tape for the first time she began running all around the house, shouting joyously. In the afternoon she did the same thing but then settled down and sat more quietly. The following day she listened quietly, while cutting paper and drawing. Then that afternoon when we put the tape on she began to cry and turned it off. The next afternoon the same thing occurred; she cried and turned it off.

"The next week Jesica was enthusiastic and turned the tape on by herself, playing and running around, making noises as if she were trying to say something, and moving her arms up and down. Many afternoons when she listens, she falls asleep. After ten days she became very familiar with the music and didn't have tantrums. At school she helps the teachers, no longer throws herself on the floor, and seems more interested in doing things. She eats her school lunch without incident. She allowed a cap to be put on her head while watching a football game; before she wouldn't allow anything to be placed on her head."

During the Hemi-Sync sessions, Jesica is more attentive, remains seated, pays attention to games, understands instructions better, and accepts interventions in her activities. She tries to imitate words by watching the speaker's mouth and says single words with better articulation. Her manual coordination has also improved.

Dante F. 3 years old.

Diagnosis: Autistic Spectrum. Therapy began in June 2002, and Hemi-Sync treatment was initiated in July 2002.

General Characteristics: Dante doesn't seem to need anybody. He wanders around aimlessly, does not respond when called, and doesn't obey any orders. He won't let anyone help him, and he searches for the things he wants by himself. He has a pleasant character but maintains little eye contact. He does not raise his arms to be lifted up, speaks only two or three words sporadically, and does not use gestures to communicate. He is not attending nursery school.

Tape Used: *Remembrance*, in the morning and afternoon.

Results: According to his mother, "Now he seeks us out more than before. He embraces his godfather whom he previously ignored. He reaches out his arms to be lifted up and responds more to his name. He looks for and calls to his father and waves goodbye. He runs to hug me when he sees me."

During Hemi-Sync sessions Dante remains seated, is more connected, and smiles, and also accepts being touched.

Federico M. 6 years old.

Diagnosis: Autistic Spectrum. Therapy began on July 1, 2002, and Hemi-Sync was integrated on July 17, 2002.

General Characteristics: Federico is a boy with attention and motivation disorders; he has a tendency to wander around and responds little to orders or requests. He does not join in games with other children, is inflexible and routine-oriented. He uses single words and simple statements in his communications, continuously repeating some of the words he hears. He is receiving treatment with a psychologist and attends a special school for autistic children.

Tape Used: *Einstein's Dream*, twice daily.

Results: According to his parents, "Day by day Federico is talking more since beginning Hemi-Sync treatment. He is more settled and does not come into our bed anymore. He responds more than before when he is called and is more attentive. He even ran to catch his brother who was falling, whereas before he never paid any attention to him."

During Hemi-Sync sessions he is more connected and speaks a lot more. He sits at play for prolonged periods.

Observations. At a home for young people and adults with different disabilities, they are employing *Einstein's Dream* in work areas, and *Remembrance* during the meal hour. Results from this have not yet been analyzed.

(Reprinted with permission from *Hemi-Sync Journal*, vol. XX, no. 1, Winter 2002.)

Hemi-Sync As an Adjunct to Pediatric Physical Therapy

Jacqueline Mast, RPT, M.S.Ed.

Jacqueline Mast is a pediatric physical therapist providing developmental evaluation and physical therapy to infants and young children at Mast Clinic, Inc., Portland, Maine. She has published many articles in professional journals and is currently writing/editing a textbook, *Pediatrics for Physical Therapist Assistants,* to be published by Prentice Hall. She lectures internationally, and her professional honors include: a fellowship with the American Academy of Pediatrics and Developmental Medicine, a Public Service Announcement Award from the California Governor's Committee on Employment of the Handicapped, and Best Practices in Pediatrics from the Maine Handicapped Children's Early Childhood Programs.

Prologue

As a child I was never particularly grounded in "Earth-time." My family's ranch was located on land that included an Indian burial ground. The spirits of these indigenous people were very real to my brothers and me. During elementary school, we regularly biked along the dirt and gravel roads that wound through the nearby Zamora Hills. Only the occasional sheepherder, his flock and his dog, and the foxes, golden eagles, coyotes, pheasants, and songbirds shared our isolation. One of my brothers called this place "a hole in the universe."

Perhaps I could have been better socialized after summer camp with city kids and attendance at a 2,000-student high school. However, my siblings and our friends from neighboring ranches had always communicated telepathically. Our behavior never seemed unusual until a visiting college friend stated, "At the Masts', you can go an entire weekend without saying a word!" A roommate once came home from shopping puzzled about why she had purchased an item I'd been thinking we needed. She accused me of "thinking too loud." I tried to use words as my primary medium of communication after that.

A number of other events contributed to disowning my paranormal sensitivities. Shortly after beginning my career in physical therapy, I angrily thought, "I hope he hurts himself," after repeatedly telling a little boy not to run. It frightened me when he fell. In a Tarot class I was unable to "walk through the card" as instructed. Instead, I slid down the rainbow on the card to its edge and found myself 3,000 miles away in my beloved Zamora Hills. The blank looks in the eyes of my teacher and fellow students discouraged further sharing. A Tarot reading seemed to foreshadow my cousin's suicide, so I stopped using the cards. I continued my out-of-body travels, however, until my daughter's birth and then shut them down completely. What if I couldn't get back to her?

By the time my children were old enough to be independent, I'd forgotten how to go out-of-body, and I'd lost my talent for telepathy. Hemi-Sync reminded me and reopened closed doors. Out-of-body travels to my parents' ranch fed my spirit and renewed my confidence. I tentatively began to give myself permission to communicate nonverbally with the pre-verbal children in my care.

Now I am once again becoming less and less grounded in Earthtime. I work with infants and young children physically, but intuitive insights also comprise a large part of my therapeutic approach. Babies cannot complain in words; infants and young children do not always recognize pain if it is chronic. I often pick up subtle clues that have been missed by many physicians. Sorting out what is going on with the child is frequently a long process that requires much mental processing on my part. While trying to figure out exactly what I've seen, felt, and touched, it is often hard to process routine daily information without feeling greatly distracted. Frequently, things will sort themselves out during sleep, and I'll suddenly awaken with an "Aha!" Listening to Hemi-Sync, particularly *Concentration,* speeds up my processing time considerably.

The Philosophy of My Practice

My clinical practice in physical therapy includes infants and young children who are "outside the norm" in terms of health, development, or body structure. I chose to work with infants because they are so clear. Babies have not learned social/emotional behavior that masks the truth of who this spirit is who has come to visit the Earth. The pure energy of babies is a lovely experience. While working with their physical bodies, it is natural to connect intuitively and/or telepathically. Infants and children have their own unique, individual patterns and paces. Even so, normal milestones occur in a slightly variable but predictable sequence. When a baby's developmental process is out of the ordinary or out of sync, caregivers generally get a gut feeling that something is not right. These are the children I see in my practice.

It is devastating for parents to learn that their baby is critically ill, has physical abnormalities, or is developmentally delayed. Parents grieve for their less-than-perfect child and for the perfect child they'd anticipated and expected to raise. Parental depression adds another challenge to the growing baby's difficulties. Parents seek me out because I've found ways to help them recognize the joy and wonder in their child and his or her capabilities. I help parents feel good about their lovely little person and about their own competence in loving caregiving.

Case Studies

Case 1. I first used Hemi-Sync as an adjunct to physical therapy while helping a boy with attention deficit and hyperactivity prepare for kindergarten. He was unable to perceive details and visually track information on paper. To lay the groundwork for reading, I tried board games and mazes. There was little change until I played the

Concentration tape as we did the activities. His inattention to details immediately changed. He followed a maze with his pencil without once being distracted. I really knew it was working when the tape clicked off and he began to make the rhythmic "shh, shh, shh" sound of the tape. The boy had no trouble learning to read.

Case 2. A newly adopted girl from China was referred to me by her pediatrician, who said, "I think she's deaf. I want you to do a developmental evaluation. We don't know how old she is but we think she's about 18 months." The child was neither walking nor crawling. It was clear to me on the first visit that she was not deaf, just shut down. The most fascinating thing about her was her accompanying retinue—a roomful of ancestors! I could see and feel them looking down on us with worry. Assuming her adoptive parents would think I was crazy, I did not mention the ancestors to them. I worked with the little girl for a few months until she was walking and beginning to talk. She developed into a typical child. As her senses slowly opened to become comfortable in our world, the ancestors gradually receded. During their final visit to my clinic, her adoptive mother offhandedly remarked, "At least the ancestors have gone. They must trust us to take good care of her."

Case 3. A two-year-old with autism flitted from one place to another in the clinic, staying with an activity for no more than a few seconds before moving on. I would follow her around until she engaged in an activity, then set a timer, hold her where she was (e.g., on a rocking horse), and tell her to stay until the timer went "beep, beep." This method was not very effective for getting her to pay attention and actively engage in the activity. She focused on the timer instead, saying "beep, beep" every so often until it went off and she was allowed to escape. One regular activity was sitting in a cone to work on balance while I simultaneously attempted to distract her by blowing bubbles. The cone is unstable unless a child uses internal balance mechanisms to remain upright. Leaning to one side or the other will tip it over. Its shape excludes extraneous visual stimuli. I sit directly in front of it and provide visual and auditory cues as needed. Bubbles are provided as a distraction as the feeling of instability is frightening for some children. Preparation involved getting a towel for each of us, moving the cone from its storage place to the center of the room, and getting the bubbles from the shelf. I would generally lose her to something else before everything was assembled. The sessions were exhausting because she required constant vigilance.

One day, in the midst of the session, I put on the *Cloudscapes* tape. She stopped, looked up at the tape deck, and stood still. The alteration in her attention span was immediate. She would begin an activity, and I'd set the timer. But now, not only did she frequently stay with the activity long past the "beep, beep," she actually began to interact with the equipment or with me. As an experiment, I waited until halfway through the next session to turn on *Cloudscapes*. The session began with the usual flitting from place to place. When the tape started playing she maintained focus on the activity she had chosen. Later in the session she looked up at the shelf and said "bubbles." Previously she had never said anything other than, "Mom, bye-bye," and "beep, beep," and those words were uttered immediately after I had used them in a sentence. The little girl then proceeded to fetch two towels, one of which she handed to me. She walked over to the cone and attempted to drag it from its storage space. I was astonished! From then on, if I did not turn on the tape she would look up at the tape deck and announce "music!" Her overall ability to engage productively continued to improve, and an obvious inner settling occurred with *Cloudscapes*. It appeared to provide an integrating mechanism for her senses.

Case 4. A 13-month-old boy with minimal visual impairment was referred to me because he was not yet crawling. He was very unhappy and would cry for entire sessions. His crying frustrated me because it was a barrier to interpersonal interaction and prevented him from making any developmental progress. One day, his mother mentioned that he liked music at home. So I let him play with bells, a xylophone, and other sound-producing toys. There was little difference. At my wits' end, I finally put on *Inner Journey*. His crying ceased within minutes. From then on, I played *Inner Journey* or *Cloudscapes* for every therapy session. Although the boy still cried occasionally, he was generally interactive with me. He frequently cocked his head with an ear toward the tape. Motor development improved and he eventually walked.

Case 5. A child who had a terminal illness characterized by normal early development, then slow deterioration, came to my clinic for four years. When she was two years old, her enormous energy filled the entire clinic. Her parents and I, as well as others who knew her, sensed that she had been a powerful but benevolent monarch in a past life. As time passed, her energy, eyesight, hearing, and motor abilities waned. She changed from an active little girl who kept me busy the entire session to one who preferred to ride in the swing or sit by her father. On one of our last days together, we sat quietly and made direct eye contact. I was transported—with and by her—to somewhere far away. I recognized Focus 10 as we passed through. She took me to a place far beyond anywhere I'd traveled out-of-body. While we were in that peaceful place, she let me know that this was where she now spent most of her time. She also let me know that although she no longer needed me, it was okay. With startling speed, I was suddenly back in my clinic. Before I could react, her father matter-of-factly stated, "She does that to me all the time now." Perhaps the experience we shared is best characterized by a quote from *Sophie's World*, by Jostein Gaarder. "They have felt themselves wrenched out of Time and have experienced the world 'from the perspective of eternity.'"

Discussion

Hemi-Sync has enriched my life and my clinical physical therapy practice in a twofold manner: by serving as a catalyst to reawaken my intuitive abilities, and by helping my young patients to be calm and to focus. My intuition indicates that Hemi-Sync modulates a child's sensory processing (and mine as well) in ways that enable us to work together more effectively.

(Reprinted with permission from *Hemi-Sync Journal,* vol. XX, no. 1, Winter 2002.)

EDUCATION AND LEARNING

Robert Sornson has had more than two decades of teaching experience and is now an executive director of special education for the public school system of Northville, Michigan. For more than ten years he has been working with Hemi-Sync as a means of helping children with learning difficulties, especially those handicapped by attention deficit disorder (ADD). In his paper he describes a project with children between the ages of six and 14 designed to discover which particular combination of sound frequencies would prove most acceptable and helpful with their learning problems.

Sornson collaborated with the author of the next paper, Barbara Bullard, a distinguished teacher of speech, in researching the frequencies embedded in the first of the Metamusic compositions that she sponsored. This composition, entitled *Remembrance,* has proved one of the most successful of all Hemi-Sync products, with a variety of applications, as Barbara's article reveals. *Remembrance* is one of the Hemi-Sync tapes employed in a research project conducted by Lisé DeLong and Raymond Waldkoetter to discover how neuro-cognitive coaching and EEG neurofeedback might help a group of special needs students with language disorders in a private school.

Finally in this section, Peter Spiro describes his work with students aged between 16 and 25 who had been rejected as lost causes by the educational system. His openhearted approach involving the use of Hemi-Sync—including *Remembrance*—resulted in a transformation in the great majority of those he taught. Sadly, however, the authorities failed to appreciate the value of his work. His inspirational account speaks for itself.

Using Binaural Beats to Enhance Attention

Robert O. Sornson, Ed.S.

Robert O. Sornson is executive director of special education for Northville Public Schools in Northville, Michigan. He coedited the book *Teaching and Joy* and regularly conducts staff and parent training on attention problems, individual learning differences, teaching and parenting with love and logic, and the development of learning potential in young children. He has been a member of the Institute's Professional Division since 1990 and collaborated with TMI to create *On Becoming a Lifelong Learner*, a four-tape album for teenage and adult students. He was a teacher for 24 years and has four children of his own.

This study contributes to the growing body of evidence showing that specific brain-wave states can be enhanced by listening to audio tapes embedded with tones that produce frequency-specific binaural beats. It is concerned with brain-wave states that enhance the feeling of sustained comfortable attention in children. The study is designed to help us understand which specific patterns of sound, and which corresponding brain-wave states, will most effectively help children feel alert. Three different patterns or combinations of sound frequencies were used behind the musical foreground, and subjective data was collected from both parents and participants in the study. The data indicates a clear pattern of preference for one of the three sound patterns used to enhance attention.

Introduction

Attention deficit disorder (ADD), a common disorder in school-age children, has uncertain, probably multiple, etiologies. It is characterized clinically by decreased attention span, impulsiveness, and—for some children—increased motor activity. Students with ADD frequently have difficulty staying on task and completing work. The broad nature of the diagnostic criteria used to define ADD has resulted in a substantially large and heterogeneous population of children being classified with this disorder. Because ADD is estimated to affect as much as 5 to 15 percent of the school-age population, such a prevalent condition may not be a "disorder" as we usually understand it, but rather a description of those individuals in our schools who have difficulty with certain forms of sustained attention. As with most children, individuals with ADD frequently show prolonged attention to television, video games, or personally interesting tasks and therefore may reflect motivation and/or other factors.

Nevertheless, there are certain truths that we may glean from recent research that apply to a large segment of the population that we describe as having ADD. We know, for example, that students with attention deficit have generally lower levels of glucose metabolism as measured across the cortical areas of the brain. We also know that individuals with ADD demonstrate a pattern of less oxygen use in the brain and that they also produce a pattern of slower brain-wave activity, with some studies specifically indicating increased theta activity in the frontal and central locations of the cortex and decreased beta activity in the posterior and temporal regions of the cortex. This research can be interpreted to indicate that many people with ADD have difficulty maintaining the high levels of brain arousal associated with sustained alertness and focused attention.

Hemi-Sync technology has been proved to be particularly effective at helping people achieve desired brain-wave states, but there is another factor that may be just as important. Usually the right and left

cortical hemispheres generate patterns of activity and brain-wave frequencies that are dissimilar. One hemisphere is often more active.
There may be more theta activity in one portion of the right cortex
than in the corresponding portion of the left cortex. When listening to
Hemi-Sync signals, there is a sustained synchronization between the
two hemispheres. The hemispheres of the brain must act in unison to
perceive the differences in signal, increasing the level of activity
between the two hemispheres and creating a balance of activity
between the hemispheres and across the cortex.

Method

This project was an effort to find the combination of sound signals
that would be preferred by children diagnosed with ADD and
described as having difficulty sustaining attention. These children
ranged from six to 14 years old. Eighteen children, volunteered by their
parents, took part in the study. They were asked to listen to three tapes
using headphones. Tape A was to be used three or more times per week
for a one-week period; Tape B three or more times for the next one-
week period; Tape C three or more times for the final one-week period.
Parents were asked to observe any changes in the children while they
were listening to a tape and engaged in an activity. Parents were also
asked to do an overall assessment of which tape the child liked the best
and which tape best helped their child stay focused. For each tape the
parents were asked to record how many times they used the tape, any
important observations, and whether the use of the tape coincided
with any changes in eating or sleeping habits. They were also asked to
note and specify any changes in behavior at school, whether the child
liked to use the tape, and to include any other pertinent comments or
observations.

Each family was given three tapes randomly labeled as Tape A, B, or
C. The tapes were blinded to reduce the influence of expectation and
possible order effects. The tapes had three variations of Hemi-Sync
tones (8–12 Hz, 12–16 Hz, 8–16–24 Hz) embedded behind a musical
score entitled *Heart Zones*, used by permission of the composer, Doc
Lew Childre, and the producer of the tapes, the Institute of HeartMath,

in Boulder Creek, California. Data was then collected from each family and analyzed to determine which of the three sound patterns was preferred overall by the student listeners, to compile anecdotal, subjective information on the willingness to use the tapes, and to assess the overall effect on sustained attention and other factors.

Results

Of the 18 families who participated in the study, seven dropped out almost immediately. Although we had discussed how to persuade children to participate consistently in this project, some simply chose not to go along. As one parent characterized it, "Trying to get him to just listen briefly became just another thing to disagree about." When confronted with this level of resistance, I asked parents not to force the issue with the child and to discontinue their participation. Those who have worked with a child or group of children with ADD will understand my reasoning.

The data collected from the 11 families who completed the study revealed the following:

Two children expressed no preference

One child chose the 8–16–24 Hz tones

Eight children chose the 12–16 Hz tones

No children preferred the 8–12 Hz tones.

The two students who had no tape preference both reported improved attention during an activity, but their parents observed no significant changes in behavior. The student who preferred the 8–16–24 Hz tones happened to be a student with no hyperactivity, but it is most unlikely that this was a significant factor. The parents of the eight students who preferred the 12–16 Hz tones made a variety of interesting comments.

Here are a few of them:

"At first he didn't want to listen because it made him tired, but after listening to it he liked the inside feeling."

"If he listens to it before school he's calmer and much easier to get along with. Sometimes he doesn't like to take the time to calm down."

"After a few days of nastiness, only a few minutes of this tape worked wonders."

"Calmed him down. Attitude changed. Was pleasant to be around (maybe because he slept better)."

"It was a positive experience for him and seemed to have a positive effect. Matt is very impulsive and explosive, and that seemed to improve."

"Mike likes Tape B (12–16 Hz) best. He uses this tape voluntarily on his own. He wants to have this one. He seems to be much happier at home—much less angry. He doesn't use the tape daily any more—but once or twice weekly."

Some of the comments about non-preferred tapes were also interesting. One mother said: "This tape isn't having any effect on him. He doesn't even like listening to it." Another mother, whose son preferred Tape B, said, "I much prefer Tape C and would like to have a copy of Tape C as well as Tape B if possible."

Discussion

It is clear that within our group, representing students aged six to 14 with diagnosed attention deficit disorders, there was a strong preference for the tape with tones reinforcing 12 and 16 Hz brain-wave activity. While there were some respondents who noted positive benefits from the 8, 12, and 16 Hz tones, and one respondent who preferred that combination, no respondents preferred an 8 and 12 Hz combination. It is apparently just too slow to provide sufficient arousal for these young people to sustain comfortable attention. I surmise from these results that something about the 8–16–24 Hz combination is also less appropriate for these students. Perhaps the 8 Hz reinforcing tones add to an already overabundant pattern of high theta and low alpha brain waves, or maybe the 24 Hz tones cause a slight level of discomfort or instability, which I refer to as over-arousal, beyond the range of desired cortical activity for this age range.

Based upon all these considerations, it is clear that the 12–16 Hz combination was preferred by students in this age range. The quote that I enjoyed most came from a mother who reported, "The problem I have now is that my son and his father are arguing over who gets to use the tape when they both have something important that they would like to do." These tapes are not a panacea for all the difficulties a student with attention problems may experience. However, they definitely offer one more tool that is likely to help a significant group of individuals within the ADD population to improve their sustained attention and to learn, over time, how to sustain attention on their own by adjusting their brains to an alert state.

(Reprinted with minor changes from *Hemi-Sync Journal*, vol. XVII, no. 4, Fall 1999.)

Facing the Learning Challenge
Barbara Bullard, M. A.

Barbara Bullard has been professor of speech at Orange Coast College for 35 years and is currently chairman of the department. She was thrice nominated as Teacher of the Year at the college and received the NISOD Teaching Excellence award from the University of Texas in 1994, 1999, and 2000. She has been selected for *Who's Who Among America's Teachers*, 2002. Barbara has been a professional member of The Monroe Institute since 1989.

Ever since the dawn of civilization, man has recognized the profound effect of music on human behavior and learning. The ancient Greeks believed that music was divinely created. Both Plato and Aristotle placed music at the core of their educational curricula, acknowledging music's power to stimulate human thought and understanding.

Modern research has given us scientific explanations for the "magic" of music that the ancients recognized by instinct and observation, as can be seen, for example, in the research described in the splendid books by musicologist Don Campbell: *Physician for Times to Come, Music and Miracles,* and *The Mozart Effect.* This research reveals that music has a powerful impact on almost every aspect of the body and mind of the listener.

Over the past 30 years, as a teacher and a parent, I have been interested in discovering methods by which my students might use music as an aid to learning faster and more efficiently. I was very impressed with the techniques of "suggestopaedia" and super-learning in the work of Dr. George Lozanov and in the studies by Ostrander and Schroeder. For more than two decades I have been recommending background music as a key element in the application of super-learning, and my students can attest to the significant impact of certain music in facilitating super-learning states. My research led to the co-authoring of a book, *Communicating from the Inside Out* (B. Bullard and K. Carroll, 1995).

The specific topic of this article, the use of Metamusic compositions that combine the synergy of super-learning musical formats with Hemi-Sync, is a more recent adventure of my research, brought about by the personal challenges of raising two children with impulsivity and attention deficit disorder (ADD). My two younger children were challenging all my parenting skills and the patience of their teachers. They were the type that walked on the classroom tables, talked incessantly, and flitted from project to project. The teachers encouraged me to try Ritalin with them. I figured there must be a less invasive alternative— and yes, there was! It was to be found in the Hemi-Sync technology, to which I was introduced when I attended the Professional Seminar in 1989.

The insights I learned in that week propelled my own research in a quantum leap. I was deeply impressed by the work of Dr. Micah Sadigh as slide after slide demonstrated the widespread neuronal effects of Hemi-Sync on eliciting desired brain-wave patterns in a synchronized manner across the cortex. This was followed by a remarkable presentation by Dr. Suzanne Morris, an internationally known speech-language therapist who works with children with developmental disabilities. Dr. Morris's research involved using Metamusic with alpha-theta brain waves on children with autism and severe brain damage. I was awed as I watched her video of an autistic child who could not even bear to be touched, yet within less than ten minutes of listening to Metamusic moved towards its source, wrapped her arms around the tape player, and allowed herself to be gently massaged by Dr. Morris while the music played on. To ordinary relaxation music the child made no response. For me this was the most dramatic image of the "magical" effects of Metamusic. Thereafter I began using Metamusic to enhance the sleep and relaxation states that would ease the stressful effects in the lives of my family. Compositions such as *Cloudscapes, Sleeping through the Rain,* and *Inner Journey* helped a lot throughout the following years.

Two years later at another Professional Seminar I was intrigued by a discussion of recent research, led by Robert Sornson, that demonstrated an insufficiency of coordinated hemispheric brain-wave pattern, especially with beta brain waves in the left hemisphere, for those with ADD. Sornson, a director of special education services, pointed out that research indicated that those with attention deficit had difficulty maintaining the high levels of brain arousal associated with sustained alertness and focused attention. He added that he had been working with Hemi-Sync using beta-harmonic sound patterns specifically designed to increase the level of awareness.

Listening to this discussion, I awoke to the idea of combining super-learning music with the beta patterns discovered by Sornson, to see if this would help my two teenagers with their issues stemming from their ADD. During the following two years, Sornson and I collaborated on incorporating his researched beta-harmonics with Hemi-Sync with a super-learning musical format that I designed myself. The music appropriate for super-learning and peak performance states had to meet many technological standards. An enchanting composition was created by J. S. Epperson, a graduate of the USC School of Electronic Music, to comply with the theoretical specifications I formatted. This "designer Metamusic" was titled *Remembrance* and was launched by The Monroe Institute in 1994.

The success of *Remembrance*, as indicated by the amount of positive feedback we received, led to the creation of a second composition in 1996. This carried similar beta-harmonics. The music itself was a modification of Mozart's *Sonata for Two Pianos in D Major*. We chose the title *Einstein's Dream*, as this was a favorite composition of both Alfred Einstein, the great Mozart expert, and Albert Einstein, the world-famous scientist. I'd like to quote two interesting comments on the effects of Mozart's music. In a *Newsweek* article on his music, Joshua Cooper Ramo remarked: "Mozart's musical architecture evokes a sympathetic response from the brain, the way one vibrating piano string can set another humming." And physics professor Dr. Gordon Shaw, a researcher on the effects of music on the cortex and on learning, says, "It is not that Mozart will make you permanently smarter, but it may be a warm-up exercise for parts of the brain."

Two more recordings were issued in 2002: *The Seasons at Roberts Mountain*, incorporating extracts from Vivaldi's *Four Seasons* (much super-learning music research has focused on Baroque selections) and arranged by Scott Bucklin, and *Indigo—for Quantum Focus*, by J. S. Epperson.

Reports received since 1994 indicate that Metamusic embedded with beta Hemi-Sync patterns may also help with other learning disabilities, specifically dyslexia and slow reading development, both of which have errors in timing between the two hemispheres as an underlying cause. As one researcher reported in *The Brain-Mind Bulletin*:

> While reading, most good readers have left-hemisphere activity in the beta range (around 13 Hz) and mid-range amplitude. Dyslexics, on the other hand, tend to have left-hemisphere measurements in alpha (roughly 10 Hz) and higher than average amplitudes, although some have unusually low amplitude . . . the cerebellum of dyslexics has not yet learned the coordination and timing involved in internal balance of the body.

It seems that the synergistic combination of designer music with the beta-harmonic Hemi-Sync-embedded frequencies helps to facilitate the necessary brain synchrony for focused attention. The musical environment helps one to study *smarter* rather than *harder*.

These effects of music make sense. All of us have had experience of the effect of music on learning. We learned our ABCs in elementary school by singing them, and we can remember the tunes throughout our lifetime. Also when the first three beats of an "oldies" song are played on the radio, you begin to remember the lyrics even if you haven't heard the song in decades. Then you may recall the image of your sweetheart at that time and the emotions you experienced when you were together. It is a truism: What goes in repeatedly with music, comes out with music even decades later.

Another reason for the effect of music on learning can be gathered from split-brain research which has found that music is the one stimulus that inherently synchronizes both hemispheres of the brain. It has been theorized that the linear-sequential aspects of music, such as the lyrics, beat, rhythm, notation, and specific details, are being processed by the left hemisphere, while the right hemisphere is processing the holistic aspects, such as harmony, intonation, creativity, and the overall flow of the musical piece. But current research has found that the impact of music on the brain is much more widespread than just the effect on the cerebral hemispheres. Brain imaging research has spotlighted the impact of music on the "convergent zones" that function in the prefrontal lobes. It is here that the interconnectivity of the two hemispheres takes place, arousing coordinated thinking patterns.

Following hundreds of studies on children and adults with ADD, Dr. Daniel Amen discovered that the frontal lobe tends to "turn off" rather than on. In *Windows into the ADD Mind* he writes, "When people with ADD try to concentrate, the frontal lobes of their brain (which control attention span, judgment, impulse control, and motivation) decreased in activity. When normal control groups do concentration tasks, there is increased activity in this part of the brain. So the harder these people try, the worse it gets for them."

Perhaps this is why the "designer Metamusic," which combines the best of music with the widespread impact on the brain of beta Hemi-Sync binaural beat technology, can be so helpful to those with ADD and dyslexia. The synergistic impact creates a side-to-side and front-to-back stimulation, a top-down process beginning from the cortex to the limbic brain where our emotions are triggered. This positive cascade of brain waves then affects the hormonal and immune systems.

There is another point to bear in mind. Earlier research indicated that the ability to switch rapidly between hemispheres might be hallmarks of higher intelligence. One characteristic of gifted children is that they have a profound switching ability between hemispheres. *Remembrance* and its companion pieces have all been specifically designed to enhance this rapid processing partnership so desirable for learning, for the gifted among us as well as for those with learning challenges. Moreover, these compositions facilitate the anchoring of studied information into a wider neuronal pathway. Wider anchoring should result in greater retention and recall—perhaps as much as five to ten times greater recall.

Here are just a few of the comments we have received from students, parents, and teachers on the effects of these compositions on learning problems.

"I was diagnosed with ADD years ago. When I first heard of the benefits that came from listening to Metamusic, I must say I was skeptical. But as I began listening to *Remembrance* I immediately noticed the difference. My breathing slowed to a steady rhythm. I relaxed naturally while staying completely alert. I was shocked to realize I'd been studying for an hour without stopping. Listening to *Remembrance* enables me to pay complete attention to my studies now."

—R. M., age 19

"Hemi-Sync dramatically improved my hyperactive son's life. Right away I noticed the calming effect while the tape was playing. Even better, my son can now usually re-create that calm state whenever he chooses to do so. It's as if his brain learned how to experience calmness and now he can move into that mental state by himself."

—M. C.

"Thank you for turning me on to Metamusic tapes. These tapes have a major impact on my life and education. I listen to *Einstein's Dream* every day, especially when I need to concentrate and energize. The other night I was studying so intensely that when the tape clicked off I jumped because it seemed like the loudest thing I'd ever heard. I turned the tape and continued. I was amazed that the difficult concepts came so easily to me while I was using it. The next day I got a perfect score on my test!"

—R. M.

"The classroom was always chaotic, and I was totally frustrated. I now play *Remembrance* as background for various activities and find a completely different level of comfort in the room. Obviously it's good for the children and I know it's great for me."

—J. A., third-grade teacher

"After five months of frustrating, largely unproductive sessions, I put on *Remembrance* while T. was sullenly fiddling with a toy. His eyes got wide, he smiled and turned up the volume. Hesitantly at first, then with increasing tempo, he began to pour out years of confusion, anger, and hurt and asked for a copy of the tape."

—R. S., counselor, speaking of a 12-year-old client

The following comments relate to the experiences of some who do not face learning challenges but have found this designer Metamusic helpful in their work.

"With only one day to study for the state insurance licensing exam, I thought it was hopeless. I'd never be able to remember a manual of 190 pages. Anyway, I decided to give it a shot. I began studying at 9 A.M. and by 1 P.M. was losing my ability to concentrate. I put *Einstein's Dream* into my continuous tape player and finished the book at 3:05 the next morning. I passed with 86 percent, thanks to *Einstein's Dream*, which enabled me to maintain concentration for 18 hours."

—B. L.

"When needing to read some highly technical papers I experimented with and without *Remembrance*. The difference really impressed me. Listening to the tape I was much more able to attend to the content, stay focused, and not have to reread sentences for comprehension. Eventually I didn't even notice it was playing. That's when the benefits started showing. I was studying for a major test requiring lots of formulas and memorization. I got a perfect score, and I know *Remembrance* helped me study more efficiently."

—E. A.

"A 60-year-old man was studying to become a minister at the Dallas Theological Seminary. He became stymied by the challenge of learning Greek and Hebrew. His mind could not wrap itself around these languages, and he was about to have to give up his dream. A friend gave him *Remembrance* to see if it would help. Within two months he mastered both languages, passed with an A, and is now Pastor at Baylor Hospital."

— W. J. Q.

Conclusion

When using Metamusic for study or attaining peak performance, it is best to treat it as a sonic background. If it is used consistently while studying, you need only allow your favorite portions of the refrain to flow through your awareness, and the information you studied will be more readily accessed. The music is especially effective when used in tandem with some other Hemi-Sync exercises. My students find *Attention, Think Fast,* and *Retain-Recall-Release* especially helpful. *Buy the Numbers* is most helpful for facilitating the learning of math. Also very supportive are the **Lifelong Learning** Program, produced by Robert Sornson, and the **Student PAL** set. Other exercises that I've found particularly helpful in assisting adults to move out of the more challenging aspects of ADD are *Brain: Repair and Maintenance* and *Off-Loading.* Played at night for about six weeks, these have been most useful when combined with the use of *Remembrance* or the other companion beta selections during the day.

Although many parents and teachers have found these beta-harmonic compositions to be highly effective tools for learning, they should not be regarded as "magic bullets." Rather, they should be treated as helpful aids to lead the brain gently into an alert and attentive state of consciousness. A 60-year-old engineer, who had suffered for many years with a medical diagnosis of "cognitive brain collapse," reported quite poetically after using *Remembrance* for two months:

"*Remembrance* is like breathing clean air; it's even better than a box of chocolates! It offers a gentle, three-dimensional support. It calms the scattering, allows the centering, like a pleasant non-noticeable incense. I find myself now able to lead the project rather than push the project.

I don't have to push logs upstream any more. With *Remembrance* I don't have to conquer tasks but can guide them simply and effectively. *Remembrance* is the difference between harmony and heartburn; as a helper, it allows me to allow."

—G. M.

Hemi-Sync in an Educational Program
Lisé D. DeLong, Ph.D., and
Raymond O. Waldkoetter, Ed.D.

Lisé DeLong, Ph.D., recently graduated from the Union Institute and University in Cincinnati, Ohio, with a degree in neuropsychology, specializing in neuro-cognitive processing. She is the founder of the Meridian Academy of the Arts Elementary/Middle School and is a neuro-cognitive specialist focusing in language disorders. Lisa organizes workshops for educators and parents in creating individualized curricula to meet specific academic needs. She is currently in private practice working with children and adolescents using the EEG Neurofeedback and Cognitive Rehabilitation techniques.

Ray Waldkoetter, Ed.D., is a consulting psychologist with an inclusive background in research psychology. He is a member of The Monroe Institute's Board of Advisors and is a founding member of its Professional Division.

Recently we conducted a controlled pilot study to evaluate the effectiveness of EEG neurofeedback and neuro-cognitive processing in a small American private school. The definition of EEG neurofeedback involves the recorded tracing of wave patterns of electrical brain activity obtained by electrodes placed on the scalp, using auditory and visual feedback on a computer display monitor. This allows individuals to observe the activity of their brain waves via a specially designed system. Neuro-cognitive processing combines EEG neurofeedback with language process coaching, using selected sound patterns to accompany a creative arts curriculum.

The study sample consisted of 24 special needs students with language disorders, some of whom had attention deficit with or without hyperactivity. They were randomly divided into two groups of 12, one for the combined neurofeedback treatment and the other to act as a control group. Both groups were pre-screened using selected academic and specialized testing devices to measure reading, writing, listening, and general cognitive abilities. The neurofeedback group was treated for two semesters for 18 weeks in all, with a total of 25 one-hour therapeutic periods using the EEG neurofeedback and neuro-cognitive coaching sessions. This coaching utilizes the premise that brain-training guidance can assist the student in creating the learning environment necessary to achieve the "multidimensional model" of brain-learning activity. Music can stimulate the creative right hemisphere, and the accompaniment of appropriate sound frequencies, pre-planned rhythms, and intensity levels can help activate the left hemisphere. The Monroe Hemi-Sync tapes have specialized in this type of combined sound support, using music in frequency-specific binaural tapes. Through EEG neurofeedback it is possible to accurately identify areas of the brain processing information and also to identify the deficit areas.

A New Start

We undertook this study of neuro-cognitive coaching coupled with EEG neurofeedback in a designed learning environment offered by the Meridian Academy of the Arts, which provided a basis of academic processing for learners with and without language disorders. The Academy provides a non-competitive, non-tested, and non-graded curriculum that is defined as stress-reduced. All students in the study received the normal curriculum provided by the Academy while the coaching group continued with an individualized one-on-one therapy program. This involved games in auditory processing, visual processing, language comprehension (verbal and receptive), and eye-hand coordination. Visual and auditory processing have been documented as common areas for neurofeedback to enhance memory, concentration, focus, and listening skills. Both groups enjoyed the full curriculum used in the Academy, consisting of music, dance, drama, literature, and the visual arts.

The proposed outcomes were to measure the academic and behavioral peformance differences between the two groups where the given variables emphasized the neuro-cognitive coaching and the EEG neurofeedback effects. Date scores were to be compared using a pre/post measurement from the full sampling of both groups. The matrix for statistical analysis required data entry units of 24 participants, times five instrumental items and their subtests.

Student Gains Achieved

The auditory processing tests reflected substantial educational gains with associated areas of cognitive receptive processing skills responsible for understanding information presented aurally while remembering the order for spelling, grammatical rules, directions, and organization of thinking. The experimental group increased in auditory skills by a factor of 2.90 over the control group, a 290 percent increase in listening skills as designated by this study. In regard to reading, this research showed the experimental group increased by a factor of 1.62, or 162 percent over the control group. The areas of reading covered were word identification, word attack, and word comprehension. The comprehension subtest demonstrated site-specific word comprehension, and a strong, rather impressive, gain was made in this area. This may suggest a viable opportunity for remediation of illiteracy in the more traditional school systems.

The global achievement rate indicated an overall increase in the experimental group by a factor of 3.41, or 341 percent over the control group, showing a substantial education improvement in a short time. The global achievement measured a nonverbal receptive knowledge base of information, highly dependent upon concentration levels and auditory processing skills. It appears that as the auditory processing skills improved, the concentration levels increased, demonstrating an improvement in overall achievement.

The scores obtained for math performance also showed an increase in the experimental group by a factor of 1.57, or 157 percent, over the control group. This increase generally correlates with the increase in global achievement, problem solving, and reasoning skills demanded in the field of mathematics. Math achievement is seriously affected by the stress level experienced by the students, with research showing that the frontal lobe performs "executive function" skills associated with mathematics. A stressed learner will "downshift" away from the frontal lobe, making it nearly impossible to access that part of the brain used for the higher functioning math skills. It would appear that the experimental group must have been taught in a stress-reduced environment to attain the distinct gains in overall math scores.

Here we would note that the experimental group had a mean of 7.5 individuals improving their performance between pre- and post-test on the ten comparative measures used, while the control group had an improving mean of 5.8. The non-parametric Mann-Whitney test for significance yielded a substantial difference (p = .008), thereby accenting via this highly significant level the power of EEG cognitive neurofeedback as a means of improving ability in this learning environment.

Findings from teacher assessments, individualized standardized tests, and parental questionnaires indicated that students in the experimental group improved in overall academic areas and behavioral aspects of attention problems: hyperactivity, internalizing problems, and adaptive skills. Auditory discrimination revealed a high level of significantly improved behavior. This study provides obvious implications for both the special-needs and normal student samples.

Brain-Wave Learning and Hemi-Sync

Augmenting EEG neurofeedback brain-wave training sessions and neuro-cognitive therapy with binaural listening stimuli (Hemi-Sync) positively improves the effects, as has been shown in this study. Increased beta brain-wave activity (13 to 30 Hz) can heighten awareness, concentration levels, and ability to focus. In contrast there is decreased eyes-closed beta for special-needs students (e.g., ADHD), allowing individuals to relax as their circadian rhythms regulate the sleep cycle naturally. The Hemi-Sync process can be observed to bring the brain into a synchronized state using blended sound patterns activating various stress-reducing brain-wave frequencies (alpha, theta, and delta).

Through his research, Robert Monroe developed audio tapes involving verbal guidance and imagery and incorporating a variety of sounds and music. These tapes elicited specific responses owing largely to the effects of the frequency-following response and the stimuli of binaural beats. With the use of an evoked EEG protocol, binaural beating was induced, measured, and monitored, with the result that increased amplitudes at desired frequencies were produced, thereby reducing amplitudes in the undesired frequency levels. The tapes used during the coaching sessions included *Sleeping through the Rain, Remembrance, Einstein's Dream, Brain Repair and Maintenance, Attention, Concentration,* and *Sensory Hearing.* Each student listened to the tapes between eight and 12 times out of the scheduled 25 sessions, for between 20 and 30 minutes each tape. Actual sessions for practicing relaxation lasted between five and 15 minutes.

The primary training employed in this research was built on findings of the sensorimotor rhythm (SMR) discovery with the 12–15 Hz activity of observed EEG neurofeedback. Initial sessions of neurofeedback in this study followed a five-minute period of SMR 12–15 Hz activity interchanged with five minutes of 15–18 Hz beta activity. This gave students more relaxed physical responses and increased alert awareness, together with overall improvement in all components of mathematics, tested reading areas, and in global achievement. It was verified that the EEG neurofeedback and neuro-cognitive coaching made a marked positive difference in students' progress, with significant gains in auditory processing, overall achievement, and the components of mathematics, including problem solving and critical thinking skills. Emphasized also is the importance of stress-reduced learning, small class size, and the structure of an individualized curriculum.

Hemi-Sync and the Self-Reflective Lover
Peter Spiro

Peter Spiro is a playwright, poet, and a former New York City school-teacher. His plays have been produced in New York City and Los Angeles; his poetry has been widely published in magazines and anthologies. Before leaving New York City for north-central Oregon, Pete taught in an alternative high school program for 11 years.

An Overview: Three Philosophies, Two Questions, One Curriculum

What we know is what we know; it means little, if it means anything at all. But to wonder, and to hold onto wonder about what we cannot know, there's Man dressed as though He were an angel. Not the most cunning among creatures, nor the most adaptable, but one sterling creature, uncertain as He may be, who can wonder that the very world He lives in exists. Wonder at existence itself. Wonder why there is something rather than nothing. The holiness of the internal experience isn't accessible to the standards of measurement and achievement to which we hold dearly in school. Having assimilated a mind-centered political/economic philosophy based on fear—fear of the unknown, fear of life, fear of death—we pass on this worldview to children through compulsory schooling and the curriculum of fear, the roots of which can be traced to the philosophies of René Descartes, Thomas Malthus, and Charles Darwin. But by using Hemi-Sync, among other tools, I've witnessed a few very troubled youngsters awaken to their own curriculum, which is self-identification and love.

Three Philosophies

René Descartes: Descartes decided he could not trust his senses to give him reliable information about the world. How could he, he wanted to know, have certainty about anything? He decided he could not. From this point of uncertainty, he realized, there must at least be the uncertain thinker. "If I can think this," thought Descartes, "I must certainly exist." *Cogito, ergo sum.* He had found his certainty and his security. He conceived of the world as a machine and himself as having no connection to it.

Thomas Malthus: In 1800, Thomas Malthus, professor of political economics of the British East India Company College, found that human population was increasing by a geometric rate while life-support resources were increasing only at an arithmetic rate. Ergo, it was universally concluded that there are only enough resources for some of us to survive.

Charles Darwin: A half-century later, Darwin expounded his theory of evolution, which believes only the fittest species, and the fittest of each species, will survive. "It has to be either you or me. There is not enough for both."

Two Questions

The mind asks "how, what, when, and why"; the heart asks only "who."

The mind seeks to understand; the heart desires experience. The mind would like to transcend; the heart wants to embrace. The mind fears for our safety and suggests ways to remain safe; the heart's promise to us all is freedom.

Does thinking precede existence, or does existence produce

thought? What Descartes, in his mystification, missed was mystery itself, the presence of wonder. What Descartes might have experienced had he gently persuaded his mind to relax was the opposite of what he had discovered; that is: "I am, therefore I think." The wonder of *who* he was preceded his thinking *that* he was. Beyond his desire for certainty, there was René's thumping heart: uncertain, unsure, and unafraid. Beyond thinking and perceiving, there is the eternal self-reflective lover, embracing what can never be understood.

While working for the British East India Company, Thomas Malthus helped propagate a philosophy of lack. It's an economic agenda to encourage competition. If we compete with each other for scarce resources, what we lose is the wealth of our connections through ourselves to each other. Instead of seeking the kingdom of heaven within, we search outward and measure wealth, not by who we are, but by what we have.

The physical form may indeed evolve, but since we are all much, much more than our physical bodies, Darwin's theories can become antagonistic to our prime concern of evolution, which is the expansion of spirit along the ever-widening spiral of life. Is life on Earth just a quest to survive? Or is it more like a laboratory in which we transform from opaque to the light of God to transparent? Darwin equates physical survival with success and physical death with failure. So much for our guaranteed return tickets Home, and the promise of the absolute perfection of eternal Love.

One Curriculum

Compulsory schooling embraces, celebrates, and helps propagate Descartes's notion that we are our minds. Only by cultivating a potent mind, children are taught, can they go out and get all those scarce resources Malthus warned us about. If they don't get those scarce resources, as Darwin suggested, they will cease to exist, thus failing in their lives' purpose, which is physical survival. This curriculum supplants the Angel's curriculum of self-identification and love with what it calls "critical thinking skills." It convinces children to reject the overflowing impulses of their hearts, to compete, to envy those who have more and to have contempt for those who have less; it encourages fear through a comprehensive curriculum of continual observation, fragmentation, disorientation, punishment, reward, grades, and provisional self-esteem. Children are taught to view themselves as necessary competitors within a worldwide economy with a premise of lack. They are drilled with the destructive notion they must "become somebody," rather than helping to remind them of the true worth of who they already are. They are taught to "achieve" an abstract goal of unattainable "success" which propels them forward into a life of chronic dissatisfaction and constant longing.

As a teacher, what I tried to do was help students to awaken to remember who they really are. Within the chaos, mind-numbing boredom, ever-present fear, and the potentially violent world of compulsory schooling, I have witnessed what I can only call "near miracles" when I've offered tools like Hemi-Sync to youngsters who can't cope anymore with the stresses of living and surviving day to day in extremely harsh and challenging physical circumstances. Within what may seem like absolute madness, one act of love can seem miraculous. With the faith of a mustard seed, indeed, we can perform miracles.

Step One: Focused Attention

I taught students who, for one reason or another, had not succeeded in either mainstream schools or other alternative settings, in parts of town where only outlaws and fools travel by foot. Year by year, I saw the students get harder, meaner, and more lost.

Every one of my students had either voluntarily dropped out or been thrown out of a previous school. Their ages ranged from 16 to 25. Most of the females had at least one child; most of the males had either been incarcerated or were on probation. If they didn't make it with me, they hit the streets and took their chances. It didn't take me long to realize that my education courses weren't doing me or the students much good. I needed something real, something that could change outlooks and modify self-destructive behavior patterns.

The year had started like any other year. My classroom was a basement room in a building in a housing project. The windows were at ground level, permitting very little light or air to enter. In the middle of the room was a large steel plate covering a sewage drain, and down the hall was the trash compactor. The room was infested with flies. Mice would scurry along the overhead pipes or inadvertently step onto glue traps where they'd wrestle mightily to free themselves of their own skin, squealing until a maintenance worker removed them. And there were the students: hot, restless, disturbed, fatigued, undernourished, fearful, and on edge.

I had already run across the books of Robert Monroe and was listening to Hemi-Sync tapes because they made me feel better. So one day I took a boombox into my classroom and attached 15-foot wires to the speakers so they could be separated for stereo. I plunked in the *Remembrance* tape and synchronized the room. Then I nearly keeled over from what I saw. One particular kid, who normally survived each day by acting like a monkey on a pogo stick, suddenly took a seat up front and quietly completed each assignment. Most of the class thought he was absent! Still, I doubted that the tape alone had helped him achieve this state of contentment.

But the same thing happened the next day, and every day thereafter as long as *Remembrance* was playing. I finally had to accept that the tape was actually performing as advertised. "You're trying to calm me down with that brain music, eh?" the kid would quip as he'd pass me with a wink. He knew. So I ordered a variety of Metamusic tapes and played them all day long. And if I forgot to play a tape I'd always get a request, "Hey, play a brain tape."

Soon I started handing out tapes for kids to play in their portable tape players. A kid would come up to me and ask for a "brain tape," then return to his seat and do the assignment.

The first time I played *Concentration* for the group, I'd given them a test to take because this was, after all, school. And in school people take tests. They obliged to take the test, I surmised, because they liked me. But damned if they didn't seem totally committed and focused. It was only after the tape ended that the focus and the commitment faded, and everyone began to get restless and drop pencils.

I have looked out into the room as a Metamusic tape played and seen a kid's face so open, so pure and innocent, so peaceful he looked like a cherub. I like to think the "brain tapes" helped get him there, if only for a short time. How much does an hour or two of Metamusic a day alleviate the stress and anxiety these kids lived with all the time? It worked well enough for a few to leave some of that stress and anxiety outside the door when they came to class.

A supervisor of mine was curious. So I gave her *Remembrance* to listen to in a portable tape player. She thought it nice, and left. But she returned the following morning to ask me where she could get that tape. It seemed her depression had mysteriously lifted after listening to *Remembrance* that afternoon. I gave her a catalog. At the end of the school year, she greeted me with a big hug. She was thoroughly pleased, grateful to have gotten off the Prozac she'd been taking.

Some teachers had expressed interest in the "brain tapes." But the administrators seemed uninterested in spending budget money for them. The prevalent view about Hemi-Sync was that it was abnormal.

What the kids could have used was something intensive, away from the city—like a trip to the Institute for a Gateway program. They needed a solid introduction to their higher selves, like the one I got during my own Gateway, where the mystery of who I am got a whole lot more mysterious.

I tried to get the kids in my classes out of the school system the quickest way possible. The school system here doesn't nurture anybody. We need a new paradigm. And I think Hemi-Sync should become part of that new paradigm in the future and should be immediately incorporated into the present curriculum everywhere. Instead of marching kids up to a stage to listen to someone sing "I believe I can fly," they need to take their own trips into the ether. Metamusic works!

The Second Step: Expanded Awareness

During the 1997/98 school year, while teaching in a literacy program at the Harlem YWCA, I tried to re-create the total TMI experience for the students with my feeble technology. "If I can't get the students to the Institute," was my logic, "I'll bring the Institute to the students." Like always, it was an ugly room with little light or air. There was a flimsy felt divider separating the room into two classes. On one side were students who had scored lower than a third-grade reading level. On my side were the students who had scored between third and sixth grade. Outside was the omnipresent harsh reality of poverty and violence. As we were all leaving for a class trip one day, we were almost trapped in a crossfire between cops on foot pursuing two fleeing men. Lucky for us all we were able to duck quickly into the Y. Life is hard here; everyone, it seems, carries at least some sort of weapon, everything from box-cutters to guns.

As the students arrived they were greeted by Robert Monroe's voice on the *Morning Exercise* tape. "Good morning," it begins, "and it is a good morning."

As the *Morning Exercise* played, I handed out paper and asked students to write whatever was on their minds. I showed them a large bucket labeled "Energy Conversion Box" and asked them to drop the papers inside when they were done. After they had converted their energy, I asked them to copy an affirmation I had written on the board. "I am more than my physical body" was the inherent message in quotes I used from various sources like *Seth Speaks, Conversations with God*, and others. The affirmations often sparked lengthy discussions about meaning and application to daily living. I supplemented the reading list with metaphysical books such as Betty Eadie's *Embraced by the Light* and other accounts of near-death experiences, out-of-body travels, and remote viewing. Hemi-Sync played nearly nonstop throughout the day. I'd mix up *Concentration, Remembrance,* various Metamusic selections, and, on occasion, some Mozart and Gregorian chants. Sometimes I'd light a stick of incense, burn a candle, or charm the students by tracing their energy fields with divining rods.

It was a momentous school year in many ways. On the other side of the flimsy felt divider the usual school madness transpired: chaos, anger, frustration, and a teacher so overwhelmed and fatigued she had to take a medical leave of absence after a few months. On my side of the divider I witnessed the miraculous: the tenderness of the human heart yearning to be exposed, shared, witnessed. At times the dichotomy became a distraction, with students from the other class flinging paper and insults over the felt divider. Yet the students in my class were, to my amazement, restrained. In fact, the rejoinder to an insult would be:

"We're more spiritual than you." Not that I equate ego-thumping with spiritual awareness, mind you, but the usual response to an insult would have been quick retaliation with a fist, a box-cutter, or a bullet. I kid you not, these kids were hungry for spirit. Their hearts were soaring!

Not everybody who attended my class transformed. But most did to some degree. And those youngsters who couldn't buy into the program quickly departed. The bond of love that had developed was that strong.

By the end of the year, most students were reading and enjoying it. Some of the kids even took extra books home. They read them, returned them, and asked for more. I had to make a supply run to Barnes and Noble because they went through books much faster than I had anticipated. It takes a lot of courage for some of them to tote a book home. Just carrying a book can be misconstrued as a symbol of weakness.

Through discourse and reading what was dropped into the "Energy Conversion Box" I discovered that most all of the kids were experiencing the nonphysical world and were frightened by the experience. A student tells me that an Indian, whom no one else can see or hear, lives in her house and beats on a drum. Why is this happening? A deceased friend visits another in her room to pass along a message for her cousin. Am I crazy? A student writes that she can see the future and wonders if this ability is good or bad. A student describes weird dreams in which he's walking around the house while his body is still asleep in bed. What does it all mean?

Most teachers I've met would probably refer them to a school psychologist. If they could not accept the unreality of their experiences, they'd be shipped off somewhere and given strong medication. Their track records of violent and maladaptive behavior can justify all sorts of malevolent therapeutic approaches. Physical reality is harsh; nonphysical reality is confusing and frightening. How do they cope? Sadly, they kill each other. And sadly, the killing is spreading to places like Springfield, Oregon, and Fayetteville, Tennessee. Why do children kill each other? What are they trying to say? Do they have a message for us? Perhaps great souls are coming through with these young ones, asking us to rediscover basic truths, to search for the intelligence of the Divine Plan unfolding in and around us.

I've been lucky enough to sit up front and watch as binaural beats, masked by sounds of surf, relax kids' minds and unlock their hearts, youngsters calm and composed, full of their own inherent sweetness, dignity, and charm.

Few things change overnight. I can tell you that by the end of the year reading scores had improved. More importantly, however, a sense of connection had developed. A connection to each other, and a connection to something even larger than that. These young ones are demanding this connection with a most impassioned appeal.

What shall our offering be?

The Third Step: Diving In and Stepping Out

During my final two years of teaching I worked in agencies where I was not allowed to use Hemi-Sync in the classroom. With the training wheels removed, I discovered how far I'd come and how much I'd learned. I taught the curriculum less and less until finally I could not, with good conscience, accept a paycheck any longer from an institution that was pressing me to demolish the inherent beauty, courage, resourcefulness, and intelligence of these young ones. The gates on my heart had broken completely open, and I could do little more than bear witness to the miraculous unfolding of life before me. Without doubt, these kids were my guides, gently (and sometimes not so gently) nudging me toward the realization of who I really was: the eternal self-reflective lover embracing what can never be understood.

Into the unknown I go.

When Class Goes Really Well

You can sometimes pass my class
and hear voices loud
as the rapid ringing of bells, see a flurry
of hands like horse tails
whipping the air.

I move through the room, blazed
with golden light, like a torch, probing,
answering questions
with questions,
shrilled on by the sound of my students'
skirls. This is fine. Some say
true learning.
But when class goes really well
you can barely hear breath flexing.
It's as if we had slipped inside a tube
of deep round silence.
And you feel as you did when you were a child,
alone, looking out into freshly fallen snow
in the sweet hush of morning
eager to make the first fresh print in the field
with your own foot.

MEDICAL

A comprehensive survey of the various ways in which Hemi-Sync may be employed in medicine is provided by Dr. Brian Dailey. An open-minded physician and a practitioner of energy medicine, Dr. Dailey is concerned with the well-being of the whole person and incorporates a variety of therapies into his practice. He designed the Hemi-Sync *Chemotherapy Companion* exercise, which is proving to be of remarkable help to those undergoing this treatment.

A graphic account of undergoing major surgery is contributed by a New Zealander Marty Gerken. Despite not receiving total cooperation from the medical staff, he managed to make use of some of the exercises in the **Surgical Support** series with the result that he required only the minimum amount of anesthetic and no post-operative pain medication at all.

Carol Sabick, who lives in Spain, is both a Monroe trainer and a teacher of Reiki. She describes how Metamusic compositions provide strong support to the practice of Reiki, enabling practitioners to work more deeply and effectively. Finally in this chapter Helene Guttman recounts her experimental work with deaf people in which she discovered that by placing headphones at certain non-ear locations the benefits of Hemi-Sync could still be enjoyed.

Hemi-Sync in Medicine to Promote Patient Well-Being
Brian D. Dailey, M.D., FACEP, FACFE

Dr. Brian Dailey is an assistant professor in emergency medicine and clinical instructor in surgery at the University of Rochester School of Medicine and Dentistry, Rochester, New York. He is a long-time practitioner and teacher of energetic medicine. This includes Reiki therapy, Hemi-Sync, crystal therapy, and aromatherapy, which he incorporates into his practice with more traditional forms of medicine. Brian Dailey designed the *Chemotherapy Companion* exercise referred to in his article and is currently working on a similar exercise for radiotherapy.

As a physician trained in both traditional and energetic medicine, I have found Hemi-Sync to be an important part of the therapeutic regimen. Using Hemi-Sync in the hospital, the hospice, and in people's homes has benefited patients on a number of levels, including relaxation and stress reduction; pain reduction; help with cancer treatment; treating specific health issues such as hypertension, asthma, and stroke; as well as spiritual growth. This article will describe our experience using Hemi-Sync for patients, suggest techniques that healthcare practitioners may find useful in utilizing Hemi-Sync in their own practices, and suggest specific Hemi-Sync exercises for treating specific health issues.

Headphones vs. Speakers

With proper speaker positioning, one on each side of the head to maximize the stereo effect, both speakers and headphones will induce a frequency-following brain response. Initially, I prefer that patients listen with headphones, to maximize the Hemi-Sync effect. Headphones are useful in noisy environments, such as hospital settings, to block out extraneous noises like loudspeaker announcements, visitors, or room-mates. There is a learned response after listening to an exercise several times with headphones. Afterwards, patients will quickly get Hemi-Sync effects when hearing exercises over speakers, even when the speakers are not optimally placed.

Patients may prefer listening over speakers so they may dialogue during therapy. Be open and flexible to this possibility, as the dialogue may be transforming. In group settings, speakers allow all to partici-pate in the experience and enjoy the group energy.

Hemi-Sync Environment

Quiet! It is imperative to have quiet during a Hemi-Sync exercise, as hearing often becomes hyper-acute in expanded states of conscious-ness. Turn off the ringers of phones, and lower the volume on answer-ing machines! Turn off timers/chimes on wristwatches.

Remove anything that may cause interruptions. Make sure you have time to complete the session. Do not schedule sessions when you know you will be interrupted.

Bathroom. The last stop before any Hemi-Sync exercise is the bathroom. Always remind the patient to go. With profound relaxation, an insistent bladder may shorten the exercise. For pregnant patients, this is even more critical. I keep treatments short (less than 30 minutes) for those in late pregnancy.

Positioning. Most patients prefer to be supine, on their backs. Any position, including sitting, is acceptable, as long as it is comfortable. In late pregnancy, place Mom slightly on her left side to displace the uterus off the vena cava.

Comfort. As patients relax, blood vessels dilate, radiating heat, so the patient may begin to feel cool. A blanket covering will keep them warm. Place a pillow behind the head *and* knees, so that the knees are slightly flexed. Darken the room if possible. Eyeshades may be helpful. Loosen clothing; remove shoes, belts, and tight jewelry.

Aromatherapy. Scents (candles, incense, etc.) and essential oils can accentuate the Hemi-Sync experience. A drop of rose or jasmine oil massaged gently beneath the nose can be wonderful!

Crystals. Crystals can add greatly to the energy and experience of Hemi-Sync.

Sleep

One of the most frequent requests I receive is for "something to help me sleep." Night-shift workers average two hours less sleep per day than day-shift workers. I worked night shifts for 16 years in a busy hospital emergency department and learned that sleep difficulties are ubiquitous among the night staff. Hemi-Sync is a wonderful drug-free alternative.

Dan D., a physician assistant at our hospital, had been using *Sleeping through the Rain* with great success after experiencing earlier sleep difficulties. As the end of a busy night shift approached, he told me how much more rested he felt. I gave him a copy of *Super Sleep* to try. The following evening he approached me excitedly. "It worked, unbelievable! I decided to put it on, keep my eyes open, just to see how long I could stay awake. I went to bed at 9 A.M., and the last thing I remember, it was 9:05."

A personal favorite of mine is *Restorative Sleep*. I use the encoding signal that it teaches at bedtime, both to help induce sleep and to induce restorative healing while asleep.

Catnapper is a wonderfully quick "pick me up" and is useful for jet lag (listen in flight, or after). I use it during a roadside rest stop, when fatigued on long driving trips. The 30-minute time will not run the car battery down, it wakes me at the end, and I wake up feeling refreshed. (Just remember, never play any Hemi-Sync product while operating a vehicle.) *Catnapper* is a hit with tired new mothers who have put the baby down for an hour nap. Mom will wake up feeling more rested before the baby finishes its nap.

Another personal favorite is *Time Out for Sleep*. When sleep deprived, I simply add an extra track 6 to increase my REM sleep.

Remember, Hemi-Sync is a drug-free alternative for sleep!

Surgery

The **Surgical Support** series is a collection of six exercises to assist patients undergoing surgical procedures, injury, and illness. Several favorable research articles have been published, among the most recent a report in *Anesthesia*, vol. 54, no. 8, pp. 769–773, 1999: "Hemispheric Synchronization During Anesthesia: A Double Blind Randomized Trial Using Audiotapes for Intra-Operative Nociception Control." Patients using the tapes in this series required a quarter of the pain medications of the control groups during surgery. Experience has shown that patients require less pain medication post-operatively as well.

Sue F. used the **Surgical Support** series for her ovarian cancer surgery. "It worked wonderfully. The doctors were amazed by the speed of my recovery and how little pain I was experiencing afterwards. I have since lent it to friends to use, all of whom found it helpful."

Maura P. underwent a hysterectomy using this series. "I was wide awake in recovery, out of bed shortly thereafter, and experiencing very little pain. I did not need or use the patient-controlled anesthesia (a morphine pump that the patient can use to self-administer pain medication). I took one pain tablet because the nurse said I should, and just Tylenol after that." Her anesthesiologist, Dr. Alan Lanni, had participated in three other hysterectomy cases that day, prior to Maura's operation, and they had encountered difficulties with patient stability during surgery with the other three cases. He stated that, in contrast, her surgery went smoothly. He was surprised she was requiring no post-op pain medication. He commented, "I wonder if it was the tapes."

Pregnancy

Opening the Way consists of eight tapes for use during pregnancy, childbirth, and nursing. It will support Mom with emotional clearing, relaxation, and visualizing a healthy baby. It includes a tape for the father, or other support person, and a tape for "Contacting the Baby's Soul."

Jackie G. found **Opening the Way** very helpful with her second pregnancy. "It was really helpful with my labor; it distracted me from any pain or discomfort I was experiencing. I had a one-hour, 20-minute labor. I was relaxed and required no episiotomy or repair."

Stroke/Brain Injury

Support for Stroke Recovery is a four-tape collection designed to assist with healing after stroke, although I have used it for patients with traumatic brain injury as well. One of the tapes utilizes guided imagery to increase energy and healing, and ends with a restful sleep. As we spend one-third of our lives asleep, using this time to promote wellness is brilliantly creative. Another exercise has an encoding signal to assist new areas of the brain to take over the function from damaged areas. Loss of speech, with an intact mind, is one of the most frustrating experiences of life. These tapes attempt to harness the tremendous recuperative power of the mind as it assists new areas of the brain in the recovery of lost motor skills.

One caveat: If using this series with traumatically brain-injured patients, advise them that although the series refers to "stroke," the "wellness" aspects are the same for a traumatic injury, recovering function from new areas of the brain. I recommended this series to a physician who had a patient with a traumatic brain injury. He contacted me later to report that the patient was frightened that he had had a stroke. He had not advised the patient of this difference, so the patient was greatly relieved to find out the mechanisms were the same for recovery, and that he had not really had a stroke.

Relaxation and Hypnosis

Metamusic compositions can create relaxation states in the listener ranging from light to deep. There are many titles to choose from, but *Gaia, Higher, Inner Journey*, and *Sleeping through the Rain* are some of my patients' favorites. The deep delta frequencies in *Sleeping through the Rain* will induce deep relaxation and/or sleep, useful for energy work, massage therapy, or hypnosis. I always use Metamusic in the background during energy work with patients. It can also be soothing when played in the waiting room of a dental or oncology office, or prior to painful procedures. Gretchen G. is a lymphoma patient who likes to listen to Metamusic over headphones while waiting in her oncologist's office. After she listened to *Gaia*, her oncologist, Dr. John Phalen, commented on how relaxed she appeared. She explained, "It's the Metamusic!"

James Richard Hughes is a master therapist in hypnosis and neurolinguistic programming at the Chrysalis Foundation. He has used Metamusic as a background for therapy to assist patients in relaxing. The expanded awareness of Focus 12 states can be useful in hypnotherapy.

Hospice

Many people have come to understand that death is a natural part of life events, not something to be feared or psychologically avoided. This change in attitude helped to bring about the hospice movement. The purpose of hospice is to bring comfort, care, and support to the terminally ill and their families. Having worked with many terminally ill patients, I have been impressed by the way hospice can contribute to the dying process. Hospice may alleviate much of the patient's anxiety and discomfort and allow them to come to terms with and accept their mortality.

Hemi-Sync is an essential tool in my work with hospice patients and their families. We have found it useful for reducing anxiety and increasing relaxation, reducing pain and discomfort, as an aid in spiritual growth, addressing specific health problems, and learning about the dying process (e.g., the *Going Home* series).

Metamusic and Hospice: Both patient and family appreciate Metamusic. I have entered numerous homes and hospices to find Metamusic being played. It brings comfort, pain relief, and relaxation. I have been present at the bedside when patients have made their transition as Metamusic played in the background. I have watched agonal respirations become easy as I started the music. The fact that family members benefit is an added bonus.

Pain Control and Hospice: My experience has been that *patients are not afraid of dying, but are afraid of dying in pain.* Through care, support, and proper management, pain can be markedly decreased or eliminated altogether. This includes appropriate pain medication in adequate doses. Hemi-Sync has become an important tool in pain management. Metamusic, *Pain Control*, *Energy Walk*, and *De-Discomfort* have proven very useful. They frequently will allow for reduced doses of pain medication for the same amount of symptom relief.

Sleep and Hospice: Fatigue is common in hospice settings for the patient, family, and caregivers. *Sleeping through the Rain*, *Super Sleep*, and *Time Out for Sleep* are extremely helpful for rest at night. *Catnapper* is very helpful during the daytime when the patient may wish to spend more time awake with family and friends.

Those of my patients who have chosen to use **Going Home** have universally found it helpful. Barney P. said, "It has brought me so much comfort and spiritual growth." My experience has been that about a third of the patients that choose to use **Going Home** have family members who decide to participate in the process by using the support tapes. Robert W. and his wife, Hazel, felt it brought them much comfort as they shared the experience together.

Cancer Therapy

Hemi-Sync is wonderful adjunctive therapy to traditional forms of cancer therapy. The **Positive Immunity** Program, inspired by Jim Greene, is a collection of eight tapes to boost the natural immune system and promote well-being. It benefits patients with conditions which weaken their immune systems, such as cancer, AIDS, rheumatic disorders, lupus, etc. It is also helpful to healthy people who wish to maintain their health.

Susan S., a lymphoma patient, had a violent reaction to her first chemotherapy, experiencing nausea, vomiting, and a severe diffuse skin rash. Reducing the dose of the agent and giving multiple anti-allergy medications resulted in a less severe reaction the second treatment. It occurred to her to put her personal Resonant Energy Balloon (REBAL) in place for the third treatment, and she had no reaction to the third chemotherapy. Thereafter, she always used the REBAL technique before any of her cancer therapies, and her oncologist was able to resume the full regimen *without* anti-allergy medications. The REBAL is a technique taught in one of the series exercises. I ask all my cancer patients to consider using the **Positive Immunity** Program because so many others have felt it benefits them physically, mentally, emotionally, and spiritually.

Traditional chemotherapy targets the rapidly growing cancer cells. Unfortunately, many of the chemotherapy side effects are related to the effects on other rapidly reproducing cells in the gastrointestinal tract (nausea, vomiting, and diarrhea), blood (anemia, neutropenia), and hair follicles (hair loss). It was apparent that Metamusic would often improve and sometimes alleviate these unpleasant experiences.

Shortly after it was first introduced, my first copy of *Chemotherapy Companion* arrived just as I was en route to see Gretchen G. at her home. She had received chemotherapy for Hodgkin's lymphoma the day before and had been vomiting for 12 hours straight, the last four hours kneeling in front of the toilet. We put her into bed, slipped the headphones onto her head, and crossed our fingers. She awoke 45 minutes later and ate lunch, remarkably improved, her nausea and vomiting resolved.

One week later, I was asked to see Ardith F. in the oncology center at our hospital. She had a recurrence of bowel carcinoma and had had a difficult time with her first chemotherapy. During the 90-minute first infusion the nurse described three "explosive episodes of diarrhea" and multiple episodes of vomiting that persisted for ten days. This caused the cancellation of her second chemotherapy. Three weeks after the initial therapy, Ardith attempted the same regimen. We started *Chemotherapy Companion* 15 minutes before we started the same 90-minute infusion. She awoke halfway through her infusion, ate a sandwich, and said afterwards, "I feel better leaving than when I came in." Two oncology patients receiving chemotherapy on either side of her, and who had been present at her initial therapy, asked, "What was that, and where can we get one?" I gave each a copy of *Chemotherapy Companion*.

Radiation Companion is designed to assist patients undergoing radiation therapy. As the CD takes 45 minutes and most therapies are completed in 5–10 minutes, most patients find it useful to listen to it before or after therapies. The Hemi-Sync frequencies assist the patient into a relaxed, whole-brain healing state. Guided visualization helps the patient in improving anemia, well being, and reducing side effects such as skin changes in the treatment areas. Energetically, radiation produces "holes" in the energy field where treatment has taken place. The visualization is used of "using your hand to smooth out the field where treatment has taken place, like smoothing the frosting on a cake." Some patients visualize putting an imaginary dressing over the site and some like to move their hand over the treatment area as well. Never underestimate the power of the mind to induce healing.

The **Cancer Support** Series is a combination of four CDs: *Chemotherapy Companion, Radiation Companion, Journey through the T-Cells* and *Sleeping through the Rain. Journey through the T-Cells* helps to boost the immune system in attacking the cancer. *Sleeping through the Rain* is useful for relaxation, meditation, or sleep. The **Cancer Support** Series is a valuable adjunct to traditional forms of cancer therapy as it will not interfere with those treatments.

I am constantly amazed at the strength and resilience of my patients. Jackie G. was a 30-year-old mother in the 34th week of her second pregnancy, when a highly aggressive cancer was discovered in her right breast. She opted to delay delivery another two weeks, against her doctor's advice, to give her baby a better chance. I met with Jackie and gave her **Opening the Way** to help with her pregnancy, **Positive Immunity** Program to help with her cancer, **Surgical Support** series to help with her surgery, *Chemotherapy Companion* to help with her chemotherapy, and three Metamusic CDs to help her relax. I was concerned that the volume of tapes and CDs would overwhelm her. She used all of them with great effect over the next few weeks. Her delivery of Michael Anthony went smoothly. Her seven-hour surgery went well, requiring little pain medication, and she has been tolerating chemotherapy well. At the same time, she has been caring for a much-loved newborn! During a recent Reiki therapy session, she expressed, "This has been a challenging time for me, but the Hemi-Sync has made it that much easier. I really feel it is contributing to my wellness."

Whenever considering therapies for patients, one has to look at risks, benefits, and costs. Hemi-Sync has no known serious adverse effects, it's inexpensive, and it is reusable. It is easy to see why Hemi-Sync remains such an important therapeutic tool in my practice of medicine.

Support for Surgery
Marty Gerken

Marty Gerken was born in Timaru, New Zealand, and now lives in Christchurch on the South Island. He worked in the food industry at a micro laboratory and then as a chemist for a major brewery. Later he established his own business in the insurance industry. He presently works in sales for a plastics company. He attended the Gateway Voyage and four subsequent residential programs in Virginia. Marty has a great affection for the Hemi-Sync process and is a Hemi-Sync distributor in his beautiful South Pacific homeland.

Prior to my spinal surgery in 1999, Hemi-Sync had been a major part of my life during the previous four years. It played an important role through the emotional challenges and acceptance of the breakup of my first marriage, and then later during the decision-making process of selling my business. Then came the travel and the life-changing experience of attending TMI and graduating from the five residential programs, all within three and a half months. Upon my return to New Zealand, Hemi-Sync again played a significant role, as I was able to support my family during my father's terminal illness and his ultimate transition in 1998.

In August 1999, I utilized another of Hemi-Sync's many applications, the support of a totally new experience for me: spinal surgery. It was to be my first adult surgical experience. TMI has many personal testimonials in support of the successful use of Hemi-Sync during surgery. Mine is not exceptional, but I want to share my personal experience in the hope that it might help others to understand how power-ful Hemi-Sync really can be, even when things don't go as planned.

First of all, I must state that I'm the sort of person who would avoid surgery like the plague if there were some other way of dealing with a health issue. In this instance X-rays and CT scans all indicated a problem that just wasn't going to go away. I was referred to an ortho-pedic surgeon, who wasn't in a hurry to operate. After ten further days of pain and no improvement in my condition, I was admitted immedi-ately for a laminectomy discectomy procedure. It didn't give me a lot of time to get prepared, mentally or otherwise, for my first time in hospi-tal. But I did make sure I took the **Surgical Support** album to the hos-pital with me! My surgeon was neither for nor against the use of Hemi-Sync tapes during surgery. The following is what I experienced.

My admission was so quick that I couldn't have a private room. I ended up being admitted to a general orthopedic ward with nine other patients. With formalities such as questionnaires, interviews, and dis-cussions with a succession of nurses, the surgeon, and the anesthetist, I had little time to myself. I was unable to successfully make use of the *Pre-Op* tape for any length of time. Added to this was the interruption of other ward patients, who I'm sure in talking with me were just try-ing to put me at ease. The problem was that I had no time at all to get relaxed, as I would have liked. By the time I reached the surgical pre-op room, my pulse was at least 100 bpm. Blood pressure was fine, but I was very nervous. Even prior to receiving my anesthetic, I was not left alone to focus. So I just went with the experience. I put my *Intra-Op* tape into the cassette player ready for the operation, then waited. I declined the offer of a pre-op sedative. My prior experience with Hemi-Sync told me that my pulse rate would be fine once I began to listen to the tape uninterrupted during the surgical procedure.

My next recollection was waking up and hearing someone chang-ing the tape in my tape player. I was immediately aware of the oxygen mask over my face and realized I was in the recovery room. I recall com-menting that the *Recovery* tape should have been on as soon as I left the operating room. The attending recovery nurse said she thought that it was too dangerous! I have no idea why she considered it was in any way a danger. Perhaps she was referring to the cord of the headphones, the

111

possibility of choking or becoming entangled with the tubes I was hooked up with. She had made the decision to go against my wishes and not play the *Recovery* tape until I was conscious! I felt disappointed, since I knew this tape would have demonstrated a successful and very quick post-op return from the anesthetic effects for all to witness. Once I began to listen to the *Recovery* tape, I became fully alert in a matter of minutes.

The oxygen mask was removed, and I was soon enjoying an ice cube to soothe my throat after the irritation of the oxygen tube. Then a nurse entered the recovery room and asked if Mr.Gerken was out of surgery. I answered, "Yes, here I am." She then asked if I was able to take a phone call. "No worries, mate!" A concerned friend had called the hospital to find out when I would be having surgery and when he might be able to visit me. I was passed the receiver and was able to talk with him in a totally coherent manner, a fact which he later confirmed. It surprised him to find I had only minutes earlier regained consciousness after back surgery.

Next, I was offered morphine pain medication. To the nurse's surprise, I declined. I knew that I would be able to control the pain myself with the help of my tapes. The next surprise was one I had never considered. Having just had spinal surgery, I had assumed I would return to the hospital ward laid on my stomach. How wrong I was! I was asked to help the nurses as they rolled me onto my back, directly onto the incision, with the drain tube still in place. Ouch! That was how I stayed for the next eight hours or so. To say I didn't feel anything while being wheeled back to the ward would be a lie. I felt every bump, consciously aware of lying on the drain tube and the packing and bandages around my incision.

Back in the ward I was asked again if I wanted a shot of morphine. I declined but asked if the nurse could change my *Recovery* tape to the *Recuperation* tape. The ward was noisy with visitors, other patients, and nurses. I found it hard to relax and focus on my pain relief, but the tape allowed me to cope in spite of the distractions. I was continually checked by the nurses for my temperature, blood pressure, O_2, and pulse. I was repeatedly asked if I was ready for pain medication yet. The nurses were showing concern and told me that it was all right to feel pain and that I didn't have to be tough. I took it from the way they were treating me that they thought I was trying to be macho by not accepting the medication. I had endured worse pain than I was feeling at that time, and the tapes were helping me control it to a level that I was comfortable with. The pity was that all the interruptions I was getting were not allowing Hemi-Sync to be as effective as I knew it could be. It still worked for me, nonetheless.

That night, before lights-out, I was turned on my side to change my dressing and to check the drainage tube. I decided to try sleeping in that position and again declined medication for pain. I changed my tape to continuously play a personal favourite, *Sleeping through the Rain*. What a night it was going to be!

My night nurse was very attentive, and it seemed to me that every hour or so she shone a light into my eyes to see if I was asleep, awake, or needing pain medication. This woman was just like a very persistent salesman. She was hell-bent on making a sale of morphine to me that night, even if it meant I didn't get any sleep until she succeeded! I did finally ask her to help me turn onto my back again. While this was being done I must have grunted at the effort. She used that as an excuse to berate me for not accepting pain medication. It was rather frustrating to say the least.

Then at three in the morning she came by again. She must have assumed I was listening to loud rock music since she was talking to me so loudly that I was sure she would wake everyone in the ward. For this reason and this reason alone, I accepted a codeine tablet. I stress not for any pain that was in my back, but for the pain in the butt that she was! I learned very quickly, just like the guy in the bed next to me. If this nurse woke you for pain medication, you should just smile and say, "Yes, I'll have a codeine tablet, thanks." She would then leave you alone, and you could get some sleep.

This night nurse's ward activities actually helped to remind me of another very powerful healing tool that we each have at our disposal—laughter. Over the next three nights, this nurse made me laugh so hard that tears flowed from my eyes as I lay in witness to her nightly rounds.

The morning following surgery, I managed to eat breakfast with no feelings of nausea at all. My wound was dressed, the drain and saline drip were removed. After lunch, I stood and walked the length of the ward. I was slow and stiff, but the only ill effect was a little light-headedness. I'm told this is a rather common "anesthetic hangover." This occurred all within 24 hours of my operation.

I know very well that I had no need for any pain medication after this surgery, even though I had ended up with a four-inch incision instead of one inch, due to the fact that the procedure was a little more complicated than expected. The anesthetist later confirmed that my need for anesthesia was at the very lower end of normal dosage. Without controls to compare me to (any previous surgical procedures), he was unable to confirm that it was due to the tapes, as everyone is different. However, he did concede that they might have helped. I had previously discovered at age 22 that I do need large amounts of local anesthetic, when a tooth removal procedure required double doses of "painless" to make it really so!

I hope this is the only surgery I will ever need. I have always been one to look at the opportunities such things present, and this experience was no different. During my time in hospital I was able to spread the Hemi-Sync word to nurses and other patients, including a teacher who was currently working on the "Uses of Music in Special Education." All these contacts will lead to opportunities to share Hemi-Sync in New Zealand.

One very satisfying experience involved the patient in the bed next to mine. Peter was a 59-year-old farmer who had just undergone a knee replacement surgery. Due to his work, he was still expected to be very active, so his rehabilitation program was quite severe. For 36 hours after his surgery his new knee was continuously moved and flexed by a machine. That was fine, I guess, while he was still on morphine. After this first treatment it was usual for him to be placed back on this machine twice every day. During this therapy he was very uncomfortable, to say the least. Peter had not managed to get much sleep due to pain in the knee, as well as "The Pain" (the notorious night nurse). I suggested that he might enjoy listening to some nice music to help him sleep during the day, so he borrowed my tape player and *Sleeping through the Rain*. He really liked it, so I suggested that he should try it while he was on the knee-bending machine. He readily agreed. Peter borrowed my tape twice while on the "torture machine," as he called it. Both times when he returned the tape he commented how relaxed he had felt while listening. He was relaxed, all right—he snored! The nurses and I could not believe that he actually went to sleep while working out on that machine!

During my 1999 hospital experiences, Hemi-Sync yet again showed me how versatile and effective it is as a support tool for healing, even when the situation or circumstances are not ideal. But of course this isn't always an ideal world!

Hemi-Sync and Reiki
Carol Sabick

Carol Sabick, born in Buffalo, New York, has been living and working in Spain since 1964, when she first visited for a Junior Year Abroad program. Holding degrees in liberal arts, spanish law, international marketing, computer science, and energy medicine, she now dedicates her time exclusively to training both weekend and residential courses with The Monroe Institute and teaching Reiki healing. She is a member of the Board of Advisors and the Professional Division of TMI and founder of the Reiki Service Association. Her home now is in a small village on the Mediterranean, but her teaching takes her all over Spain and to the United States.

The word Reiki now forms part of modern vocabulary. A large percentage of people recognize Reiki as some form of healing, even if they aren't acquainted with any other aspects of its history, development, or use. So to start, a brief overview of this technique seems appropriate.

Reiki is a form of energy healing in which the practitioner passes energy, often referred to as unconditional love, to the recipient for what he/she most needs at the time. Reiki differs from some other forms of healing in that the practitioner does not use his own energy, but in effect channels or gathers universal energy into himself and passes it on to the recipient. This can be done by "laying on of hands" or by using a non-contact approach. Reiki, as with other healing methods, can also be effectively sent at a distance, as has been shown by several controlled studies.

Although in 1980 there were only 23 Reiki teachers, or "Masters," in the Western world, in the short time since then the practice and teaching of Reiki have mushroomed all over the world to include tens of thousands of people from every culture and walk of life. Many different Reiki schools have developed, all based essentially on the original teachings of Mikao Usui, who rediscovered this healing method at the end of the last century. Brought to America in the 1930s, the simplicity and power of Reiki have attracted many people who would not otherwise be inclined to delve into the healing arts.

My first acquaintance with Reiki was at the pilot Lifeline class at The Monroe Institute. Some of the participants were conducting a Reiki session for another participant who was not feeling well. I looked in and saw a fully clothed person lying peacefully on a table, while five or six others silently held their hands on or near his body. I thought to myself: "They probably think that this stuff really works!"

Little could I have imagined then that three years later I would not only be practicing and teaching Reiki, but also heading up a volunteer Reiki center, where every day 35 to 40 people sought healing or help with many diverse ailments. And daily, 25 to 30 Reiki practitioners volunteered their time and skills to help those in need. From this healing center came many experiences that I would like to comment on with regard to the use of Hemi-Sync technology together with Reiki healing energy, a dynamic duo.

As background music in our center, *Inner Journey* and *Sleeping through the Rain* were alternately and continuously playing. A receptionist received each visitor, who was shown to the waiting room after filling in a registration form and signing a release. When their turn came, the recipient was led to one of the five healing rooms. There they relaxed onto a massage table, and two to four practitioners transmitted Reiki healing energy in silence. Pillows which incorporated speakers were used to gently soothe the recipient with the surf sounds of *Soft and Still*. Each session was approximately a half hour long.

We found that the recipients who came to us for healing quickly entered a state of relaxation, even while in the waiting room, as they were immersed in the background music. They would comment that the good vibrations from the center had them feeling a lot better even as they walked in the door. When they reclined on the massage table to receive the Reiki energy, the soft surf sounds from the head-pillow speakers usually had them deeply relaxed or asleep in a few moments.

Research has shown that the delta state of deep sleep is when the body regenerates from daily stresses. The Hemi-Sync Focus 10 state used on these tapes incorporates delta signals, and it follows that the music alone permits the healing mechanisms of the body to become more active. Our experience shows that due to the relaxed state attained by Hemi-Sync, the healing energy of Reiki could be directed to purposes other than relaxation, and a more profound healing could be possible.

We had many remarkable healing results from diverse physical and emotional problems, some very serious such as different cancers, and others of lesser magnitude such as skin lesions healed in one session. One lady experienced a complete realignment of body weight, with the loss of 35 lbs. in a short period of time. She made no effort to change eating habits or diet. Her husband was so impressed that he took up Reiki also!

There were several interesting cases regarding hypertension and angina. One of the patients came after a bout of angina. He was taking five different pills to control pain and blood pressure. After the first session of Reiki and using Hemi-Sync tapes at home, he called the doctor because his blood pressure was very low. The doctor told him he could eliminate one of the medications. About a week later, he called again, because his blood pressure was again quite low. This time the doctor did not want to reduce medication over the phone and asked him to wait until his appointment two weeks later.

Due to the action of the four remaining medications and the Reiki/Hemi-Sync combo, he had to drink coffee every day to maintain a reasonable blood pressure. On his next visit, the doctor said: "I've seen a few others who were receiving this Reiki stuff at the same place as you, and they all eventually came off their medications completely. Could you ask them if they would accept a doctor as a patient?"

Many of the Reiki recipients borrowed or bought tapes to use as homework between healing sessions. Daily use of the tapes for a relaxing siesta encouraged the healing mechanisms of the body to stay active. Many also used tapes to recover proper sleep patterns, providing another nudge in the right direction.

Seeing these people on a continuing basis revealed some other benefits: an important change in perspective regarding life in general and especially their illness. Many began to see it as a path to getting in touch again with themselves and their families. Some even mentioned how thankful they were to have an illness that led them to Reiki/Hemi-Sync and eventually to a whole new understanding—a different overview, as Monroe would say. New priorities emerged as they contacted deeper levels of Self.

More balance in their lives seemed to be one of the benefits of the hemispheric synchronization facilitated by the Hemi-Sync tapes. Recipients commented on how their work relationships improved, their families were more united and spoke about their problems, and obsessions and feelings of neediness decreased. Others said that just the contact with so many caring people and so much loving energy had changed them forever. One I remember said: "I knew there were loving and good people in the world, but I never expected to find so many, so good, all together." Many claimed that coming into contact with the Reiki/Hemi-Sync combination was the most important thing that had ever happened to them in their whole lives.

The practitioners also benefited greatly from the experience and continued to come to the center for months or years, even those that lived a considerable distance away. Practitioners came from many backgrounds: housewives, businesspeople, an admiral in the navy, a college law professor, three secret-service policemen, students, one person who didn't know how to write. Their ages ranged from 18 to 89, men and women, sometimes whole families.

I recall one man would come to pick up his wife but refused to enter the building because he didn't approve of these "weird things." His daughter and son also became Reiki practitioners. Then one day, I found him among the students in a first-level class. He commented that after seeing the results over a year's time, he was very impressed how his family had changed. His wife was more understanding, his children were more loving, even his dog became nicer and didn't bark so much. He decided that only good things were coming from this center and he wanted to see if it would work for him too. The following year he was teaching Reiki.

The practitioners noted that with the music of *Inner Journey* and *Sleeping through the Rain*, they were able to get into deeper healing states also. It supported them to quickly enter into the silent meditative style of Reiki that we used. "Cool-down time" was reduced. They indicated that the intensity of the Reiki energy that they were able to channel was much greater. Their hands were hotter, vibrating, or felt more tingly.

Twice, to spread the good news of the dynamic duo, we rented a stand at a large ecological exposition. Six garden chairs substituted for massage tables. Each was equipped with headphones where our subjects listened to ten minutes of *Inner Journey* while receiving Reiki energy from a practitioner who stood behind the chair. As word got around, a long line of people formed. I think some just wanted to sit down somewhere and rest their swelling feet after hours of wandering through the exhibition halls laden with exciting things they had acquired. Our sessions were free—another powerful incentive! Others stated that they came because they felt a loving energy and peace flowing from our stand, and they wanted to experience it firsthand.

Amid the loud ambient music, announcements, and general clatter, the calming music emanating from the headphones provided a special kind of oasis—far from the madding crowd, though right in the middle of it. Recipients relaxed, and quite a few even fell asleep during their ten-minute session. Several of the most extraordinary cases were children whose mothers claimed they were hyperactive. In one case, the mother became very concerned. She had never seen her nine-year-old so relaxed, even when he was asleep. She was convinced we had hypnotized him or performed some other magic. The child, very happy to feel so calm, was reluctant to leave the chair, and it wasn't until the mother received a session herself that she could understand what a gift it was for both. She left determined to continue the experience, purchasing several Hemi-Sync tapes for home use and planning to learn Reiki herself.

We wondered if these benefits could reach into the community. To explore the possibility a group of practitioners met weekly to do distant healing and special projects. Accompanied by Metamusic, we sat in a circle to offer Reiki to many different personal situations and health problems. At the time the unemployment in our small city was severe—somewhere around 29 percent according to statistics—and summer was coming, which would make things worse. We decided to offer Reiki to the job situation for ten minutes every week. We started at the beginning of June. Much to our surprise, at the end of July, a short article in the local paper announced that for the first time, employment had increased during the month of July by 10 percent. Maybe our dynamic trio—Reiki, Hemi-Sync, and us—had something to do with it!

All this happened between 1994 and 2000. In the beginning I taught Reiki, and now most of my time is spent facilitating Hemi-Sync programs. Many of my participants are finding the reverse: They want to study Reiki and use unconditional love as a complement to their inner exploration work with the Monroe technology.

It seems that Reiki and Hemi-Sync form a perfect duo from whatever angle you approach it!

Preparing to Use Binaural Beat Sounds with Deaf Clients

Helene N. Guttman, Ph.D.

Helene N. Guttman, Ph.D., is currently president of HNG Associates/ Sound Balance, Bethesda, M.D., where she has a private transpersonal counseling practice and researches states of awareness (see www.soundbalance.net). Previously she was a professor in medical and graduate schools where she researched widely, published in several multidisciplinary areas, and held various administrative appointments. More recently, Helene held administrative positions in federal science agencies, including the National Institutes of Heath, the U.S. Environmental Protection Agency, and the U.S. Department of Agriculture, where she was associate director of a human nutrition research center.

People with normal hearing, as well as those who are profoundly deaf, sense sound vibrations. These sensations do not always "enter" via the ears. How can we utilize this ability so that profoundly deaf individuals can utilize binaural beat audio tapes, such as The Monroe Institute's Hemi-Sync, to stimulate beneficial changes in states of awareness readily enjoyed by individuals with normal hearing? Some clues are in the way profoundly deaf individuals sense sound vibration.

An example of a profoundly deaf person is the internationally famous musician Evelyn Glennie, the percussionist who performs barefooted (so that she can sense her own instruments and those of the rest of the accompanying orchestra). Is this a special trait reserved for gifted, trained musicians? No!

For example—in July 2002 a major international festival called Deafway II was held in Washington, D.C., at Gallaudet University, the premier educational institution for the deaf and hard of hearing. Many people with normal hearing were surprised to learn that the program included dancing to rock bands—whose beats were easily followed by the deaf dancers through the vibrations of the music coursing up from their feet through their bodies. Deaf non-dancers clustered around loudspeakers, with their hands on the speakers, and swayed to the beat coursing through their bodies from their hands.

So, must deaf individuals either place their feet or hands on loud-speakers to enjoy the benefits of Hemi-Sync? As will be shown, all people, hearing or deaf, sense sound via several routes, the ears being just one.

The objective of this study was to locate *convenient and comfortable* placements for inexpensive, readily available headphones on deaf individuals so that the beneficial effects of using Hemi-Sync to move into different states of consciousness and achieve the benefits enjoyed by hearing individuals (e.g., relaxation, pain control, etc.) could be realized. Since Hemi-Sync-induced changes in states of awareness are usually accompanied by synchrony between the left and right sides of the brain at the same frequency, these electrophysiological changes were used to determine the best non-ear placements for headphones.

In this study, hearing individuals were the subjects. Using a 16-channel EEG ("brain mapper"), brain responses (EEGs) were measured while sound was delivered through headphones placed over the ears and at different head locations. The purpose of the "brain mapper" was to ascertain whether there were specific electrophysiological responses to the tape being played that were independent of the anecdotal reports of the individual being tested. When non-ear locations were tested, subjects were fitted with ear plugs to prevent sound sensation via the ears.

Tapes used included the meditation music tape *Inner Journey* with Hemi-Sync, the *Inner Journey* tape without Hemi-Sync, and the Hemi-Sync tape *Touring the Interstate* from the **Going Home** series.

Both subjects and operator were unaware of which tapes were being played. Therefore, subjects were not given "clues" to what they might experience during the playing of the tapes. During playing of a tape, the operator viewed the computer screen that showed the "brain map."

Results showed that left-right brain synchrony could be achieved with headphones placed at several non-ear locations. The best locations—judged both for comfort and ease in keeping headphones in place—were approximately one inch above, and slightly behind, each ear. In addition, subjects reported relaxation and "feeling of lightness" with both versions of *Inner Journey*.

Anecdotal reports of subjects fitted with headphones at non-ear locations during the playing of *Touring the Interstate* were particularly interesting because although they received no clues as to what to expect (either from the operator or from the vocalization of the tape) they replicated the essence of reports by individuals who listened to the instructions on the tape and also read the instructions that accompanied the tape series *(Going Home)*. These reports included moving through different colors (that represented different focus levels) and then visualizing or hearing deceased relatives or "non-earthly beings."

Subsequent to the completion of this series of experiments, an American Sign Language (ASL) translator, who also is a hypnotherapist, suggested still another placement of headphones that might be more comfortable to subjects. This placement, roughly over the carotid (neck) arteries, can be perceived by first feeling the pulsation of the arteries and placing the headphones over those pulsations. Using the *Touring the Interstate* tape, a client generally replicated the same report as with headphones located over non-ear, head locations. Proof that this was indeed due to the Hemi-Sync sounds delivered through the nerve close to the carotid arteries came when, inadvertently, the headphones slipped from their placement. The subject (an experienced Hemi-Sync user) then reported that the "experience" was ending and that she was returning to her usual conscious state.

As a result of this study with control subjects, I am in the process of including various Hemi-Sync-embedded tapes with deaf clients in my transpersonal counseling practice, and I encourage others to do so, too.

THE MIND: PSYCHIATRY AND PSYCHOTHERAPY

The Monroe audio technology is proving increasingly helpful in psychiatry and psychotherapy. Dr. Jonathan Holt has had extensive experience in psychiatry and reports on his use of Hemi-Sync when working in consultation-liaison psychiatry at a hospital in Albany, New York. He describes five cases, three of them from a hospice unit where patients in their final days listened to tapes from the *Going Home* series that appeared to ease their transition.

Dr. Gary Chaikin, currently a director of psychiatric education, discusses the experiences of both therapist and client when working with a combination of psychotherapy and Hemi-Sync. In his second paper he develops his concept of healing of the Self, with Hemi-Sync as the essential element in the practice.

Nora Rosen, a personal development trainer based in Argentina, focuses on what she describes as the "Inner Therapist," finding that Hemi-Sync enabled her to communicate with the inner therapist within her clients. In contrast, two highly experienced psychologists, Dr. John Milligan and Dr. Ray Waldkoetter, report on a study using six Hemi-Sync tapes with military patients suffering from depression as a result of alcohol dependency. Lastly, Patricia Martin, a graduate of the Paris medical faculty, gives an account of an experience of one of her clients while listening to the Metamusic composition *Inner Journey*.

Hemi-Sync in My Medical Psychiatric Practice
Jonathan H. Holt, M.D.

Jonathan H. Holt graduated from Yale University in 1980 and received Yale's Lidz Prize in psychiatry. Jon also did his residency at Yale and completed a fellowship in consultation-liaison psychiatry (medical psychiatry) at Mt. Sinai Medical Center in New York. He was on the clinical faculty at Albany Medical College and was on staff as consultation-liaison psychiatrist at St. Peter's Hospital in Albany, New York. In 2001 he accepted a position with SUNY as Associate Professor of Clinical Psychiatry doing consultation-liaison psychiatry at the Buffalo Hospitals. Jon is a third-level Reiki practitioner and a practitioner of therapeutic touch and other subtle-energy methods. He also utilizes eye movement desensitization reprocessing (EMDR), thought field therapy (TFT), and EEG and peripheral biofeedback. He has been a member of The Monroe Institute Professional Division since 1996.

An interest in exploring consciousness long predated my psychiatry career and was partly responsible for my choice of profession. I decided on an eclectic training program at Yale University and subspecialized in consultation-liaison psychiatry, sometimes known as medical psychiatry. In that subspecialty, one consults with patients under treatment for various medical problems about their coexisting psychological problems and psychiatric disorders. During my tenure as program director of consultation-liaison psychiatry at the Veterans Administration Medical Center in Albany, New York, I joined the

Professional Division of The Monroe Institute and started to integrate Hemi-Sync into my psychiatry practice.

When shrinking funding resulted in organizational difficulties, I left the Veterans Administration and affiliated with two private-practice groups. This allowed me to specialize in outpatient medical psychiatry and conduct a general psychiatric outpatient practice as well. I hoped to combine standard psychiatry techniques, e.g., psychopharmacology and generic psychotherapy, with less traditional therapies: Hemi-Sync, EMDR (eye movement desensitization reprocessing), TFT (thought field therapy), peripheral and EEG biofeedback, subtle-energy treatments, psycho-spirituality, and transpersonal psychiatry. After a year and a half of private practice, I returned to consultation-liaison psychiatry, first at St. Peter's Hospital in Albany, and now at SUNY, Buffalo. The work referred to in this article took place at St. Peter's Hospital and opened up two somewhat different areas of "play."

In my hospital consultation work I can be called in to evaluate any patient admitted. These patients may be under the care of any internal medicine subspecialty: surgery, obstetrics and gynecology, neurology, rehabilitation medicine, hospice, or the substance-abuse detoxification unit. Since there is no inpatient psychiatry unit in the hospital, all patients requiring concomitant medical and psychiatric care must be treated on one of the medical units. Once their medical conditions are stabilized, they are transferred to psychiatric hospitals if inpatient psychiatric treatment is indicated. Patients requiring, or to be more accurate, accepting of or eligible for residential substance-abuse rehabilitation programs are transferred elsewhere. The patient's personal physician, also termed the attending physician, is the primary initiator of psychiatry consults. Prompting by the nursing or social work staff often plays a part in the physician's decision. Occasionally, patients will request consultation themselves. Thus, urgent psychiatric conditions or perceptions of a problem that would benefit from psychiatric care determine which cases I will see.

In almost every instance involving agitation, anxiety, or depression, I offer Hemi-Sync tapes. My two standbys are *Surf* and *Cloudscapes,* which offer a gentle, neutral background. A few people request tapes with verbal guidance. In such cases, *Guide to Serenity* and *Deep 10 Relaxation* have been very useful. *Pain Control* obviously has good hospital applicability.

Turnaround time in hospitals is generally quick nowadays. However, the readmission rate is climbing rapidly. Speedy turnover means limited feedback. This scenario is particularly true in the detoxification unit. Unless patients manifest severe withdrawal, they are often discharged within 23 hours. The more seriously incapacitated are usually discharged shortly after they become clear enough to process what I'm saying. In those circumstances I'm launching my assistance out into the void, a twenty-first-century version of casting bread upon the waters. Despite these sub-optimal conditions, I still try to discuss psycho-spirituality with most of my detoxification consults and offer Hemi-Sync tapes where and when they are likely to be accepted. My negotiations with the substance-abuse treatment department have focused on expanding the availability of Hemi-Sync and other complementary modalities.

On rare occasions, I receive feedback from hospital units that experience rapid patient turnaround. The first clinical case is a good example.

Case 1: Surgery and Gastrointestinal (GI)

An 18-year-old woman with a family history of cholelithiasis (gallstones) went to her college infirmary with acute upper abdominal pain and fever. She was examined, sent home, and received further diagnostic studies. She was diagnosed with cholelithiasis, so an endoscopic retrograde cholangio-pancreatography (ERCP) was performed to remove the stones. A cholecystectomy was planned but was postponed because the ERCP had induced pancreatitis. I gave her the *Pain Control* and *Surf* tapes with directions for using them, plus some positive imagery exercises. In addition, I performed subtle energy healing (combining techniques from Reiki, therapeutic touch, Barbara Brennan, and the Dolphin Energy Club). The patient and her mother were also instructed in a simple Huna-based healing exercise. The patient was discharged the next day, and the cholecystectomy was scheduled for the following week. She later wrote me a letter saying that the techniques were effective for both the pancreatitis and the subsequent surgery and recovery.

Case 2: Rehabilitation Medicine

Mrs. A., a 70-year-old widow, was first hospitalized in December 1999 after an overdose of sleeping medication. I performed her psychiatric evaluation in the intensive care unit. Upon stabilization, she was transferred to a nearby psychiatric hospital. In addition to depression and suicide attempts, Mrs. A. had abused pain medication for some time, which had resulted in a chronic organic brain syndrome (OBS). After being weaned from the analgesics and anti-anxiety medications and cleared from her OBS, she had spinal surgery and then was transferred to rehabilitation. Depression, anxiety, and persistent GI (gastrointestinal) symptoms complicated her recovery. Antidepressants helped with her depression, but her anxiety persisted. There was a suspicion that the GI symptoms were psychosomatic. The detrimental effect of past substance abuse on her cognition ruled out conventional anti-anxiety medication. I prescribed *Surf* and *Guide to Serenity*. The patient played the tapes for several hours at a time and reported feeling much calmer while listening. She had some return of anxiety afterward. With repeated playing of the tapes, her general anxiety level improved markedly from her pre-treatment state. Her physical and occupational therapy performance also improved. The GI symptoms did not change in response to the tapes, indicating the strong possibility of a non-psychosomatic component. The patient was discharged after a week and a half.

Two settings maximize my chances for more extended interaction and better feedback: the medical rehabilitation unit and the hospice unit. Both units screen referrals from the rest of the hospital and from outside sources and are technically separate from other inpatient treatments. Stays in the rehabilitation unit tend to be shorter than in the hospice unit. Rehabilitation receives orthopedic patients, cardiac and cardiac surgery patients, and some neurological patients dealing with conditions like post-stroke, multiple sclerosis, and amyotrophic lateral sclerosis.

Case 3: Hospice

An 80-year-old widow, Mrs. G., had lost her husband to cancer seven months before admission. She had multiple medical problems, and an occult malignancy was suspected. She had been hospitalized due to acute shortness of breath and was found to have a pleural effusion. As her condition worsened, a pulmonary embolism was feared. Mrs. G. was anxious and depressed. After an extensive interview, I mentioned the possibility of using Hemi-Sync tapes for relaxation, as well as the *Going Home* series. We talked about her fear of dying and her uncertain beliefs about death and the afterlife. As I described the series, *Going Home* (a collaboration between The Monroe Institute, Professor Charles Tart, and Dr. Elisabeth Kübler-Ross), and related topics like near-death experiences (NDEs), Mrs. G. remembered a crucial piece of information. Many decades earlier, complications during labor and the delivery of her second child had caused cardiac arrest. Mrs. G. then had an NDE that included an out-of-body component and a visit "in the light." Listening to her story gave me an opportunity to support that memory and suggest that she return in her mind to the sensations of the NDE, while listening to *Cloudscapes*. Mrs. G. passed on peacefully the next day.

The Hospice Inn, St. Peter's inpatient hospice setting, has been the most receptive to complementary interventions. It is also the inpatient unit with the longest stays.

Case 4: Hospice

Mrs. K., a 54-year-old woman with advanced breast cancer, was admitted to the Hospice Inn from the home hospice program. She had completed a significant number of life tasks and repeatedly told hospice staff that she was ready to go. She soon lapsed into a light coma but had persisted for several weeks in more or less the same state. Two visitors were present as we reviewed her case in a team meeting. One of them was a freelance writer doing an article on hospice for a local newspaper; the other was a representative of the hospital's public relations department. I raised the question of unfinished business and the possibility that Mrs. K. was being held back by some fear-based belief. The public relations representative wondered why I wanted to rush her if she wasn't suffering. I replied that I had no preference about her timing, but what if she was suffering quietly with her fear? After a brief explanation of *Going Home*, the freelance writer volunteered that her grandmother had experienced an NDE. The nursing coordinator requested suggestions, and I offered one of the later *Going Home* tapes. The nurse coordinator called me later that same day to say that she had played *Homecoming* for the patient. Mrs. K.'s breathing had quieted, and, by the end of the tape, she had peacefully expired.

Case 5: Hospice

Mrs. L., a 58-year-old mother with grown children, had a diagnosis of advanced lung cancer when she was transferred from home hospice. She was in considerable pain and had been admitted in order to optimize pain management. It was soon clear that Mrs. L. and her family would need the Hospice Inn for an extended period. Mrs. L. was a practicing Catholic and a former nurse. She was also terrified of losing control. Several weeks elapsed before her family permitted the hospice team to request a psychiatric consult. On interviewing Mrs. L. and her family members, it became clear that she had clinical depression and intermittent delirium with paranoia. I suggested a mild antidepressant and a small amount of anti-psychotic medication. The latter is fast acting and was particularly helpful. The success of that intervention led the patient, the family, and the personal physician to become more accepting of my involvement.

Mrs. L. had a complex and ambivalent attitude toward complementary therapy and spiritual issues. On the one hand, she accepted Reiki and therapeutic touch from friends and caregivers. On the other hand, she focused on medication as the key to her treatment. She described herself as religious, yet when I asked her about her afterlife beliefs, she admitted to being very unsure and scared. I played several of the later *Going Home* tapes and performed a mixture of subtle energy techniques as she listened. During that process, I perceived an internal component of the self in the process of clearing and readying for transition. However, residual parts and energies were still entangled. I left the **Going Home** tapes with Mrs. L.'s family, who eagerly welcomed them. Her husband feared that she was holding on for the anniversary of her diagnosis, a date that was more than a month away, and thus faced the prospect of much additional suffering. The day after the healing session, the patient remained unconscious while the tapes played. The next day, Mrs. L. had some periods of wakefulness and anxiety, but she passed peacefully away early that evening with her family in attendance.

These and similar experiences inspire me to work and hope for more complete integration of psychiatric and psychological services into the hospital system. Both patients and their caregivers stand to benefit from a partnership between standard interventions and complementary resources.

Enhanced Intuitive Psychotherapy
Gary D. Chaikin, M.D.

Dr. Gary Chaikin is a 1982 graduate of Emory University School of Medicine in Atlanta, Georgia. He completed a psychiatric residency in the U.S. Air Force at Wilford Hall Medical Center, Texas, in 1986. Gary is currently employed at Gunderson Lutheran Medical Center, La Crosse, Wisconsin, as director of psychiatric education. He is an associate professor at the University of Wisconsin, La Crosse. Gary has a special interest in the application of integral psychology and has recently begun to incorporate altered states of consciousness into a biopsychosocial model.

I have often wondered what it would be like if I could do psychotherapy by getting into my clients' heads. Like most therapists, I have had to settle for their verbal and nonverbal communications. But is this enough when working with those who come to us with spiritual issues? I glimpsed an answer to my questions during a presentation by Dominique De Backer at The Monroe Institute Professional Seminar in March 2000. Mme. De Backer took us inside her consulting room for a look at clinical cases in which she used Hemi-Sync to enter certain altered states with her clients. The depth, rate, and intensity of treatment were accelerated, and apparent spiritual breakthroughs occurred.

For some time I've been developing a clinical model for working with clients at different levels of awareness. During this period I came across the work of Ken Wilber, whose theories concerning the

Spectrum of Consciousness closely paralleled my own clinical principles. The majority of my clients have come into treatment with issues at what I characterize as the moral level. Therapy is oriented toward growth and stabilization in awareness at what may be termed the ethical level. However, as treatment draws to an end, or sometimes even at the beginning, deeper spiritual concerns come to the forefront. Psychotherapists are usually not taught to work at the spiritual level. This compounds the client's difficulty in accessing this deeper buried and unacknowledged core material. How are we to get at this level of awareness?

The Spectrum of Consciousness, Ken Wilber's theory of the evolution of human awareness, is based on the classic Perennial Philosophy. Its central premise is that consciousness evolves in a holoarchy, with the higher/deeper levels transcending and including the lower/superficial levels. Wilber defined these levels as progressing from Pre-conventional to Conventional to Post-conventional, and ultimately to Trans-conventional. My clinical model, also based on the Spectrum of Consciousness, is a holoarchy proceeding from Narcissistic to Moral, to Ethical, and to Spiritual. Reality is constructed through the lens of self in Narcissism, right and wrong in Morality, what is best in Ethics, and soul in Spirituality.

Reading Joseph McMoneagle's book *Mind Trek* contributed to the resolution of the question of how to reach those deeper levels. McMoneagle claims it is possible to target politically important people and remote-view their thoughts, feelings, and attitudes. If his natural ability and training enabled him to do so, why couldn't I develop a similar capacity? After all, my patients have often accused me of "reading their minds"! McMoneagle states that the presence of a protocol to eliminate front-loading (providing information in advance) differentiates remote viewing from psychic functioning. In contrast, successful psychotherapy depends on front-loading the present therapeutic context with everything that has preceded it in treatment. Therefore, what I was going to do could not be characterized as therapeutic remote viewing. As empathy is to emotion and as understanding is to thought, so intuition is to spirit. I was going to attempt enhanced intuitive psychotherapy.

Eriksonian hypnosis taught me a principle that became very important at this juncture: In the course of hypnosis, the best trance inductions and guidance occur when both the therapist and the subject are in an altered state of consciousness. What better way to achieve that objective than by using Hemi-Sync and sharing the same Focus level? Each spiritual tradition has its unique technology. Shamans since antiquity have utilized drums, plants, and fetishes; modern healers have computers, compact discs, and Hemi-Sync.

The candidates I selected to work with using a combination of psychotherapy and Hemi-Sync were drawn from two groups: those who had reached and could maintain an ethical level of awareness as a result of our prior work, and those just beginning therapy who still responded primarily from a moral level of awareness. The equipment was set up in a quiet, comfortable, distraction-free environment. A split-out line from the sound equipment powered our open-air headphones, which allowed us to hear each other clearly. I controlled the volume and selected Hemi-Sync material to suit the treatment task.

The first point to determine is whether the therapist or the Hemi-Sync recording will guide the work. When the therapist is directing, nonverbal material such as *Transcendence* or *Remembrance* is employed. For Hemi-Sync-guided sessions, the **Gateway Experience** and album sets such as **Positive Immunity, Opening the Heart, Going Home,** or **Human Plus** titles are used. Throughout the exercise the therapist maintains ever-hovering attention—that is to say, open to the experience, actively listening, postponing assignment of meaning. The patient learns to achieve and sustain a Focus state, find a "kind and wise" spiritual guide, receive three messages from the Universe, or recapitulate a memory. The practitioner mentally files symbols and imagery encountered during the process for later interpretative use. As the end of the exercise approaches, the client is assured that he or she will remember and understand only what the conscious mind can handle. It is also suggested that feelings of relaxation will carry over into the rest of the day.

When both therapist and client are alert in C1 (everyday consciousness), the headphones are removed, the room is illuminated, and the client is asked to talk about his or her experience of the exercise.

The therapist writes down any intuitive metaphors. Therapy then proceeds based on the therapist's psychodynamic model of choice, e.g., Freudian, Jungian, or Transpersonal. With enhanced intuitive psychotherapy there is a significant addition: The therapist's metaphors are introduced into the process. The patient free-associates to those images or uses an instrument such as Arrien's Preferential Shapes Test. This is a cross-culturally validated test using archetypal symbols (spiral, circle, square, triangle, cross) which have universal meanings. The patient's ranking of the shapes from one to five gives deep insight into the unconscious via the language of images rather than words. It is important to avoid literalization during interpretation because both the client's and the therapist's productions in the Hemi-Sync ambience are from unconscious sources and obey the rules of dream psychology. I prefer to use Wilmer's Jungian dream analysis, in which the client relates the experience twice and then free-associates to significant elements. Ultimate meaning rests with the subject, and the therapist stays alert for verbal or behavioral cues from the client that confirm the analytical interpretation. A typical session runs approximately 70 minutes and includes an intake interview, 30 to 40 minutes of Hemi-Sync, and a post-session discussion. Based on the session, further experiential "homework" is assigned utilizing Hemi-Sync to extend awareness.

The following case studies demonstrate the possibilities for enhancing the psychotherapeutic process.

Case 1. S.R.

This 40-year-old woman had had spinal muscular atrophy for more than 14 years. She was in a wheelchair and suffered from significant depression. Antidepressants had been prescribed, and the patient had been seen in psychotherapy every other week for about 11 months, in order to work on transforming her awareness from the moral to the ethical level. She used the *Positive Immunity* series at home for several months in hope of engaging her T-cells to repair nervous-system damage. Failure to progress led her to abandon the program, and sessions using enhanced intuitive psychotherapy were initiated. In one session, hypnotic induction was used to initiate an altered state of consciousness. Using the system as presented in the **Positive Immunity** program, hypnotic induction progressed from C1 through Focus 10, 12, and finally to Focus 15. Once in Focus 15, classic guided imagery of a meadow was introduced with the intention of contacting an inner guide. While both participants were experiencing Focus 15, the therapist—remaining open to intuitions from the patient—visualized a coil or spiral and an arch. Once beforehand he had interpreted the arch as a mountain in an experience with another patient. Upon returning to C1, the client was asked to free-associate to those elements. The spiral reminded her of the spring on a door. She then began to cry and spoke of a place in Heber Springs, Arkansas, that she had gone to at age 17. S.R. had been dating then and could "do things that I can't do now, such as climb to the top of Sugar Mountain with a young man." The session was a breakthrough, for this patient had never been willing to discuss her life prior to her illness.

Case 2. R.J.

A 30-year-old female physician's assistant student, divorced, with a seven-year-old child, was being treated for depression. She was going to school out of state and dating a young man back home, with the difficulties attendant on a long-distance relationship. In this meeting the therapist decided to use *Flying Free*, instead of the exercise previously planned. At the point where the listener flies with Robert Monroe, the therapist got an image of the client flying hand in hand with a woman who was blond like herself. He wondered if this was her sister, and "heard" the response, "No, my sister does not have blond hair." Back in C1, he asked, "How was your experience?" She replied, "Relaxing," and described clouds and a rainbow. She then recalled becoming angry at the instruction to fly alone. "I didn't want to fly by myself," she said.

The therapist then asked if she had a sister. "Yes," she replied. "Two years younger and she's a redhead." When she was told of the therapist's images, she responded, "That would be my best friend since first grade. She's blond. I was flying with her during the exercise because I did not want to be alone. I share all my spiritual experiences with her." She was asked why she did not want to be alone and replied that it was depressing to her. She added that she was also afraid to die alone. Questioned about her belief as to what happens after death, she replied, "You rejoin people from the past, maybe. I feel I don't deserve that."

R.J. was assigned homework with *Release and Recharge*, during which she was to remember times when she felt alone. Work with *Free Flow 10* was initiated to find an inner guide that could help deal with R.J.'s inner loneliness. This patient had never talked about her loneliness or spiritual beliefs until the therapist's intuitive insight created an opening for her to do so.

Case 3. G.V.

A 51-year-old woman, with insulin-dependent diabetes and a history of stroke that caused a mild decrease in concentration and vision, was originally seen for depression due to job stress. She was on antidepressants and underwent therapy with the goal of elevating her level of awareness from the moral to the ethical level. Achieving this goal resolved her depression and led to significant improvement at work. The client then expressed a desire to explore a spiritual path, which she had experienced after her stroke and from which she now felt disconnected because of the work situation. G.V. was loaned the *Discovery* and *Threshold* albums from the **Gateway Experience**. She felt that these exercises helped her "reconnect with God," although she was still unable to bring compassion into relationships at work and held onto resentment for "what they did to her."

We began by discussing the boss's favoritism toward another female employee. The client wanted to detach from what she saw as the unfairness of the situation. Using *Free Flow 12*, therapist and client entered Focus 12. The therapist visualized himself floating in front of the patient; then he opened her eyes and began looking out from her point of view. He saw an image of chickens, then a farm with a red barn. A question flashed into his mind: "Who was the favorite in G.V.'s family while she was growing up?" He speculated that it might have been her brother because of the rural environment. When he later asked, "How was your experience?" G.V. replied, "Okay, but my eyes wanted to move; they wanted to open." To the question, "Who was the favorite child in your family?" she replied that her older sister was her mother's favorite after they left the farm. She added that she loved the farm and had lived there until she was five. It transpired that her mother had raised chickens and that the patient had became the father's favorite after the family relocated. This led to a very constructive conversation regarding G.V.'s relationship to her mother and its association to the current scenario at work. Afterwards, G.V. was able to develop compassion for her coworkers and felt she had progressed further along her spiritual path.

Case 4. C. J.

This 40-year-old man with obsessive-compulsive traits and chronic mild depression works in the medical field. Another therapist referred him for Hemi-Sync-enhanced psychotherapy. In his third session, while using the exercise *Advanced Focus 10*, the therapist received images of Bryce Canyon, which he had visited many years before. Back in C1, the patient was asked if he had ever been to Bryce Canyon. He answered, "No," with a smile, and said, "I was just talking to one of my patients about Bryce Canyon. I'm going there when I retire." (This is an event far into the future.) The therapist commented, "When you're able to relax?" with the tacit meaning, "What are you waiting for?" C. J. replied, "Yes," with an overtone of "aha!" From that point on, he has been happier, improvements are continuing within his marriage and family life, and he no longer brings up the past. He just wants to experience more Hemi-Sync. The therapist hadn't thought of Bryce Canyon in years.

Discussion

Do we therapists actually get inside our patients' heads or is this just an interesting metaphor? The answer will depend on the theoretical model employed to filter the information, and on one's own level of awareness. Ken Wilber and other philosophers maintain that consciousness is an evolving process. If consciousness evolves, then therapeutic techniques must keep pace in order to serve clients' needs. By combining natural talent and learning with practice, we can develop the skill of intuiting or knowing information about our patients. This is information not ordinarily available to us which we can utilize in the therapeutic care of our patients. The source of such presentiments may be controversial, but their value has proven to be pivotal in many cases. As long as we heed the warnings to avoid taking our intuitions literally, and to validate our metaphors, the insights obtained through this process are a beneficial part of treatment. As stated in the introduction to this article, additional tools are necessary for clients with spiritual issues. According to Wilber, spiritual transformation requires a consistent spiritual practice. That viewpoint might be taken as a mandate to "do this and take the experience that comes." Hemi-Sync embedded in enhanced intuitive psychotherapy provides experiences of deeper layers of the Self and builds a bridge between the levels of awareness through interpretation of those experiences.

Although the need for front-loading prevents validating enhanced intuitive psychotherapy by the same criteria as remote viewing, these case reports show that the process has substantial worth. It can be employed across a wide variety of subjective and consensual models of therapy. It is a mental/psychic skill that can be learned and strengthened with practice and experience, from symbols to images, through intuitions, and finally to knowing. Deeper insights into the Self, sometimes obtainable only through intuitive mental processing, can assist clients to move past internal blocks, as well as open new paths for growth. Most patients find that this client-centered approach fulfills their needs and provides a much-needed connection to spiritual essence.

Critics may say of enhanced intuitive psychotherapy, as they have said of remote viewing and psychic functioning in general, that mistakes can be made, erroneous interpretations advanced, and that the process is not 100 percent accurate. I would respond in the same vein as Joseph McMoneagle, that nothing in life works perfectly. All one has is a greater or lesser probability. As one of my hypnosis training supervisors said, "If you use good judgment, you will not hurt anyone, and you may certainly help a lot of people."

Hemi-Sync: A Healing of the Self
Gary D. Chaikin, M.D.

Many times in therapy I've said, "You need an ego to get on the bus; and then it will be your ego which will keep you from getting off the bus." What I'm alluding to is our identification of self with mind or ego, while forgetting larger Self or Spirit. In this article I will be examining the evolution of the therapist's ego towards a deeper connection with the transpersonal soul. This process will be called a healing of the self.

The self, for the majority of people, has been narrowly defined as an identification with the persona: the collected, socially acceptable, mental images of our experiences. Soul or Self is a trans-egoic bridge linking Psyche to Spirit, called "essence" by Stephen Wolinsky. Healing, then, is the discovery of, and a journey through, the Gateless Gate, to Unity Consciousness or Spirit. The primary boundary of self and not-self must be transcended and included by the process of moving the ego out of the driver's seat and telling it to go to the back of the bus. (Egos are very good at balancing checkbooks but are lousy at knowing who you really are.) Healing, then, is finding the connection or relationship to all, or "going through a door of discovery" and finding that "I am Thou."

In my work I began to notice myself growing exponentially. This was especially important for three reasons. First, as a psychiatrist I knew that statistically we had the highest suicide rate of any profession.

I believed that the reason for this was that many of us had entered the field of mental health looking for answers to our own emotional questions. Upon becoming professionals we were cut off from the quest, putting aside our own needs in service of our clients. Here at last was an opportunity to restore the process of healing. Second, through my training it became apparent that when working with clients I could only take them as far as I had been myself. The limiting factor in treatment most of the time was not the client's limitations but my own lack of personal growth. Third, the spiritual path was my preferred journey, as ultimately it is with everyone.

If healing is a transcendent and all-embracing connection between mind and spirit, why does Hemi-Sync lead to a healing of the self? The answer lies in the concept of the development of a practice. A practice has been described by Ken Wilber as being like a recipe for baking a chocolate cake. No one can adequately tell you what a chocolate cake tastes like. But if you mix together eggs, flour, butter, chocolate, etc., pour it into a pan, bake it, and then try it, you will know what a chocolate cake tastes like. This is what a practice does. It is an experiential method to connect with soul or the deeper layers of who we are. In my work, I discovered how the use of Hemi-Sync and its shifts in consciousness provide a much-needed connection to spiritual essence. Because therapist and client are experiencing the same states of consciousness, which create the possibility for enhancing the psychotherapeutic process, each session provides the opportunity for both participants to take steps along the spiritual path. What started as a development in therapy became a practice. Through the use of Hemi-Sync the care provider is transformed from ego psychologist to spiritual counselor, a techno-shaman. Hemi-Sync is a gateway to a place of no boundaries, beyond time and space. You can discover who you are and move past the threshold of human limitations, finding freedom in being more than your physical body.

The same skills and techniques used with clients can be employed in a healing of the Self. Healing is different from being cured. To be healed is to become whole, while to be cured is to become functional. It is often said that all is energy, and many a time I've told a depressed client, "To have energy you have to use energy." Spirituality is an inquiry into one's energetic nature. Most of our clients, as well as ourselves, are running on empty. We barely have enough personal power to do the basic processes involved in living in ordinary reality. Consequently, a significant part of the beginning of a practice is the tracking of the self and the reclaiming of the energy to be used in the process of transcendence towards becoming whole, connected, without boundaries.

There are many ways to remove energetic obstacles and reclaim our personal energy, or pieces of the Self. Preference probably depends on our experiences and level of awareness. My predilection is a Quantum Psychology approach (see Note, page 147), where identity and the observer are realized to be of the same energy as Essence and therefore are intra-convertible or re-absorbable. What matters most is not the method or content but the state of consciousness commensurate with the practice. As has been well documented, mystical sensibility can be compared with Hemi-Sync's Focus states. Spiritual acumen necessitates this state-dependent learning.

Methodologically, I employ a three-step process. It must be clear, however, that the steps are often not orderly nor sufficient for progress to occur. Growth is punctuated with peak experiences and even at times with regression. Spirit knocks on the door, as Castaneda says, and cares little for our agenda. As previously noted, the work commences with a practice, which ousts identity/persona/ego from the driver's seat. I initially utilized exercises in Focus 10 and 12, including *Release and Recharge* and Metamusic, while practicing the Toltec technique of recapitulation. More recently the work has extended into explorations in Focus 21 and 27 while re-absorbing identity. As this transformation proceeds, a connection through Soul to our Higher Self begins to become more evident. Many names have been given to this unfolding: connecting with intent (Toltec), cleansing the vessel (Kabbalah), or Focus 21 (Hemi-Sync), to name a few. Energy body training, contact with guides, and education about chakras is of particular assistance at this juncture. Practices utilizing the **Gateway Experience, Wave VII,** and the **Opening the Heart** series have been of significant benefit. The final level, for this section of the path, of finding out who you are, of becoming whole, engages issues surrounding such concepts as prior lives, soul retrievals, and Dolphin Energy. Through practice, the spiritual Self is continually experienced. Nothing is wasted; all leads to a method to help yourself while helping others. Is this not why most of us went into our professions in the first place?

To illustrate this healing journey of discovery, let me highlight the experiences of both client and provider. The key question that kept coming to mind in this process, often unbidden, was "And what am I supposed to do with this new awareness?" The first encounter I would like to share involves H.W., a female who had made exceptional progress through working with the *Opening the Heart* series, initially at my office and then almost daily at home each morning.

The session I'd like to describe involved the client working with a medical student instead of me. Her task was to send a message to the student, to demonstrate for herself how we relate at different vibratory levels. The client reported that when she had been experiencing Focus 21 she had "a dream or image, where I saw the student riding a motorcycle. It was a Harley." During discussion, the student, who was himself dealing with role and identity issues, said, "I always wanted a motorcycle, but was unable to get one." I asked him what make he wanted. "A Harley," he replied. He then revealed that while in Focus 21 himself, he had repeatedly had an image of the patient as a young girl jumping rope joyfully. H.W. reported that she worked with the *Opening the Heart* CDs each morning and added that for her assigned task she had projected to the student her experience of joy and love. She also said that she had never ridden a motorcycle, didn't know anyone who owned one, nor had any desire for one herself.

H.W. found the connection with the student very validating of her spiritual work and her search for compassion. The next week, upon returning for her appointment, she remarked, "As a child I was happy, carefree, and was always jumping rope," and laughed.

A 43-year-old man, B.W., was followed for depression and obsessional anxiety associated with significant obesity. No psychotherapeutic modality attempted had been able to relieve his symptoms. He had been involved in psychotherapy, an eating disorder program, biofeedback, and was taking medication with minimal success. One day, after

I had told this client about my own past despair and subsequent transcendence by connection to spirit, B.W. revealed that he had a deep conviction regarding his faith that he had never told anyone before. We discussed Hemi-Sync, and I proposed an experience, which he readily accepted. To begin with, we listened to the first two exercises in **Opening the Heart**. During the instruction to extend love, I moved to Focus 12 to interact with the client. I sensed an anomaly in the client's crown chakra. I decided to use the mental construct of Dolphin Energy to revitalize his system. Upon returning to everyday consciousness, I asked B.W. about his experience. For the first time since treatment had begun, B.W. smiled. "Nothing," he said. "I wanted to try too hard. Then I experienced for the first time being totally relaxed. I suddenly understood everything you've been trying to tell me about control of my mind. I'm not going to quit. This is the first time I know that I'm smart enough. I feel happy. I feel like I can do this." I gave him a hug. "Once the door is open you can never go back. The only way is up," I told him. B.W. left happy and grateful, saying, "This is what I always wanted." He continues to this time feeling significantly better.

The last case I'll call "Physician, heal thyself." After all the clinical experiences and all the times I've asked myself the question, "And what am I supposed to do with this new awareness?" I decided to take my own advice. It was November 2001, and I had returned to TMI to attend the Lifeline program. Exploration of my Higher Self, using Hemi-Sync, had slowed down to an occasional early morning exercise of receiving guidance or reconstruction of what may be called a prior life. About a week before, while preparing to go to Lifeline, I was working with Metamusic *Visitation*. In the process of returning to everyday consciousness I clearly heard the name "Ari." I knew I had heard that name many years ago while studying Kabbalah. I was determined to find the roots of this recurrent theme during my time at the Institute.

During the program, in Focus 21 I encountered "The Ari." He was Isaac Luria, a 15th-century Kabbalistic Rabbi. He became my new inner guide for the investigation of higher Focus states, where I intended to find out more about who I am and what my purpose is, beyond the boundaries of my smaller separate sense of self. As we advanced to Focus 23 and 25, my knowing deepened, culminating in a retrieval of a part of myself that was constrained in Focus 23. With this new insight into the nature of my makeup, many older limiting questions about life in general began to dissolve within the process of transcending and including, leaving me with a feeling of connection to Higher Self Purpose, a true healing of the Self.

In therapy, as in life, we must all continue to grow, transcend, and include. This leads to healing of the Self. We need our egos to get on the bus, but it will be our egos that keep us from getting off. A significant pitfall is the tendency to become so enamored of the bus journey that we miss where we are going. This tendency is so common that in Zen Buddhism they have a saying, "Don't mistake the finger pointing at the moon for the moon."

The goal of healing is to go through the Gateless Gate, the Boundaryless Boundary, beyond technique and the concepts of illness and cure. Only when we move beyond ego, beyond boundaries, will we encounter the true Essence. Hemi-Sync is the key to the gate for our day and age. It is a practice that is efficient, consistent, repeatable, and rapid. I now know what I'm supposed to do with this new awareness!

Note

Quantum Psychology is a form of psychotherapy developed by Stephen Wolinsky, Ph.D., in which the client's subjective reality reflects an underlying unity with the universe, seeing everything as made of the same energy. A quantum approach to consciousness provides an experiential pathway (a practice) by which one can begin to perceive and relate to a universe in which the "facts" of observer-created realities and the inherent interconnectedness of all things are recognized and experienced. This is accomplished by progressive exercises, which assist the individual to see how our experience is observer-constructed and can be de-constructed through the same observer processes. Identity, or self, is seen as a set of deep trance phenomena, which can be assimilated, allowing discovery of what is behind. Boundaries between foreground and background disappear and all is experienced as Self, Void, or Essence.

Hemi-Sync and the Inner Therapist
Nora Rosen

Nora Elisa Rosen is a personal development trainer and a hypnotherapy trainer (Harte's School, New York). She is the director of the Creacción Personal Experience Training Center, Buenos Aires, Argentina. She works in association with Dr. Martin Koreztki, a cardiologist who recommends her to patients with stress-control problems, and with Dr. Alejandro Carra, who was director of the toxicology department, The Clinics Hospital, assisting people who want to control cigarette addiction. Both projects are utilizing Hemi-Sync—Nora is an accredited Outreach Trainer—with very good results.

Hemi-Sync was a discovery that had the virtue of fulfilling a personal search of many years. For fifteen years I worked as a trainer in the area of personal development, and during that time one of the techniques that I liked to use was hypnosis. The use of hypnosis with individuals opened an endless number of doorways into the extraordinary potential of each one of them. But in many ways I felt that the people were depending too much on me and on my judgment while guiding them.

When I first began to experiment on myself with Hemi-Sync, I felt that I had finally found the necessary tool to communicate with the inner therapist within each person. It provides a way for each one of us to be guided toward our own inner wisdom. After numerous experiences with my workshop participants, I continue to be amazed at the results I have witnessed.

The common format for the Outreach Excursion Workshop is to present it over a two-day period, usually a weekend. Some Outreach Trainers split the two-day event into separate weekends, to offer more flexibility to the participants' schedules. However, I found that not all participants are able to use an entire day away from their commitments. So these people complete the sessions by experiencing one exercise each week until the Workshop is complete. In this way, we find we are able to explore each exercise more fully. The rest of the week, until the next session, they are processing what they have experienced, and practicing with the tools they have learned, thus further enriching those experiences. Both ways of presenting the Workshop are different. Doing the whole thing in one weekend is a great way to surge ahead with the unique perspectives offered: whereas doing it over several weeks allows for more profound awareness of the process of each exercise in the series.

Let me tell you about some of the participants' experiences, in a sort of potpourri of manifestations.

Case 1

A young woman, 30 years old, was suffering with a phobia of water. Even to take a bath was torture for her. Simply coming in contact with water would put her into a panic. She experienced feelings of panic every day to the point that she neglected her personal hygiene.

She was doing the exercises during the Gateway Outreach Excursion Workshop, along with 35 other people. Every Hemi-Sync exercise begins with the sounds of ocean surf, and she was surprised to find that instead of feeling afraid at the sound, it actually relaxed her! When we did the exercise *Release and Recharge,* a tape designed to help the participants free themselves of their limiting fears and reclaim healthy energy, she awoke in tears. She remembered during the exercise that her mother had submerged her head in a bucket of cold water when she was a small child. She was having a tantrum and her mother did that to snap her out of it.

Later on in the Workshop, while listening to the exercise *Quantum Self,* she saw herself during one scenario of the guided imagery actually enjoying her submersion in warm water. Then, when the imagery took her to a doorway, she was met by a gentle and loving guide who took charge of tending to her emotional hurt.

Following this experience she let go of her panic and fear of water and gained greater self-esteem. Even her body posture reflected a secure and confident person.

Case 2

Ana came in search of something, without really knowing what that "something" was. At the same time, she brought a certain skepticism with respect to the Hemi-Sync technique, and even to the existence of that "something." She attended weekly, doing the Workshop exercises with regularity. During the first exercises, she was surprised to find herself perceiving something that felt to her like a kind of electricity, which inundated her entire body.

The first time that it happened in Focus 12 she was unable to speak for several minutes afterwards while the tears flowed silently down her cheeks.

"I can't describe what I felt or where I was," she told me, sobbing. "I can only describe to you that I felt a strong sensation of being loved, of being surrounded by a love that I have never known in my entire life. A love in which there is no place for fear of loss, a love that has existed always, and which is without end. An unending peacefulness."

Ana stated that by some inexplicable means her focus on the events in her life had been changed. Everything appeared to be illuminated by purpose and a reason for being. Argentina at that time was going through difficult economic and social times. People were expressing great discontent and hopelessness. Ana was subsequently able to move through this chaos as if protected within a bubble.

The Workshop exercise *Release and Recharge* helped her to face a longtime fear of her father. She believed that she had worked sufficiently with the paternal issue during psychotherapy and that she was over it. However, this exercise demonstrated otherwise. At first, she felt uncomfortable with the discovery that the issue had surfaced and was still unresolved. She thought she had already moved past it. To her surprise, during the week between workshop exercises while listening to other taped exercises at home, she had felt the presence of her late mother. She told Ana about certain events that had happened in her father's life, which clarified things about him and helped her to begin to understand him on a deeper level. This new understanding allowed her to forgive him at the same time. Amazingly, these revelations also helped her to reduce the resentment that she had held against her mother.

"I feel like my mind has been cleared of its cobwebs," she told me. "I was able to see the images as if they were photographs. I've never been able to visualize anything! The images appeared clearly and in color." Her personal growth continued in a cascade, week by week. At home, while using the tapes *Nostalgia* and *Visitation,* she perceived herself as a small child with her mother. She realized how this little girl began to close a curtain between herself and the chidings and constant complaints of her mother. This began a progressive distancing between herself and others. Now she finds it easier to allow herself to listen to people without closing off her mind and emotions.

This last case perhaps does not reflect so much the work of the Inner Therapist, but I chose to include it because sometimes it's good to remind ourselves of the inner magic that occurs in our lives. I fervently believe that Hemi-Sync is a tool that gives us the ability to encounter that personal magic.

Case 3

Mabel, during one of the Outreach Workshop exercises, saw a white antique car with a registration plate that ended with the numbers 520. The sharpness of the image caught her attention. Next to the car, a man stood watching something attentively. She didn't recognize this man, the car, or the plate number, but in some way the image left her with a feeling of calm and relief. I asked her to make a note of all the details. A month later, she excitedly called me to tell me of an experience.

Two years previously, she had tried to sell an old shed that was beside her house in order to pay off some bills. Nobody had wanted to buy the shed, and so it remained there. Great was her surprise when the week following her Workshop she saw, parked next to the shed, a white car. It had plates ending in 520. Then the man in her Workshop vision got out of the car! He had come to buy the shed and paid the price that she had been asking for it. Magic and Hemi-Sync!

(Adapted with permission from an article published in *Hemi-Sync Journal*, vol. XVIII, no. 1, Winter 2000.)

Use of Hemi-Sync to Reduce Levels of Depression for Alcohol-Dependent Patients

**John R. Milligan, Ph.D., and
Raymond O. Waldkoetter, Ed.D.**

Dr. John Milligan is a clinical and research psychologist currently employed as a clinical psychologist with a military alcohol and drug treatment center. His experience includes university teaching and research and administrative experience as the director of a large community health center. Dr. Ray Waldkoetter is a consulting psychologist with an inclusive background in research psychology. He is a member of The Monroe Institute's Board of Advisors and a founding member of its Professional Division.

Introduction

This study evaluated the use of Hemi-Sync as a supplemental treatment procedure for outpatients diagnosed as alcohol dependent with mild to moderate levels of depressive feelings. The subjects were enlisted military patients indicating various levels of depression as measured by the Beck Depression Inventory (BDI). The BDI was given before and after treatment as a measure of effect. A comparison group of outpatients was also given before-and-after BDIs, but not the supplemental tape treatment. Both groups received primary psycho-educational therapy.

Many studies have documented the common presence of depressive symptoms among patients seeking treatment for alcoholism.

Depressive symptoms are frequently reported as comorbid factors in such treatment, which must be addressed for long-term relapse prevention and acceptance of treatment in the short term. Effective treatment programs for substance abuse are no longer dependent upon the 12-step Alcoholics Anonymous model as the only treatment modality. More often, substance-abuse programs have now moved to models emphasizing cognitive-behavioral approaches and to somewhat decreased reliance on the AA model, except as an ongoing support function after formal treatment. Such programs recognize that cognitive thought patterns have contributed to and reinforced dysfunctional lifestyles and lifelong behavioral patterns leading to alcohol dependence or abuse.

Modern programs are frequently patterned after models such as that of the American Society of Addictions Medicine. These programs emphasize individualized, flexible treatment with specific criteria guiding the level of care and the length of services. These criteria result in the patients being placed at less intense treatment levels than do programs with fixed entrance and levels of care, allowing many of these programs to substantially reduce the cost of treatment. The savings result from shorter lengths of stay during the actual treatment phase, with generally longer aftercare or follow-on supportive services once the person completes the treatment phase. This study was designed along these lines, emphasizing flexibility and the unique differences in individuals who have developed substance abuse problems requiring treatment.

New techniques in substance abuse treatment include the use of brain-wave training with biofeedback and the increased use of cognitive techniques in federal prisons. More programs are moving to shorter lengths of treatment due both to improved flexible models and to pressures from managed-care organizations to limit costs. This move to shorter training periods increases the importance of developing self-paced and self-administered techniques as adjuncts to the primary program. The innovative use of Hemi-Sync audiotapes targeting brain-wave synchronicity using designed sound patterns has been reported in certain select publications and studies. Further exploration relating to the use of this method for synchronizing brain-wave patterns, altering mental imagery, and enhancing relaxation appears warranted in connection with substance abuse. This was a major purpose of the research reported here.

Method

The study involved 42 male naval military personnel referred for treatment to an outpatient military alcohol and drug treatment facility. Ages ranged from 22 to 38, and all were diagnosed as alcohol dependent. Half of the subjects were assigned to a control group and half to an experimental group. Assignment to each group was alternated based on order of admission. All completed a comprehensive biopsychosocial assessment following approved healthcare and military standards. Each was administered the Beck Depression Inventory as part of this assessment. The BDI is a 21-question, multiple-response screening instrument and is widely used because it is cost-effective, easy to administer and score, and usually takes less than five minutes to complete. Those scoring at or above a cut-off score of 13, indicating minimal depression, were included in the study. They were also screened by a medical health professional to ensure that those in need of a particular treatment for a depressive disorder were provided with such care.

Subjects in the experimental group were given an album of six Hemi-Sync tapes, stereo headsets, and instructions on their use. The instructions included listening to one side of each of the six tapes on a daily basis for 12 days. The tapes were to be used within two hours of scheduled bedtime each evening, and the subjects were to refrain from any stimulant consumption beforehand. Previously, brain-wave training in a biofeedback protocol with alcoholics had identified positive reaction to alpha-theta brain waves, with increased alpha and theta brain rhythms, less reported depression, and longer abstinence post-treatment.

Hemi-Sync brain-wave stimulation—increasing hemispheric brain synchrony, altering mental imagery, and promoting relaxation—has increasingly been employed in therapy. This auditory stimulation uses specific mixes of sound frequencies, e.g., alpha, beta, theta, and delta. The brain resonates with this stimulus by producing similar EEG patterns as the listener follows the audio-guidance program. The six tapes in the album were: *Morning Exercise, De-Hab, Energy Walk, Moment of Revelation, Winds over the World,* and *Surf.* The control group did not receive the tapes.

Both groups followed the same primary treatment program. The content included two psychosocial skills-building lectures/discussions each day and two group treatment sessions per day, five days a week, with the experimental group receiving the augmented tape therapy. The length of treatment varied for each individual in both groups depending on progress in meeting treatment goals. The average length of stay was three weeks, followed by a structured aftercare program. Each subject worked with his counselor to develop an individual treatment plan tailored to his needs, including aftercare considerations such as referral to community resources for non-alcohol problems. With regard to the use of the tapes, some studies have suggested that tape effects are cumulative and different for each individual, and after initial exposure the tape sequence may be varied to support individual choice.

Results

A simplified version of the results is presented here.

The Beck Depression Inventory score of the control group before treatment began and expressed as an average or mean was 15.10. The comparable post-treatment score was 8.67.

The BDI score of the experimental group before treatment was 19.95. The comparable post-treatment score was 4.90.

These results reflect highly significant differences between the two groups. The large difference between the scores at the end of treatment would be expected to occur only by chance less than once in 1,000 such measures if the groups had received identical treatment.

Previous studies have explored the possible applications of The Monroe Institute's sound technology and audio-guidance systems, and the authors have discussed how formal learning and behavioral change could occur. As now appears from the experimental group's markedly lower level of alcoholic depression in the results of this study, the Hemi-Sync audio tapes—a largely self-administered and self-paced treatment technology—proved clearly useful, suggesting that existing substance-abuse treatment programs may benefit from including them as part of their therapeutic regimens.

(Adapted with permission from an article in *Hemi-Sync Journal*, vol. XVIII, no. 1, Winter 2000.)

Note

The complete statistically expressed results of this study may be seen in the *Journal* article in which the full report appeared.

Journey into Symbolism
Patricia Martin

Patricia Martin is a psychotherapist, alcohol and addiction therapist, and graduate of the Paris Medical Faculty. She is a member of the Professional Division of The Monroe Institute. Patricia transmits the knowledge she has gained by delving deeply into the sources of European tradition. Following years of research into ethno-medicine and medieval anthropology, she shares her interest in symbolism, mythology, and archetypes.

I facilitate group and individual sessions using Monroe Institute techniques. During an individual session, one of my patients began to relate an interesting journey that she was experiencing. She had previously progressed in sessions with me through the consciousness states identified as from Focus 3 to Focus 21. She had frequent "journey" experiences. In her journeys she had encountered master builders from the Middle Ages. In this session we used the Metamusic composition *Inner Journey*.

This client has no ties to, or previous knowledge of, Freemasonry, the compagnons, architecture, mathematics, physics, or mystic symbols. She is 50 years old, a secretary working in the French Public Service. She is Catholic, but not a churchgoer.

She was deeply relaxed by the Hemi-Sync, lying snugly under a blanket. She began to describe her journey.

I feel I am sinking in water. I see a man who is holding out his hand to me, asking me to come with him. Now I see a lion, and we form a triangle, the man, the lion, and myself. From the base of this triangle to its center, a plumb line is strung. This line is to be used to see the right place, the right being, the right competence. Right to receive this transmission. The connection between the plumb line and the base of the triangle is made through a being who belongs to another world. Between the base of the triangle and the line, the word "Mary" is written.

A voice says, "This woman worked. She was a woman builder." She is young and dressed in long, dark-colored clothes. She is alone, without a husband or children. Now her clothes are changing color. They have become blue, gold, and silver. On her head she wears a headband and a transparent veil. The voice tells me that she used to belong to an order or lodge, which is not in any European country. The place is hot; there is sand; there are horses, camels, and donkeys. The horses are black, but it is a symbolic black. They look as if they have been waxed, shiny black, which reflects the sun. This order or lodge was associated with the stars and light.

The voice continues: "You have signed the book and made the oath with your blood. Blood has been spilt by the sword, because it was required to be written. The sword has cleaved; this is the word. Thus you have left a trace of your passing on the floor of the lodge. I see the signs that mark the stains. In this lodge there exists a bond of brotherhood, passed on from generation to generation. The courage and perseverance you have now comes from this bond."

Now I see the triangle again. The voice says, "The moment has come to form the triangle again. It is up to you to transmit your knowledge. You will see the mark. Take it.

Now I return, and I see a being dressed like a pharaoh. He has been watching all of this experience. I see a bird, flying away. It is over, and I return to ordinary reality.

This experience contains some very significant symbols.

1. Water: one of the four elements of Masonic initiation. Also found in the ritual of baptism in the Catholic church. It purifies.

2. The lion: symbol of strength, and corresponds to the level of apprentice among the Freemasons and compagnons. The lion is also the eleventh Arcanum of the tarot. There is a woman and a lion—femininity and strength.

3. The triangle: a significant Masonic symbol.

4. The plumb line: still used by builders to this day. It brings rightness, justice, centeredness.

5. The name Mary: used by Templars in their rituals. Freemasons are a branch of the Templars.

In the European tradition, there are many women builders. Chartres was the first religious place to be dedicated to a goddess, as early as the fourth century. Vezelay was built by a famous woman, Berthe de Roussillon, as related in the "chanson de geste," a ballad of the troubadours.

The dress color changes from dark to light, in alchemical fashion from lead to gold. The great cathedrals and sacred places are often the starting points for pilgrimages like the Compostella pilgrimage. In many cathedrals, black is represented by black virgins, virgins from the underworld, as seen at Chartres for example.

In my client's experience, a black horse appears. The horse gives added significance to the experience, as it represents the Kabbala.

The lodge is an assembly of builders, and today the term is used to denote the meeting place of Freemasons. The Freemason initiate makes an oath on the Bible and signs his oath with his own blood. He wears a sword across his chest. If he betrays his brothers, the sword will pierce his heart. The sword cleaves and carries the word.

Before they would begin to carve the stone, builders would draw the building plans onto the ground, then erase them. Theirs was an oral tradition, with oral transmission of information. Each stone worker signed his stones with a mark, which we call the mark of the compagnons. One of the qualities of builders and Freemasons today is perseverance. The aspiring Freemason learns of this at his initiation.

This session demonstrates the usefulness of Hemi-Sync as an important tool for the practitioner, aiding in the access to traditions that are anchored in a country's culture, although still in a secret way.

SLEEP

One of the first discoveries Robert Monroe made in the early days of the development of Hemi-Sync was that it was very effective in sending people to sleep. Several exercises were designed to help listeners to achieve a good night's sleep, and "sleep signals" were incorporated in other exercises so that the listener, having absorbed the content of the tape or CD, would then fall into natural sleep. Scott Taylor shows that various immune dysfunction conditions affect the normal sleeping pattern, and he illustrates that exercises such as those in the *Positive Immunity* series have the dual purpose of working to affect the immune system and easing the listener into deep, healing sleep.

Edward and Mary O'Malley are directors of a sleep disorder center where they study the causes of insomnia. They have received positive feedback on the effect of the *Super Sleep* nonverbal tape and are seeking to obtain objective findings by launching a double-blind, placebo-controlled study to evaluate the efficacy of binaural auditory beats (as embedded in this tape) with insomnia patients.

Lastly, Dr. Brian Dailey describes his own experiences with the *Lucid Dreaming* series. He defines Lucid Dreaming as "the conscious awareness that one is dreaming" and indicates several ways in which this kind of dreaming may prove of value.

Hemi-Sync Intervention for Insomnia and Immune Dysfunction Syndromes
Scott M. Taylor, Ed.D.

Scott M. Taylor, Ed.D., is founder of the Expanded Awareness Institute in Edina, Minnesota, and a residential trainer for The Monroe Institute. He is a member of the faculty in the small business management department at South Central Technical College. Scott earned his BA from Coe College, his M.M. from Kellogg Graduate School of Management at Northwestern University, his M.S.C. from the New Seminary, and his Ed.D. from the University of St. Thomas in St. Paul, MN.

I was immersed in re-watching the film *Top Gun* with my new larger-than-life surround sound system when my fiancée appeared in the room, tears streaming down her face. Pain searing down the entire right side of her body made it impossible for her to stand, sit, walk, or lie down. Her pain and her frustration were unbearable. My feeling of helplessness and powerlessness left those minutes burned into my brain as if branded there, a memory not soon, if ever, forgotten. Sharon could not be still, and she could not move to escape the agony. When she finally sought help, her doctor patted her on the knee telling her, "We all have a few aches and pains now and then." We knew better. Sharon had to do something. We were fortunate in securing an appointment at a regional medical center within the next few weeks.

After weeks of anxious waiting and more tests than I could remember—and more than Sharon wanted to endure—we received a definitive diagnosis: fibromyalgia, a muscle pain syndrome that is not degenerative but is extremely painful and can be debilitating. They said they were sorry but Sharon would have to learn to live with it. A nurse gave Sharon a pamphlet and some stretching exercises, sending her home because there was nothing more to do. "Maybe biofeedback and exercising daily would help," medical personnel told her.

Secluded in her bedroom, Sharon read the pamphlet that explained more about learning to live with the pain of fibromyalgia. She fell into a depression and cried for three days. Then, as quickly as the depression hit her, she sat bolt upright with sudden, new conviction and said, "What do you mean I have to live with this? I don't think so." She did not yet know what that meant. She just suddenly knew the answer was somewhere and that she was certainly not going to learn to live with this kind of pain.

Fast forward one year to the fall of 1995. Sharon and I married in September. The stresses of wedding preparation, a honeymoon trip, and her job induced a major flare-up. At the same time, Sharon planned to attend a Gateway program one month after our marriage. The travel, new situation, new people, and new, unknown experiences helped compound her pain into a severe attack at The Monroe Institute during the first couple of days of the workshop. In spite of the discomfort, she found the people interesting and the journeys during Gateway compelling. By the end of the week, Sharon awakened to the realization that her body was no longer in pain.

Why? What could a week at The Monroe Institute be providing that created this turnaround? Research indicates, and both the Expanded Awareness Institute and Sharon's experience verify, that persons afflicted with fibromyalgia, chronic fatigue, and other immune dysfunction syndromes do not sleep well. They have trouble getting to sleep, staying asleep, and achieving restorative sleep. Indeed, research shows that their EEG sleeping patterns are abnormal and that unless sleeping patterns get better, the patient won't get better. Therefore, Hemi-Sync tapes become uniquely suited to assist these persons in sleeping better.

Sharon returned home. Within two weeks, pain again began to flare. I suggested she use a sleep tape each night as The Monroe

Institute does during the Gateway course. This was the beginning of a full recovery for Sharon.

Getting to Sleep

Hemi-Sync technology assists a willing participant in getting to sleep in numerous ways. First, the tones gently lead the brain from normal "beta" consciousness to deep "delta" sleep via the frequency-following response. Any tape that has Focus 10, the state of "mind awake/body asleep" assists in this function. Second, on some of the sleep tapes, verbal instruction assists listeners in reducing "mind chatter." Many of our clients have overactive minds that try to solve all the world's problems when they go to bed. After finishing that list, overactive minds frequently seek out potential new problems, attempting to solve them or, at least, worry about them. Third, some of the sleep tapes have a progressive relaxation exercise. This exercise allows users to identify where stress is stored in their body and begin learning how to identify it and let it go. Fourth, some of the sleep tapes use an enjoyable, verbally guided tour that acts like a "bedtime story for big kids." Fifth, some persons hurt so much that the act of lying in bed is too painful and doesn't allow them to get to sleep. The *Pain Control* tape addresses this issue directly, helping reduce the pain signals and subsequently dropping the listener off into deep sleep.

Hemi-Sync sleep tapes also help break the habit of expecting to not fall asleep. After a few successes, the tapes reinforce normal sleeping behavior, and the task of falling asleep becomes easier and easier. The expectation of sleeping well then becomes the norm. Sleeping confidence returns.

This "new" positive sleeping-expectation habit becomes central to reinforcing other behaviors. After many nights of putting one's troubles into an imaginary receptacle called the "Energy Conversion Box" clients begin to do it automatically, and mind chatter becomes markedly reduced and eventually almost nonexistent. After many nights of progressive relaxation exercises, the very act of getting into bed triggers a relaxation response. Storing stress in muscles becomes a behavior of the past. In addition, users begin using techniques to reduce mind chatter and stored stress during their waking hours as well.

The range of sleep tapes offered by The Monroe Institute suits our clients' varied needs in getting to sleep. The varied exercises on these titles help reduce mind chatter, reduce stored stress in the body, and help alleviate pain signals. Some create guided visualizations for those who react better to stories than exercises. Others contain sounds of rainstorms and music for those who prefer non-voiced tapes. Also available are exercises containing Hemi-Sync signals mixed with pink noise for those who need a quiet environment.

We augment the Hemi-Sync materials with an instruction sheet on tape use and sleep hygiene. Stereo placement, nutrition, exercises, bedtime ritual, bed activities, consistency, and attitude all play a part in helping persons to learn to sleep better. Making a habit of proper pre-sleep behavior assists the body/mind to remember, "I am locking the doors, putting the cat out, brushing my hair . . . it is time to sleep."

Staying Asleep

Our experience has shown that most clients, once introduced to Hemi-Sync, slide from normal consciousness to deep restful sleep and need no further reinforcement to stay asleep. The body/mind seems to remember what to do and kicks into an "automatic" sleep cycle. Most persons then sleep in normal 90-minute sleep cycles the rest of the night and awake refreshed.

Some, however, do not. These persons may have a condition called A-spiking, where, as research has demonstrated, the brain emits a burst of alpha waves in the midst of the deep sleep cycle. The body interprets this as wake-up signals and begins the arousal sequence. In these cases, we recommend that clients use one of the auto-reverse sleep titles available from the Institute. These titles re-create the normal 90-minute sleep cycle. When played in continuous auto-reverse mode (repeat for CDs), the exercise provides reinforcement to the brain. This helps the brain to remain in the appropriate stage of the sleep cycle for the appropriate duration and in the appropriate sequence, in effect overriding the brain's desire to release alpha waves.

Sometimes A-spiking persists even under the influence of Hemi-Sync, and users wake up periodically throughout the night. Hemi-Sync tapes playing softly in the background help users fall back asleep quickly. Using an auto-reverse tape also applies to persons who awake to urinate frequently during the night. We recommend this trip be accomplished in as little ambient light as possible. Night lights work well. Bright overhead lights stimulate the body to a more awakened state. Over time we see A-spiking reduced markedly due to the entrainment effect Hemi-Sync offers. The brain relearns to operate more normally.

Restorative Sleep

Persons with fibromyalgia, chronic fatigue, and other immune dysfunction syndromes do not receive the deep "delta" sleep that is necessary for good health. The affected brain seems to lack the ability to enter delta sleep, or once entered, does not stay in the cycle for the proper amount of time. Our clients and others such as those reported in Dr. Goldenberg's article in *Hospital Practice* ("Diagnostic and therapeutic challenges of fibromyalgia," vol. 24, no. 9, pp. 39–52, 1989) describe this pattern of waking up unrefreshed as "feeling like a truck had hit them in the night, even though they may have slept 8 or 9 hours." During a normal 90-minute sleep cycle, we should be spending 20 percent of the time in delta sleep, as Stanley Coren explains in his well-researched book *Sleep Thieves*. It is during this critical 18 minutes that the body releases hormones that play an important role in muscle maintenance (see *Arthritis Today*, Sept–Oct 1993). Without this time in delta sleep, the body may go unconscious, but the restorative work is left undone. Symptoms of sleep deprivation set in. If lack of delta sleep persists, the result is fibromyalgia-like symptoms—persistent and severe muscle pain. Restoring proper delta sleep reduces or eliminates fibromyalgia symptoms (as reported in the *British Medical Journal*, Feb. 1995).

Hemi-Sync technology assists the brain to enter and maintain the delta wave patterns necessary for restorative sleep. Sleep can be a learned behavior. Consistent use of the tapes every night upon retiring entrains the brain to this restored way of being, and the change seems to be permanent. Thankfully, once Sharon was on a program of using the tapes every night, she achieved immediate improvement within two weeks. It took nine months for Sharon to achieve consistent normal sleeping patterns without the use of tapes. Most clients relearn this sleep skill much sooner. After two years, she became pain free.

Use of Hemi-Sync sleep technology provides a drug-free solution, a technique that is gentle and easy to administer, and a permanent effect. Hemi-Sync is cost-effective, portable, and teaches additional healthful living skills.

The Expanded Awareness Institute also created workshops around the use of the **Positive Immunity** Program (PIP). PIP tapes provide additional layered benefits. As people learn to sleep and move into the rhythm their bodies normally function within, they learn how to boost their immune systems. We augment the PIP with the *De-Discomfort Human Plus* exercise for off-tape pain control.

L. B. and her husband are caretakers of a senior citizen high-rise apartment complex in Middledale, Minnesota. Diagnosed with severe fibromyalgia by a regional medical center, she recalls their medical advice to her: "You will never work again. Go to Social Security, get disability, and learn to live with it the best you can . . . fibromyalgia will never kill you, but you may wish it did." She came to us in desperation after finding limited relief from standard and alternative medical approaches. In a follow-up letter (within one month after attending a sleep workshop) L. B. writes:

> . . . I have experienced [more] full nights sleep, free of medications, for the first time in one and a half years. I came to the workshop excited about getting some help for my severe insomnia, yet apprehensive and full of concerns that this would work for me. I am a Christian, raised in a Missouri Synod Lutheran background, which as you know, forbids "hypnosis," certain types of meditation, etc. I talked to some people about this workshop, and with all the gross ignorance out there, was warned that this might be "Satanic"! Your straightforward, scientific approach calmed my anxieties.
>
> I had been to the major clinics for health problems, starting with Lyme disease, since 1992, and even to the psychiatric clinic to obtain help after being told that this was "all in my head." We

even tried biofeedback to help with the pain. No one, and I repeat *no one*, was able to help with the sleep disturbance. My doctor was giving me sleeping pills and Trazadone, an antidepressant, which has a major side effect of sleepiness. He told me that if I refused to take the medications to finally get some sleep, I would end up in the mental hospital *soon!* Desperate, I tried these too, and finally was able to get some "drug-induced" sleep. The side effects were terrible! I quit the Trazadone and cut the sleeping pills in half. I just had to continue taking them in order to fall asleep.

Imagine my surprise and delight to realize that I had actually "clicked out" for part of one of the tapes on the first day of your workshop!! Since then I have been using the tapes every night and find that I have more energy and am getting back to my "pre-sick" work abilities. I need to learn to pace myself, however. I've had pain from overdoing as a result of this new burst of energy I feel. [L.B. washed every window in her complex two days after the workshop!]

I am very much aware that Hemi-Sync is not a "magic bullet" but a progressive process. If there were any magic bullets, I think with all the clinics I have been through, one of the doctors would have discovered it! I know I have to work consistently with the tapes to benefit from and feel more comfortable with all these new tools you have provided me with for healing, pain, etc . . ." [used with permission, May 1996].

In a two-year follow up with L. B. (June 1998), the Hemi-Sync brain entrainment permanently changed her sleeping pattern. She now sleeps almost every night ("like a log!") without using Hemi-Sync tapes. L. B. estimates that she averages seven hours of sleep, without interruption, awaking refreshed. L. B. occasionally has a "bad night"; she can usually pinpoint the cause to increased stress in her life. In those cases L. B. puts on a sleep tape and has a "refresher course" for that evening.

L. B. has not seen a doctor since the workshop. "No reason to," she says, "I feel wonderful. I now do everything I did before. I work a regular day, and then some. I can lift everything I could before. The docs told me I would never be able to lift much again. I may have an occasional pain from overexertion, but it's like the old days before fibromyalgia, normal aches. Never anywhere near as severe as before. Essentially I am now pain free!

"The *Positive Immunity* Program is so helpful. When I was in the midst of the fibromyalgia battle, I would be susceptible to every bug that went around. Now I hardly ever get sick. Tell those doubting Thomases that my sister is married to a Missouri Synod (Lutheran Church) minister. They now have the tapes (PIP) in their church library!"

I leave you with this note: the first exercise of L. B.'s workshop witnessed her being roused from sleep by the beta signals ending the tape. To our surprise, she awoke expressing anger. She turned to C. C., the patient in the bed next to her, and exclaimed, "Your snoring woke me up!" She and C. C. both paused and started crying because neither had been able to fall asleep without the aid of drugs for the past 18 years.

Insomnia and Hemi-Sync
Edward B. O'Malley, Ph.D., and
Mary B. O'Malley, M.D., Ph.D.

Dr. Ed O'Malley completed his B.S. degree in psychology at SUNY, Stony Brook, in 1985, his Ph.D. in neurobiology from Cornell University Graduate School of Medical Sciences in 1992, and returned to human brain studies at NYU Sleep Disorder Center (SDC). He received his board certification in sleep medicine in 1995 and is presently director of the Norwalk Hospital SDC. He headed the insomnia section at NYU for several years and developed his own behavioral treatment approach. His current research interests include brain-mapping arousal from sleep and other states of consciousness, and evaluating sleep and fatigue in medical training programs.

Dr. Mary O'Malley completed her B.A. in chemistry at Oberlin College in 1985, the M.D./Ph.D. joint degree program at Cornell Medical College/ Rockefeller University in New York City in 1993, her internship at Yale University/Norwalk Hospital, and completed psychiatry residency at NYU/Bellevue Medical Center in 1998. She is currently an attending psychiatrist at Norwalk Hospital, and is also the sleep fellowship director at the Sleep Disorders Center, establishing an academic/clinical program in sleep medicine. She has extensive experience in the treatment of narcolepsy, and her research interests include dreaming sleep and its potential for healing.

Insomnia is generally defined as the subjective sense that sleep is difficult to initiate or maintain, or that sleep itself is non-refreshing. Prevalence studies have shown that about one-third of the adult population experiences insomnia (nearly 10 percent as a chronic problem). Many sufferers report daytime consequences similar to those associated with chronic sleep deprivation: fatigue, performance decrements, and mood disturbances. The daytime impairments result in decreased work productivity, higher accident rate, and increased morbidity with augmented use of medical facilities. These findings present an obvious cause for concern in today's 24/7 society.

A combination of factors often underlies insomnia. These can be generally grouped under the five "Ps": physical, psychological, pharmacologic, psychiatric, and physiologic. Physical factors like pain, illness, hormonal changes, or environmental disturbances can play a causative role in insomnia by acting to heighten the arousal system. Psychological stressors and active psychiatric disease can directly affect the body's ability to initiate or maintain sleep. Pharmacologic factors may cause insomnia in several ways: as a side effect of medications prescribed for other illnesses, through the arousing properties of caffeine and other central nervous system (CNS) stimulants; as a direct effect of alcohol ingestion; or indirectly as a rebound effect following withdrawal of CNS depressants initially prescribed as sleep aids. Finally, physiologic, or circadian, changes such as those involving jet travel or rotating shift work can severely disrupt the sleep/wake cycle.

It is important to note that the complaint of insomnia is a symptom, not a disorder itself. Thus, careful evaluation of potential medical, psychiatric, and environmental causes is indicated. Duration, accompanying symptoms, and prior health status are all critical factors important for accurate diagnosis and treatment. Sleep studies may be used to exclude other physical causes of sleep disruption, or document the individual's complaints, but are not routinely indicated for psychological insomnia.

Once insomnia is diagnosed, treatment should be addressed toward correction of the underlying cause, particularly when there are associated medical/psychiatric issues. Simple changes in routine, living situation, and food intake may be effective. In all cases, sleep hygiene education regarding the mechanics of sleep is important: i.e., sleep promoting or interfering behaviors. However, specific treatment regimens are generally implemented in accordance with the time-course of symptoms. Transient insomnia, lasting a few days to a couple of weeks, is usually associated with trans-meridian travel, a brief illness, or a stressful event (e.g., next-day exam or presentation). This rather mild form of insomnia may be managed effectively with a brief course of sleep aids; over-the-counter agents such as herbal preparations, sedating antihistamines, and nighttime versions of common pain relievers, or prescribed mild hypnotics can be used as the main therapy. Short-term insomnia, lasting several weeks to a month, is usually associated with more traumatic life events that can be negative (death of a loved one, divorce, or sudden hospitalization) or positive (marriage, job promotion, birth of a child). Although medication may be useful over the short term, behavioral therapies and sleep hygiene education are important corollaries necessary to prevent the development of chronic insomnia. The longer insomnia persists, the more complex causes and treatments become.

Long-term or chronic insomnia may last months to years. There are well-recognized effective behavioral treatments available to address the symptoms of chronic insomnia: sleep restriction, cognitive therapy, relaxation therapies, stimulus control, and biofeedback. These therapies have common modes of action and relieve insomnia by reducing emotional/somatic arousal (cognitive and relaxation therapy, stimulus control, biofeedback) or improving sleep efficiency (sleep restriction). Behavioral therapies are typically implemented during a six- to ten-week program administered by competently trained therapists. Notably, hypnotics should not be viewed as the sole source of treatment, particularly in the case of chronic insomnia. Rather, medication should be utilized as reinforcement for the education and behavioral techniques.

Current behavioral treatment regimens for all forms of insomnia require the expertise of specially trained healthcare providers, and unfortunately there are too few of these available. Furthermore, implementation of a six- to ten-week program may preclude the treatment of many people due to scheduling conflicts, available time, restrictive health insurance coverage, etc. Any intervention that reduces the therapeutic time window and can be administered by almost any healthcare provider has the potential to vastly increase the number of insomnia sufferers treated. We feel that Hemi-Sync holds promise as one such intervention.

Insomnia patients have been shown to exhibit a hyperaroused state reflected by increased fast and decreased slow brain frequency activity. Specific Hemi-Sync frequencies have been postulated to be able to drive the brain activity, or EEG, towards a less-aroused state. A special sound stimulus is embedded in a "pink noise" background and listened to via stereo inputs. The sound stimulus, termed binaural auditory beat, is generated when slightly different sound frequencies are presented separately to each ear. The auditory system processes this information and actually induces a third frequency beat, perceived by the listener. When a subject "hears" a sound beat in the frequency range of EEG activity, the resulting EEG pattern eventually mimics the sound frequency. If the sound stimulus is presented in the slower EEG frequency range, it can produce drowsiness and sleep by entraining the EEG. In fact, Bob Monroe, founder of The Monroe Institute and creator of the Hemi-Sync technology, related to me that many program participants at the Institute complained that they fell asleep too often while desperately trying to remain alert! Given the sleep-inducing properties of Hemi-Sync, the Institute produced several tapes particularly designed for this purpose. Using these tapes, many people reported longer or better (i.e., deeper, more efficient) sleep. Although numerous anecdotal reports attest to the efficacy of Hemi-Sync technology to induce sleep, no "scientific tests" had yet been conducted. Consequently, we are rigorously testing this in a double-blind, placebo-controlled research protocol (see Appendix for detailed description of this work in progress).

Briefly, the research protocol calls for subjects to have an initial sleep study to rule out the presence of organic sleep disorders. Following a normal study, the subject then has a second study to establish baseline parameters. The morning after, subjects take home a stereo pillow, auto-reverse tape player, and an experimental tape (either Hemi-Sync embedded in pink noise or a placebo tape of pink noise alone), wear a device to monitor sleep/wake activity, and keep logs. After two weeks, subjects return to the sleep center for one last sleep study, listening to the tape throughout the night while brain activity and multiple physiological signals are recorded. To assess improvement, objective and subjective measures are made of sleep parameters and extent of brain entrainment.

Until the data is fully analyzed and the blind is broken we won't have objective findings. However, we have received interesting comments from most of our subjects. To date, approximately half the participants have reported improved sleep over the course of the protocol with the experimental tape. In fact, one subject canceled her final follow-up appointment several times and when requested to come in would only return to the office if she didn't have to return the tape, stereo pillow, or auto-reverse tape player. I assured her that she would be allowed to keep the apparatus but needed to exchange the experimental tape for the commercially available one, which proved satisfactory. Generally, once the protocol is completed, subjects who report no significant improvement are given a trial of the commercially available *Super Sleep* tape. Those who've tried the commercial tape have also provided positive feedback, and none have returned the tape, pillow, or tape player. We take that as an indication of effective treatment afforded by the Hemi-Sync sleep tapes and are looking forward to completing the study and the final data analysis.

Appendix

Title: Double-Blind Placebo Controlled Study of the Efficacy of Binaural Auditory Beats to Improve Sleep in Primary Insomnia

Investigators: Edward B. O'Malley, Ph.D., and Mary B. O'Malley, M.D., Ph.D.

Facility: Community-based teaching hospital sleep disorders center

Introduction: Insomnia patients have been shown to exhibit a hyperaroused state reflected in heightened physiological measures. There is well-documented evidence showing increased fast and decreased slow EEG activity, during both wakefulness and sleep. Several interventional therapies have shown that a reduction in this hyperaroused state facilitates sleep in these patients. Recent research has shown that a specific auditory sound, the binaural auditory beat (BAB), may be able to drive the EEG towards a less aroused state by entraining, or resonating with, the EEG. These signals are generated when two tones of slightly different frequencies are presented to each

177

ear, creating the subjective perception of a wavering tone that varies at the frequency difference between the two tones. When presented in the slower EEG frequency ranges, BABs are reported to induce drowsiness and sleep. We hypothesize that the presentation of BABs in the slow EEG range will reduce fast EEG activity, enhance slow activity, and consequently improve sleep in insomnia patients.

Objective: This study will evaluate the efficacy of binaural auditory beats for improving sleep in insomnia patients presenting to a community-based hospital sleep disorders center.

Design and Procedure: The study will employ a double-blind, placebo-controlled between and within subjects design comparing delta/theta pure tone binaural auditory beats embedded in "pink noise" (experimental group) with a placebo condition of pure tones and pink noise alone (control group). A minimum of six subjects will be enrolled in each group. Following an acclimation night sleep study to rule out organic sleep disorders and to accustom patients to the procedures, subjects will then return for a baseline sleep study. After returning home, all subjects will then listen to cassette tapes with or without binaural auditory beats presented through pillow stereo speakers nightly for the 14-day duration of the study. Subjects will be monitored with an actigraph, an unobtrusive movement detector (size of a wristwatch) worn on the wrist to serve as a surrogate measure of sleep/wake recording, and daily sleep logs for subjective estimation of sleep variables with visual analog scales (VAS) for mood and alertness. After two weeks, subjects will return to the lab for a post-treatment sleep study. Actigraphy and topographic brain mapping (TBM; full 10-20 EEG montage) will be performed during baseline and experimental sleep studies. Following the study, subjects will be offered continuation treatment with the commercially available version of the experimental sleep tape for an additional one to two weeks. If no improvement, subjects will be offered standard behavioral therapy for insomnia.

Subjects: Subjects will be recruited from patients presenting to the community-based hospital sleep disorders center with a clinical suggestion of insomnia. After IRB-approved informed consent, a minimum of six sex- and age-matched insomnia patients in each group will be enrolled. Subjects with a recent history or presence of psychiatric illness, use of psychoactive substances, neurologic abnormality, or other primary sleep disorder will be excluded from the study.

Intervention: Subjects will listen to experimental or placebo tapes nightly for two weeks.

Outcome Measures: The primary outcome measures are NPSG-derived sleep onset latency (SOL), wake after sleep onset (WASO), and sleep efficiency (SE). Secondary outcome measures include NPSG-derived total sleep time (TST), sleep fragmentation index, percent NREM sleep stages 1–4 and REM sleep; EEG data collapsed across frontal, central, parietal, temporal, and occipital sites, and in four frequency bands (beta, alpha, theta, and delta); daily actigraphy data-SOL, WASO, SE, and TST. Subjective measures include daily sleep log data-SOL, WASO, TST, and VAS scales for alertness and mood.

Statistical Analysis: Multivariate statistics and post-hoc analysis, where appropriate, will be performed.

Lucid Dreaming
Brian D. Dailey, M.D., FACEP, FACFE

Lucid dreaming is the conscious awareness that one is dreaming. Lucid dreaming may be useful therapy for nightmares, to improve physical health, for problem solving, for artistic inspiration, and for the experience of transcendental states. By consciously participating in and programming lucid dream states, it may be possible for one to manifest thoughts into physical reality.

The *Lucid Dreaming* series is a set of four taped exercises to aid both lucid dreaming and dream recall. It differs from other dream programs in several ways. Hemi-Sync frequencies are used to induce states of hypnogogia, the deeply relaxed state experienced right before falling asleep. These frequencies also allow one to create a natural 90-minute sleep cycle, ending with rapid eye movement (REM) sleep, when dreaming occurs. This is of major significance as one can then easily learn to recognize REM sleep to initiate the lucid dreaming process. This is perhaps the most difficult aspect of lucid dreaming—learning to recognize, program, and recall the dream state. However, since Hemi-Sync technology allows REM sleep to be attained in a reliable and consistent manner, a major impediment to lucid dreaming is eliminated. Stereo headphones with an auto-reverse cassette player are generally required, but a foam pillow with enclosed speakers may also be effective and may be more comfortable for some.

Several points raised in the booklet accompanying the *Lucid Dreaming* series are worth emphasizing. I'd like to illustrate this from my own experience. Lucid dreaming is learned through practice and intention. I had great difficulty in the past with dream recall, so I set a goal of learning these skills over one month. I listened to each tape three times. I then selected one of the series' second, third, or fourth tapes at random to listen to at bedtime each night for about two weeks. I then spent one week listening to tape four each night. After approximately two weeks, my dream recall had remarkably improved so that I could record my experiences in a dream journal. Many important insights will become apparent if a journal is kept that would otherwise be lost to memory.

It is recommended that the listener set intentions, goals, or dream scenarios in writing before going to sleep. For example, last night I wrote, "Please give me assistance in writing the article on lucid dreaming and Hemi-Sync." Today, the article was easily written after my conscious and unconscious mind had time to process this request. Also, one week ago my wife and I had $3,600 to pay in unexpected expenses. That night I wrote, "Please help me to pay these bills." Next day my paycheck arrived with an extra $4,000 we were not expecting. Coincidence? Perhaps, although I prefer to call these events synchronicities.

In my work with patients, lucid dreaming may provide insight into their illnesses that I might not have considered otherwise. Sue S. is a delightful person challenged with lymphoma, with whom I had been doing energetic work using Hemi-Sync, Reiki, crystals, and aromatherapy, in addition to her conventional chemotherapy. Unfortunately, during the last several treatments I had become less holistic and more physical, focusing directly on the tumor in her chest, abdomen, and lymph nodes. I had totally neglected treating her head and emotional well-being (she had no brain involvement and is emotionally well adjusted despite her challenges). In a lucid dream I saw myself focusing on her head. The next day I was seeing Sue, and as I placed my hands in the energy field around her head I felt a huge infusion of energy. Sue had recently started chemotherapy and had lost her hair. Much to our surprise, her hair grew back during her chemotherapy with this and subsequent treatments.

I see several other patients in a group session with Sue. Even those who had their hair had the same energy draw about their heads. In subsequent dream sessions I relearned the importance of treating the whole patient (I have to remind myself time and again). We weren't only treating Sue's hair loss—we were treating emotional, spiritual, and multiple other components. Sue reminded me to do this with all my patients. Sue and *Lucid Dreaming* reminded me of this insight: treat the *person*, not the problem.

Utilizing the four tapes in the *Lucid Dreaming* series allows you to learn lucid dreaming and improve dream recall. The Hemi-Sync frequencies are a crucial component of this process, changing a hard-to-learn process into one readily achievable by anyone.

NURSING HOMES

Debra Davis's presentations at Monroe professional seminars are always enlivening and full of energy—an energy she displays also in her work in nursing homes, where she trains staff in the use of Hemi-Sync and distributes cassette players and tapes far and wide. Her paper is full of examples of the many ways in which Hemi-Sync can relieve pain and anxiety among the residents and also create a calm atmosphere for staff members and visiting families.

Richard Staudt and Judy McKee are occupational therapists in a long-term care facility and work with residents age 65 and over. They have created a multisensory room where Metamusic is played, and residents also have stereos at their bedsides with several Metamusic tapes available. This has proved so effective that they are now planning to use Metamusic in the dining areas, and they also envision Hemi-Sync relaxation rooms on each floor.

Bridging the Communication Gap: Hemi-Sync in Nursing Homes
Debra Davis, M.Ed., LPC, LMFT

Debra D. Davis joined the Professional Division in 1995. She has maintained a private practice in Fort Worth, Texas, more than 20 years as a licensed professional counselor and marriage and family therapist. Her primary counseling contract has been with the Parenting Center, whose clientele is a mixture of referrals from the Texas Department of Protective and Regulatory Services and Child Protective Services.

In early 1997 I began working in nursing homes. A fellow counselor at the Parenting Center told me that a company called GeroCare needed more counselors, and this attracted my attention. At first I wondered if I could handle the environment without passing judgment or fighting with staff over how people were treated. I surprised myself. I like the environment, and I'm usually able just to be there and advocate appropriately. My occasional anger is directed toward getting problems corrected.

GeroCare was founded in 1996 by David Dickson, now its CEO. David is a licensed professional counselor who has provided geriatric consultation to long-term care facilities since 1989. He was counseling at two nursing homes during downtime in his professional practice, and when he recognized the enormous need, it occurred to him that designing a program whereby other professionals contracted to provide such a service could expand coverage exponentially. Within two years of that insight, GeroCare was serving 50 nursing homes in Texas. I came on board just as he got a contract for the second 25. I am contracted to train GeroCare therapists, psychologists, and other staff members to utilize Hemi-Sync.

The overall population is aging, and the frequency of depression among the elderly living at home is estimated at between 40 and 60 percent. In a nursing home setting, excluding those with dementia, it soars to 70 to 90 percent. The traditional view saw aging as the end of adult development, and "warehousing" seemed logical. Back then, nursing home stays were fairly short. Now they may run from five to 20 years. Depression leads to withdrawal, staying in bed (which increases the risk of decubitus ulcers), behavior problems, and a generally lower quality of life. David thinks that on-site preventive measures to address depression alone will significantly reduce costs and improve the environment.

Many times I walk into a situation that is already chaotic. At these times, I just plug in the tape player and start *Concentration*. Before long, the atmosphere changes. Things come back into focus, the noise level drops, and staff and residents calm down. Smiling to myself, I go off to visit my next client. Some of the homes now play Hemi-Sync in the common areas, and problem behaviors have dramatically declined.

Success Stories

A 93-year-old woman was living independently in her own apartment. She got up one night to go to the bathroom and remembers nothing until she woke up in the hospital with a broken hip! She went directly from the hospital to the home. At first she had a private room. She had some physical therapy but still walked bent over. Instead of socializing, eating in the dining room with others, she withdrew. I saw her after she'd been there a month and had deteriorated into anxiety and panic attacks. She talked fast and nonstop to keep me there. I explained that other people were waiting to see me but I would leave some special music to help her relax. I asked her to "test" the music and promised to return.

Over the next three hours I came in to change the tape or CD several times, ending with the *Inner Journey/Sleeping through the Rain* CD. The nurse told me to keep it up. The call light had not been on since I went in that morning, and it normally flashed several times an hour. Later, the resident came out into the hall and yelled, "Help! Help!" When the nurse ran to her, she pointed to the boom box and said, "It stopped, and it was working!" It was just between items. She had gotten so mellow that the absence of the soothing music and tones upset her.

Another resident in her late 50s has many psychiatric and physical issues. She took to Hemi-Sync right away and has five favorites. I occasionally offer others, but she is satisfied with her choices. She can sense when she is getting unbalanced and just listens to a Hemi-Sync tape for a while. Before, she had to sleep for days to overcome that shaky feeling, or maybe avoid a full-blown emotional crisis. She has since been elected president of the residents' council, does a little gardening, waters the plants, and is very nurturing towards others.

Glenda Green's tapes about the information she received while painting a portrait of Jesus have also been useful. The material is practical, universal, and free of religious bias. It is now published as *Love Without End* (Spiritis Publishing). I used Glenda's tapes and Hemi-Sync with a 50-year-old with multiple physical and psychiatric problems. Her daughter had committed her to the state hospital because she went off the deep end with religion. For several months Metamusic worked well, then her medications needed adjusting and she did a nosedive into borderline personality disorder. She raged constantly and reviewed past wrongs.

Finally she started listening to a religious radio station with an apocalyptic slant. I thought that one of Glenda's tapes might introduce a bit of balance. Well, over the weeks something got through. *Energy Walk* had been left with her for many weeks, and she eventually listened to it the night before my last visit. Her whole countenance was different—more peaceful. She sheepishly said, "You know, I listened to that *Energy Walk* last night, and I really like it. Do you have more like that?" "As many as you want to try," I said, "I have them in my car, and I'll get them now." She now has two more Hemi-Sync tapes and has finished Glenda's tapes. To help her present her complaints differently, I advised her to listen to the tapes to get into a clear frame of mind and speak up concisely. It seems to be working.

I provide the tape players. They are $15 tape players with headphones and continuous play—a rare feature at that price. Some people can't tolerate headphones, but my search for a cheap, compact boombox with continuous play and a tape deck plus CD capability has so far been unsuccessful. Space is also at a premium. If the rolling tray for food is uncluttered, I put my equipment there to introduce Hemi-Sync. I tell them it's some special "sound stuff" with music and ask them for their opinion. Some residents didn't like tapes with talking but now that they know Hemi-Sync works they'll try whatever I have.

One 70-year-old man was quite angry with his wife for getting sick and admitting him to the home. He was a sailor in World War II, and his incredible bigotry causes certain aides to avoid him. Old wounds and stroke damage cause this man a lot of pain. I've tried to convince him that when one entire side of your body won't work and you are dependent on others for care, it is desirable to maintain productive communication. In the last few months he has taken to Hemi-Sync. He listens at night to manage the pain and sleep better. *Midnight* is a favorite because it's light jazz and reminds him of drinking at VFW gatherings. Also Glenda's tapes are helping him with a spiritual crisis, as he's not sure he believes in anything. Now he drives the social worker crazy changing batteries.

A woman in her 80s is in a cosmetically nicer home, although all of them are basically the same. She was evidently pampered by her late husband. Problems with her daughter and conflict between her daughter and granddaughter cause her anxiety and tension. When she said, "I can't believe things like this can happen to people like us," it gave me a clue. I selected *Surf* for her. To begin with she insisted she couldn't hear it. I shrugged and said, "Don't work at trying to hear it." Each time, she was asleep within five minutes. The nurse said, "Whatever that is, I've got to have some," and bought one for the resident and one for herself. She had just moved to Texas from Florida and missed the ocean.

Another resident has emphysema. She is on oxygen and struggles for every breath. I suspected that headphones would be irritating and used my boombox instead. Attempts to persuade her family to acquire a tape player resulted in a dictating cassette recorder with a mono speaker. I popped in a Metamusic tape anyway. She cradled the player to her like a stuffed toy, and it seemed to work. Maybe her brain remembered the stereo effect. She really took to the auto-reverse player I gave her because the staff had been neglectful about turning the tape for her despite my urging.

I received a profound lesson from a Hispanic woman whose stroke had paralyzed one whole side. She sat in the front lobby each day, looking out of the window and crying—behavior that didn't help the general atmosphere. I would plug in my boombox, start the Hemi-Sync, and pull up a chair. She told me she had cleaned houses for a living and earned enough to purchase a nice house where her daughter and grandchildren now lived. She was confused, and so sad. Medicaid, which pays me, allows only a 30-session limit per patient each year. As the limit drew near, I dropped back to checking on her every other week. In the meantime, she suffered a massive coronary and died in the dining room. When I learned of this, it dawned on me—who cares if the session isn't covered? Check on all of them every week, if only for eye contact and heart-to-heart communication. Let them know someone cares. This lady enjoyed that time with Hemi-Sync and me. Hemi-Sync assists patients with speech and occasional bursts of clarity that give insights into their thoughts and needs.

Another woman's loneliness was intensified by memory loss and confusion. She couldn't remember the names of her four children, and ten minutes after one of her niece's infrequent visits, she had forgotten the event. On bad days she calmed down with Hemi-Sync, personal contact, and reminiscing. Interestingly, listening to Hemi-Sync seemed to trigger positive and nurturing memories.

I was called in during a time of decision for a 60-year-old man who was wasted away from a life with hard drugs. He couldn't quite understand that hospice was for assisting the dying process, not for heroic rescues. His family provided a tape player and I started *Super Sleep* at once. He was in excruciating pain and dramatically sleep-deprived. Pain relief was almost instantaneous, and he slept

189

immediately. I used only *Super Sleep* and *Concentration* because he couldn't tolerate words or music. I saw him three times, then educated the hospice team about Hemi-Sync with a demo and literature. I later heard hospice caregivers discussing the challenge of insuring a medication level that would keep the patient pain-free. I approached the issue from another angle by playing Hemi-Sync at the nurses' station. The nurse got the point and even bought Hemi-Sync for herself and her family.

A coworker at the Parenting Center used the **Surgical Support** series with great success. Later, she introduced *Pain Control* from that album to her mother, who was still hurting and sleepless three weeks after surgery. Relief was rapid on both counts, but her mother grumbled, "It's just too easy." Now, two years later, Mom is living with her daughter and has become quite forgetful. She will use the tape to sleep and to relieve pain and restlessness when she is reminded. And she still protests that it's too easy!

Only one woman actually introduces me as her counselor. I usually say that I'm visiting, to avoid loaded terminology. Say "counseling" and a resident will say, "Well, I'm not crazy!" I spent weeks working up to a visit with this 80-year-old woman. She had been hospitalized and felt confused, isolated, anxious, and she practically apologized for living. I started by taking dictation from her and writing to her family, because she was unable to answer letters and that had bothered her. Making a list of family names and addresses in big, easy-to-read type got her motivated, and now she's in the thick of nursing home activities.

I recently saw a resident in her late 70s. She was never married and her family lives far away. She likes the home, but poor eyesight keeps her from reading and doing the needlework she loved for years. I set her up with *Masterworks* the next day. By noon, she was saying that she loved it. She put the tape in her dresser drawer at supper time, so I had to explain that it was for everyone's use and she could borrow it from the Social Services office. She was reassured by that and by my promise of other tapes to try.

A resident in her 50s had a heart condition. Her rapid decline after a medication change alarmed the social worker. A call to our consulting psychologists got medication recommendations, but she needed help immediately. This woman had cried frequently for days and wept throughout her evaluation. Although she had always been careless of her appearance, the degree of despair was frightening. I offered her *Remembrance* the next day. Her demeanor was hopeless and skeptical. I was insistent. She claimed to have broken three cassette players. I said, "This is cheap, so break it," and showed her how to clip it onto her wheelchair tray. About ten minutes later she appeared mesmerized and *way* into it. She returned the tape player before lunch without comment. I found her attending an activity after lunch and asked for her opinion. She smilingly told me she had relaxed and fallen asleep. Later she was observed laughing in the midst of yet another activity. Early that morning, when she was still down, she had resisted the social worker's offer to go shopping. But by mid-afternoon she was joyful and shopped like crazy at the Dollar Store. To the social worker's delight, she even bought makeup!

A Hispanic male resident was very angry about his declining health and abilities. He was either verbally abusive or he ignored all attempts to engage him. A colleague tried to evaluate him and was shouted out of the room. That night I dreamed that the social worker and I took my boombox and Hemi-Sync tapes in for this man's roommate. The roommate was practically frozen into position. Next morning we acted on the dream. I left *Remembrance* playing. As we left, the roommate was smiling and visibly relaxing. At least our "target" did not yell or protest about the music. A subsequent walk-by and visual check revealed peace and quiet. About midafternoon, my colleague returned for another interview attempt and to pick up the boombox. However, it was now tuned to a radio station, and the men had reverted to being angry, yelling, or frozen. Unfortunately, it's not unusual for the cleaning staff to switch to something they themselves prefer.

Hemi-Sync has been a bridge with another Hispanic resident. Each week we talk with the aid of an interpreter. At our second session, I introduced Hemi-Sync to alleviate her depression and frequent crying. Her daughter and granddaughter visited daily. After I explained about Hemi-Sync and the cheap cassette player, they brought one in the next day. I'd ordered Hemi-Sync tapes in Spanish, and now she asks for "Español" or "música" when she feels agitated.

The Mission

GeoCare has a special orientation. We attempt to give residents a sense of belonging and being important to at least a couple of people. We also try to create a sense of purposefulness to fill the void left by the loss of their former roles. GeoCare makes recommendations to the nurses, who pass them on to doctors as their trust and confidence in us increase.

Being there is easier for me than for the families because I've never known these people any other way. It's the comparisons that are so painful. By getting to know them fresh, I bring them the present moment and allow them to be present with me. I deal with and for them around what's on their minds right now and look at how to change the situation. The nursing home social workers are my primary source of referrals. In all that I do, Hemi-Sync is a real bonus. No one else has an intervention that can relieve pain non-invasively (without interfering with medication), and also calms the staff, residents, and visiting families.

(Reprinted with minor changes from the *Hemi-Sync Journal,* vol. XVII, no. 2, Spring 1999.)

Hemi-Sync As a Complementary Treatment with Long-Term Residents

Richard Staudt, MOT, OTR/L, LMT, and Judy McKee, COTA/L

Richard Staudt earned concurrent B.A. degrees in biology and psychology from Texas Lutheran University in 1989, followed in 1992 with an MOT in Occupational Therapy from Texas Women's University, Houston campus. He and his wife, Katie, pursued travel therapy positions in long-term care settings across the United States. After settling in Carlisle, Pennsylvania, Richard attended massage therapy school and passed the examination for national certification and licensure. Richard is also a full instructor of the John Barnes Myofascial Release approach. He is currently the occupational therapy supervisor at South Mountain Restoration Center near Waynesboro, Pennsylvania, the sole remaining state-owned long-term care facility in Pennsylvania.

Judy McKee currently holds the position of certified occupational therapy assistant at South Mountain Restoration Center. Initially employed as a restorative aide, Judy graduated from Penn State, Mount Alto, and returned to become an integral part of the occupational therapy department. During her 21 years in healthcare, Judy has also acted as a therapeutic activities service worker. Richard and Judy work together at South Mountain striving to provide a stimulating environment for the long-term residents under their care.

After working with a population of adults with physical and cognitive disabilities, Richard began to yearn for more than textbook interventions, which usually brought only limited success. His heart and senses were opened by a new treatment of the whole person, which satisfied this inner conflict. The John Barnes Myofascial Release approach, together with craniosacral therapy, used music to stimulate the right brain while manually releasing soft-tissue restrictions of the body. Recipients entered altered states of consciousness and sometimes re-experienced old childhood traumas or delved into emotional past-life episodes. Richard felt they were making connections between their bodies and minds that led to a "thawing" of their conscious perceptions. Myofascial Release sensitized him to the possibilities of hemispheric synchronization with occupational therapy interventions.

Richard found that long-term care residents with physical disabilities benefited from a combination of approaches. However, South Mountain Restoration Center offered heightened challenges. This Center has a 100-year-old history of evolving service to the community. The median age for residents is 65, and all are unique. Along with age-related illness requiring nursing care, they also have underlying psychiatric illness. Many are on psychotropic medication. Functional levels range from minimal assistance to total assistance.

Judy McKee says, "I'm an occupational therapy assistant, Richard's assistant. I've only known him for two years, and his ideas have positively changed my life. I was doing the traditional things that occupational therapy school teaches you, and Richard has broadened my horizons." Judy has 20-plus years of service at South Mountain and a simple yet profound philosophy of occupational therapy. She feels that a resident cannot benefit from whole-person therapy unless his/her mind instinctively accepts and assimilates what it is receiving without fear or coercion, regardless of cognitive capacity. This is the goal Richard and Judy set for themselves, using Hemi-Sync as the facilitator.

First, Richard and Judy met with the Medical Health Services Board of in-house physicians. After playing Hemi-Sync, Richard explained, "This is just to help relax." The next step was to screen the residents. Those who were yelling out, who were considered difficult, were the ones they wanted. "We got our first referral from the behavioral health expert and started in the therapy clinic using a small CD player, with about eight or ten inches between the speakers. The stereo system was on a table, and the residents sat in front of it, probably four to six feet away. We finally got funds and purchased a CD stereo with detachable speakers, which can be placed at opposite sides of the room. Residents have small stereos by the beds in their rooms. *Sleeping through the Rain, Inner Journey, Remembrance, Midnight, Nostalgia, Surf,* and *Cloudscapes* are the most frequently used Metamusic selections. Judy says, "*Cloudscapes, Sleeping through the Rain,* and *Inner Journey* are my three mainstays."

The occupational therapists also created a multisensory room, much like what every 16-year-old wanted in the '60s. Black lights, glow-in-the-dark mobiles, hand-held fiber-optic toys, and Hemi-Sync are presented at various "stations." A dark background was chosen because it's much easier for residents to perceive the contrast of light on dark. Judy tries one thing at a time, and whatever the person resonates with becomes the facilitation.

The following four case studies illustrate the dramatic effectiveness of Hemi-Sync within the challenging environment at South Mountain Restoration Center.

Case 1. N. W.

N. W. is a 94-year-old female with undifferentiated schizophrenia, which began at 11 years of age. She was institutionalized at the age of 19. No history of physical or sexual abuse was noted. N. W. was referred to Occupational Therapy because she would constantly pound and slap her face every day until it was beet red. She had indentations on her skull from all the years of pounding. During self-care, she would cry out and could not tolerate touch. We hoped to see a reduction of self-abuse and more acceptance of care. Once in therapy, she would not accept any tactile stimulation. Initial treatment consisted of behavioral modification, neuromuscular re-education, and traditional soft music approximately three times a week. Tactile defensiveness was reduced by 50 percent after implementing craniosacral techniques to the parietal and temporal bones. After approximately eight visits, with Metamusic incorporated into the sessions, head-striking ceased for between 30 and 60 minutes of a one-hour session. This dramatic change was difficult for staff to believe. After about another eight sessions, N. W. made eye contact. After the third or fourth month, she actually started reaching out to her environment, extended her right hand to greet us, and would reach out and hold the hand of her caregiver. She eventually tolerated grooming and skin management without self-injurious behavior. A learned response also appeared to have developed. She would automatically cease or reduce her abusive behavior and become more relaxed when brought to the occupational therapy department. To optimize carry-over, a portable stereo was placed in her room with her favorite Metamusic selections.

Case 2. R. Y.

After seeing these dramatic results, we felt obligated to try Hemi-Sync with R. Y. This resident possessed a long history of self-abusive behavior and a habit of screaming so loudly that she could be heard in the parking lot from the sixth floor! R. Y. is a 73-year-old female, severely retarded since birth. Her mother cared for her until she was 36; then she was institutionalized. R. Y.'s diagnoses are dementia and behavioral problems that include screaming, pulling her hair, and scratching herself to the point of self-mutilation. She would rub her face, eyes, and lips repeatedly, until they were raw. She did not communicate and was considered to be legally blind. We brought her to the multisensory room and played *Sleeping through the Rain* two times a week. One of R. Y.'s eyes seemed to have some sight, and she responded to the overhead mobiles. Following the first month, she spontaneously said, "You're red," to Judy. Three months into occupational therapy, she accepted and would lift her foot for massage. R. Y. usually resisted touch by hitting, kicking, or bouncing in her chair. Soon, her compulsive self-injurious pattern was reduced to occasional light stroking that didn't cause irritation. Yelling out was reduced to one or two times per one-hour session, and eye contact was maintained during conversation with staff. Within approximately five months of sessions including Hemi-Sync, R. Y. was calm and quiet for up to 40 minutes of each one-hour session. She also made a complete, relevant statement regarding the softness of a plush stuffed rabbit given to her by the activity worker—an unprecedented event. A portable CD player with Hemi-

Sync, overhead mobiles, and colorful banners were placed in her room for their calming effects.

Case 3 M. A.

We monitored residents who could not express themselves verbally by observing their body language, frequency of vocalization, and intensity of any movements. We had to look for really subtle changes, and hoped for an opportunity to learn from someone who could verbalize their thoughts about Hemi-Sync.

Our wish was answered when the secured unit received a new admission. This 81-year-old woman had a diagnosis of chronic schizophrenia with psychosis, Alzheimer's disease, and anorexia. Recurrent major depression and self-reported auditory hallucinations were also recorded. M. A. was referred to occupational therapy because she would walk out without finishing meals and sometimes remained in her room for entire shifts. She could express herself verbally but unemotionally. She would also strike out at staff and other residents. She was initially wary of the multisensory room, so we started Hemi-Sync in the open clinic during simple cognitive tasks. Developing trust allowed Judy to start sessions in the multisensory room using the *Remembrance* CD, which markedly decreased M. A.'s anxiety. After a month of sessions three times weekly, M. A. would seat herself in a beanbag chair without hesitation and remain there for craniosacral techniques. During one session, the *Inner Journey* CD was being played when she let out a loud scream and exclaimed, "I didn't do it! I didn't do it!" She refused to elaborate on her statement; however, since that "release" she has been more relaxed both on and off the unit. She recognized Judy off the OT floor and requested to attend sessions at scheduled times.

Case 4 N. F.

N. F. was diagnosed with end-stage Huntington's chorea and epilepsy and is essentially immobile and suffering from multiple contractures. At admission, she cried and moaned almost constantly without observable response to environmental stimuli. She received Tylenol for pain. She was brought to the Multisensory Room and put under the space mobile with glow-in-the-dark stars, just on the chance she could see them. Judy kept talking to her and touching her. N. F. was doing a lot of moaning and crying and was really restless; then after 15 to 20 minutes with Hemi-Sync there was no more moaning and crying. Now she responds with "baby coos." Massage work on her arms has loosened one of them up, and she can move one finger. Many times now she's not making a sound when she comes down for therapy, and the moaning and crying aren't as frequent on her unit floor. Historically a challenge for maintaining adequate nutritional status with dysphagia, she demonstrated a significant healthy weight gain of 24 pounds since initiating Hemi-Sync, although her meal regimen hasn't changed.

We'd like to pursue research and documentation in situations like N. F.'s. In individuals who have long-term or short-term contractures, joint mobility and range of motion would be measured. Then, after incorporating Hemi-Sync with the neuromuscular manual therapies, we'd check to see if there was a difference. Presently, we check the chart for decreases in medication each time a resident improves. Most of the time there's no decrease; however, we're heartened that usually there's no increase either.

Case 5 R. B.

R. B. was a 50-year-old diagnosed in 1998 with a severe chronic progressive irreversible neurological disorder called Pick's Disease. A CAT scan revealed significant frontal and anterior temporal atrophy of the brain and presenile dementia. Prior to admission, medical assessments stated that R. B. did not engage in tasks nor follow one-step commands. Upon admission, R. B. made eye contact, vocalizations, and simple rote movements with extremities associated with donning clothing, but could not execute one-step commands. After approximately 25 visits incorporating Metamusic with multisensory environment he demonstrated significant and observable progress. Presently he possesses a focused gaze on visual stimuli, is able to vocalize, and physically interacts with the environment using gross grasp patterns. Most amazingly, he initiated a structured multi-step task of stacking a cone with verbal and visual cues only! This is from an individual who was considered to be incapable of learning or engaging in any new or functional tasks due to his disease process. His further progress remains to be seen, as he continues to be treated by Occupational Therapy.

These cases are pioneers in the integration of complementary and traditional interventions at South Mountain Restoration Center. The Occupational Therapy Department, encouraged by these successes, plans to investigate the utilization of Hemi-Sync in the dining areas. The dining rooms are like school cafeterias. The residents get supplements, protein powders, and everything they need. They just do not want to eat because of the disruptive atmosphere. Responses could be measured through weight gain, number of different foods accepted, relaxation, and focus of attention. We also envision Hemi-Sync relaxation rooms on each unit. The rooms would be a sanctuary away from the hustle and bustle on the floor—somewhere residents could go on their own or be taken by a staff member if they are agitated. There's a lot of wonderful work waiting to be done!

WORK AND BUSINESS

It may be that the value of Hemi-Sync has not yet been fully appreciated in the business world. These three papers in their different ways show how useful a knowledge of the resources of the audio technology can be.

Lynn Robinson's paper, drawn from her experience in marketing and consultancy, provides a blueprint for its use in business seminars. James Akenhead gives a detailed account of using Hemi-Sync to enrich the workshop environment for a two-day program on conflict management. Finally, Douglas Black reveals how the use of one *H-PLUS* function enabled him to make a valuable contribution to a high-powered naval planning exercise in a situation when, as he says, he realized that he needed a miracle!

Business Seminars and Hemi-Sync
Lynn Robinson, Ph.D.

Lynn Robinson is an emeritus professor of marketing with a business consulting career spanning three decades. She has spoken at and facilitated workshops in a number of countries on four continents.

Straggling into the auditorium, alone or in small groups, were professionals and staff of a private hospital. They'd come to attend a seminar that would satisfy their continuing education requirements. They walked slowly, shoulders bent. Some sighed as they sat. They seemed tired. They had varying degrees of interest. They just wanted to do what must be done and return to their incessant daily demands. The speaker began. Before she could say much, an audience member seated nearby interrupted, "What is that music? It's so relaxing." Playing softly in the background, Hemi-Sync had introduced itself. It wasn't the focus of the meeting, though it could have been.

After a day and a half of intense team building and strategy work, six senior energy executives jokingly expressed the need for a nap. Having anticipated their fatigue, the facilitator agreed. While they had been at lunch, she'd set up the sound and earphone equipment for listening to *Catnapper*, a 30-minute Hemi-Sync experience that provides a full 90-minute sleep cycle. Though some were more comfortable than others with the experience, all achieved a more rested state. Revitalized, they completed the day of work.

A program for a corporate client demanded design time, and her office screamed for some housekeeping attention. To clear her desk and her mind, the consultant put *Concentration* into the tape player. She remained focused, putting enough things in order to begin her more favored creative work. She switched Metamusic selections to include *Inner Journey* and *Sleeping through the Rain*, and she was off into the far reaches of discovery and ingenuity in the design of the program that would satisfy her client's objectives.

Hemi-Sync in business situations makes good sense. Each of the three examples above really happened. The applications are as limitless as imaginable—and there are Hemi-Sync choices that can expand the imaginable.

Using Hemi-Sync with Client Groups

Depending on the topic, Hemi-Sync can work as support or it can be an integral component of a program. Either way, participants will ask for more information and give feedback on their response to Metamusic. For corporate trainers, speakers, and consultants working with groups, this audio technology is a very effective aid. Once used, Metamusic and other Hemi-Sync recordings can become an essential component of the work.

For successful use of Hemi-Sync, room setup needs to include the means to play both audiotapes and CDs through stereophonic speakers. In medium- to small-size rooms, there is no need for sophisticated sound systems. A portable boombox is quite satisfactory, though it is often helpful to bring along an extension cord if the room where you'll work is unfamiliar to you.

For a variety of reasons, participants of seminars or workshops are often uncomfortable. Hemi-Sync makes the facilitator's job easier. Having Metamusic playing softly in the background as people enter the room begins a stress reduction process for them, preparing them for pleasurable work. *Inner Journey* and *Cloudscapes* are proven relaxation winners.

At break time, it's common for a seminar participant to ask about the music. The comments are generally favorable. You can expect a few participants to feel distracted by relaxing background music, especially those persons who have high control needs. For this reason, it's important to consider the composition of the group and the goals of the workshop in the choice of Metamusic. *Remembrance* and *Baroque Garden*, for instance, will help participants to focus, and those with control needs no longer feel the need to fight relaxation. Even so, there are times when using no background music will be the appropriate choice.

When the work lasts for a day or more, it's always a good idea to have both brain and body rest breaks. Breathing, stretching, and laughing exercises are good for the body. Quick meditations and guided imagery are good for the brain, and either is improved with the use of Hemi-Sync.

When the work has been intense and protracted, the use of *Catnapper* provides a "power nap" that can prolong high-quality productivity. It is best followed by a physical moving-about exercise of some kind, to ensure a return to full attention.

Hemi-Sync and Metamusic Choices

Have several tapes and CDs with you for each work group. You'll begin to get a sense of which selections work best for you and for the types of groups with which you work. Then you'll be able to set up a rotation of selections for seamless changes, as you'll probably need alternating types of Hemi-Sync. You'll want one or more that are relaxing, such as *Inner Journey* or *Higher*. Also, bring with you a variety that help participants to focus, such as *Baroque Garden*, *Remembrance*, or *Einstein's Dream*. Each of these appeals to listeners quite differently.

Sometimes participants appreciate taking home a tape that they have heard during the workshop. A tape or CD is a wonderful "take-away" for you to give to participants.

Synergies

Any brain-related assessment or procedure is an opportunity to talk more specifically about Hemi-Sync and its relationship to your training materials. There is a natural flow between applied brain function research and the consciousness studies of Bob Monroe and the Institute. Two specific fits with Hemi-Sync are Tony Buzan's mind-mapping techniques and Ned Herrmann's whole-brain technology.

Intuition training of any kind benefits from the use of Hemi-Sync. Even so, be aware and cautious of the still-prevailing bias in industrial, scientific, and many educational settings for linear approaches and exterior solutions. Often the preference remains for the reductionist, controlled, linear, materialistic approach to learning and problem solving. Hemi-Sync is an in-reaching technology that provides for more holistic conceptualization but continues among many to elicit resistance. Consider framing Hemi-Sync as a technology for facilitating expansion of sensory input, or as an option that results in greater use and recognition of intuitive faculties. It is often easier for many people to talk about what they sense than to talk about what they intuit, though the two may be the same.

Corporate values clarification is an opportunity for using Hemi-Sync. Talking a bit about the technology can ease people into the depths not present in a typical discussion of what to do and how to do it. Then playing Metamusic in the background assists in the discovery of what matters. Hemi-Sync is a guide to the inner realms, those places less frequently visited in boardrooms. It supports, for good or otherwise, the pragmatic practices of daily business decisions. Successful corporations are value-driven, and among the more important values is that of learning.

Personal Use for Business People

Consciousness expansion and learning are keys to building and expressing your expertise. Experiment with tapes such as *Moment of Revelation, Transcendence,* or *The Visit.* Prior to use, take a moment to establish your intention for using a tape experience to improve your work. Establishing intention is like creating a gently floating objective, a suggestion to the subconscious. For a more intense experience, listen to the tape or CD (without headphones) while submerged in water.

And, don't forget to take *Catnapper* along on trips. Using it is good insurance for being refreshed, enthusiastic, and energetic.

Though business may take you by train, plane, or other conveyance to places far and near, your mind transports you to the realms of possibility. Your destinations are limitless, and Hemi-Sync is an excellent travel companion. However, don't listen to any Hemi-Sync product while you are in control of a vehicle. The relaxing aspect can distract you from your responsibility as a driver.

The more familiar you are with Hemi-Sync, the greater will be your appreciation of the options for use and application. You'll develop your personal preferences and your own recommendations.

Team Development Strategies: Looking at the Frontier
James Akenhead, Ed.D.

Jim has earned five university degrees including a doctorate in education and a master's degree in counseling. He served 23 years as a school superintendent and 20 years as a university instructor and consultant. In 1995 Jim was acknowledged by the Alumni of Bowling Green State University as a distinguished graduate. In June 2000, Jim and his wife, Charlene, backpacked Alaska's Chilkoot Pass, noted by some historians as the meanest 33 miles in history. Jim is also a certified canine trainer.

In today's organizations, the development of work teams becomes a formidable undertaking. Even more difficult than the initial establishment of a work team is the challenge of keeping a team vibrant over time. As a work team becomes more sophisticated, the task of providing new growth experiences requires finding a new focus each year. That focus becomes the driving force for training and integrating new skills and new understanding into the team's operation. Here is an overview of one such effort to take a team into less charted territory.

Finding out what is happening at the frontier of research on human potential can be demanding and sometimes confusing. There are many so-called experts who profess ideas that, when checked closely, have a questionable, untraceable, or even nonexistent scientific basis.

One organization whose members perform such research is the Professional Division of The Monroe Institute, which is involved in the study of human consciousness. These members include psychologists, psychiatrists, medical doctors from several specialty areas, physicists, biologists, chemists, geneticists, college professors, educators, administrators, counselors, and a host of others from various countries around the world.

The Professional Division holds regular symposiums to share proposed research projects, review results of prior efforts, and exchange ideas on how to increase human potential. As an educator and consultant for more than 30 years, one of my primary interest areas at these conferences has centered on those features that might help tired, burnt-out people get more from their time in seminars, workshops, and presentations. Typically, adding an element of humor, varying instructional methods, and attending to creature comforts are the conventional methods that receive attention in this regard. However, as a result of involvement with the Monroe professional group, I decided to take a different approach to help these "tired, burnt-out" people obtain more from their time and effort.

The project I designed involved using Hemi-Sync for enhancing the delivery of a workshop on conflict management. The overall intention was to investigate how this audio-technology system might enhance instruction in an otherwise standard training program.

Objectives

A primary objective was to provide a group of school administrators with the skills and understanding to make them better conflict managers. In addition, we used the Hemi-Sync technology to improve the workshop learning environment by helping participants maintain a centered state in which they would be able to deal more effectively with conflict situations. This centered state or focus could be thought of as similar to "the zone" that athletes and other performers refer to and credit with their ability to perform under pressure.

Content

The curriculum for the workshop included a study of how the individual personality style of each participant might relate to conflict situations. Each person's style was compared with a hypothetical style deemed to be productive in managing conflict. Following this analysis, participants were given lectures, structured activities, and simulations that further acquainted them with the nature of conflict and methods for conflict resolution.

At the beginning of the workshop, we told the participants that Hemi-Sync would be used to enrich the workshop environment. Various audio tapes and CDs would be played in the background while the workshop was being conducted. We briefly explained the technical aspects of Hemi-Sync, together with information on brain-wave changes. We also included information on the frequency-following response and its capacity to support productive brain-wave patterns. We pointed out that the use of certain sounds embedded in music or pink noise and conveyed via a stereo system is able to induce predictable brain-wave patterns. The idea is that this allows us to exert some control on our mental focus.

During the workshop we employed four approaches.

1. *Concentration.* The nonverbal *Concentration* tape was played during the lectures and debriefing sessions. We explained the technology and rationale of this tape and ensured that the volume was sufficiently high so that the sounds could be distinguished. Then the sound was turned down so that it faded into the background. Our purpose here was to make it easier for the participants to stay focused during the seminar.

2. *Metamusic.* During small group discussions and breaks, Metamusic selections were played. We assured participants that neither on these nor on any of the other tapes or CDs were there any subliminal messages. The selections we used included *Cloudscapes* and *Daybreak.*

3. *Exploring.* The tape *Exploring,* from the series ***Journeys into Creative Problem Solving,*** developed by Applied Creative Leadership Systems in conjunction with The Monroe Institute, was introduced in the last phase of the workshop. This tape employs guided imagery as an

additional resource for creating and exploring options for use in problem solving and planning relative to conflict situations.

4. *Relaxation.* We introduced **H-PLUS** *Relax* to help bring about full-body relaxation by repeating the function command on a deep breath. The effect of this may be compared to what happens when we hear a favorite song that brings about relaxation, exhilaration, or general good feeling. We suggested that once it had been practiced, this personal code would initiate the relaxation response on cue and this could help regain a centered focus in stressful situations.

Reactions and Perceptions

We decided to evaluate the Hemi-Sync technology by asking the participants about their perceptions. Each participant was asked to complete a form giving reactions to each situation in which Hemi-Sync had been used. Thirteen of the 15 participants completed the form. The other two had to leave early owing to other commitments. We also undertook a statistical analysis of the replies.

Conclusions

1. *Concentration.* The participants themselves did not think that the *Concentration* tape helped them to maintain alertness or focus. However, we are aware that owing to the nature of this tape, personal perception may not be the best method to evaluate its effectiveness. A formal test to assess actual increase of knowledge or skill might be more appropriate. Our own observation led us to think that the tape did help participants to maintain a more intense focus on the material presented. We thought this because even though the environment for the workshop was unusually hot and humid, participants stayed on task when normally these conditions would reduce their attention span and energy level.

2. *Metamusic.* The participants reported that the Metamusic selections had a positive effect on their levels of productivity and also relaxation during small group discussion sessions and breaks. We felt that

the music was enjoyed by all. We used standard stereo equipment with speakers in the four corners of the room, and no problems were experienced.

3. *Exploring.* The use of this tape for guided imagery and enhancing creativity was not regarded as helpful by the group. We felt that the negative response might have been caused by the use of this tape only at the end of the workshop, when time was short and the room was especially hot.

4. **H-PLUS.** The Prep side of **H-PLUS** *Relax* was perceived by participants to have a marked impact on their state of relaxation. About half of them said they could not believe that anything could relax them to the degree that was accomplished by listening to this tape.

Summary and Personal Observations

We concluded that the elements of Hemi-Sync technology that were employed in this project enhanced the delivery of the conflict management seminar. The problems were minimal, and careful orientation resolved most questions about the nature and intent of the tapes. Some participants perceived the tapes as being similar in effect to hypnosis, while one had a conflict with personal beliefs regarding the use of the creativity and relaxation tapes and was provided with alternative activities. In general, we feel that the technology succeeded in demonstrating its value in support of a seminar setting.

Waking ... Knowing
Douglas M. Black

Douglas M. Black, Colonel USMC (Ret.), has worked in the commercial and defense information technology industries and has studied the Monroe technology for more than a decade. He has attended four residential programs and is an active member of the Dolphin Energy Club and the Professional Division. His memoir *Finding My Way* highlights his personal journey of spiritual discovery through his training in and application of the Monroe technology. He currently lives with his wife in Salisbury, North Carolina, where he writes.

During the early 1990s I served as the senior communications staff officer at Headquarters United States Marine Corps, for Command, Control, Communications, and Intelligence. During that period, one of my duties was to participate as a staff planner and discussion leader in an annual naval exercise hosted by the chief of naval operations at the Naval War College, Newport, Rhode Island. This was a weeklong technology and staff planning exercise focused on the deployment of U.S. and allied naval forces in various global war fighting scenarios. Members of the U.S. Defense Department, various agencies, the State Department, and members of the defense industry, among others, were in attendance, lending their particular expertise to the issues under consideration. The importance of this event lay in the development and verification of future naval war fighting strategies. Key among the many topics reported on as a result of the exercise was the accurate identification of areas of technical weakness that required attention and investment to ensure that future war fighting strategies would be successful and able to support various foreign policy scenarios.

I reported to Newport with several of my colleagues from the Washington area. My specific assignment was ground battle commander. I would work in close coordination with two senior Navy officers who would act as the surface and amphibious ready group commanders. The three of us, with advice from a retired admiral, a well-respected and amiable submariner, would run our portion of the exercise and interface with other groups such as air warfare.

Meeting our team as they reported on day one of the exercise, I recall being very impressed with the large number of credentialed professionals from nearly every aspect of the war-fighting community. We occupied a large 1940s-style classroom, blackboards and all, with floor-to-ceiling windows. When all the straight-backed oak chairs were filled, I estimated that our team numbered nearly a hundred experienced and eager professionals. Our immediate task was to quickly get organized and then address how we might achieve our primary goal: to identify the essential or core key technology weaknesses in joint and combined war fighting (United States alone, and with allies). It was a tall and frankly never-ending task. Given the personality types, experience level, and dedication of the individuals sent to these events, we organized very quickly, and by the end of the day we had a fairly clear idea of what we were about.

I was very pleased to see this progress but was quite disturbed to learn very late in the day that my two co-commanders were being called away to handle unexpected and unavoidable crises. Although one said he would be back, I did not expect to see either of them again that week. In short, I was virtually on my own! I felt abandoned, and I was terrified. The admiral and I looked at each other, sighed, and shrugged our shoulders. We knew all too well that operational priorities must come first. The key people who attended these exercises had real-world assignments that occasionally overrode the needs of such exercises. In quiet desperation I put my papers in my briefcase and walked slowly down the hall and out the front door.

That night, after a dinner I hardly tasted, I returned to my hotel room wondering how in God's name I was going to pull this one out of the fire. I knew that I was not experienced enough to play the surface warfare role successfully, although I could handle the amphibious role and my own. But that was not the key issue in my mind. The key issue was what process I was going to use to arrange the many technology issues that I expected to surface over the next several days. How, among all these experts with their own strong opinions, pet programs, and issues, would we be able to determine which was most or least important? After all, budget decisions would be based, in large part, on our recommendations. More importantly, in the five to ten years to follow, the success of foreign policy and the lives of uniformed and civilian service personnel would depend on us getting it right this week.

I had completed my first resident class at The Monroe Institute a few months before and had purchased and was beginning to apply some of the Hemi-Sync tapes sold by the Institute. I had also brought some TMI reading material with me just in case there was extra time— silly me! But among that material was a tape entitled *Wake/Know* from the **Human Plus** series. I had purchased this tape as an experiment. Early in my regular job assignment as the chief communications staff officer for the Marine Corps, I had quickly realized that I was faced with a tremendous workload and the requirement to learn a mountain of new material. I felt inadequate and not up to the task, but failure was not an option. So, along with working long hours, finding and keeping talented people on the staff, and trying my best, I also began to explore Hemi-Sync materials in hopes of enhancing my productivity. *Wake/Know* had arrived in the mail the week before, and I had brought it along with the intent to read up on it and possibly try it out during the exercise.

As I considered my options that evening I realized I needed a miracle. Other than doing my best and inspiring others to do the same, then sorting out the results, I desperately wanted some idea of what might be the "right" answer to be looking for at the end of the week. I made some notes concerning how I wanted to proceed in the morning. I recall looking at the clock on the dresser. It was ten at night. I was beat and knew I needed a good night's sleep and answers, but since I was fresh out of ideas, I put the *Wake/Know* tape on and climbed into bed.

Trying to relax, I asked the question: "What is the key technology requirement that needs to be fulfilled, which will drive all other essential future war fighting processes?" And then I slept.

Vaguely, I became aware that I was waking up. I opened my eyes to find the ceiling over my head was deep black. It filled my vision. I was faintly aware that I could not see my hotel room. "This is odd," I recall remarking to myself. "God, it's dark in here for morning." I stared at the blackness above me as it began to change. Slowly but steadily the center of the blackness in the middle of the ceiling began to extend downwards in an inverted mound shape. The action was slow and deliberate, as if the protrusion were working against substantial resistance. It reminded me of the tar that I had once pulled from city sidewalks as a child in Indianapolis. On summer days the normally hard tar between the sidewalk sections would become hot and pliable, and my friends and I would pull it loose in chunks and then throw it at each other or chew it like gum!

Then in the blackness of the growing mound there were bright orange-red fracture lines appearing and radiating out from the center of the protrusion. As the protrusion grew, the lines of fracture lengthened in all directions. I watched, mystified, in my early morning half-dream state. After what seemed like only a few minutes, the mound stopped growing and a voice said, in what I perceived as clear and deep resounding English: "Data base management."

The mound immediately retreated upward until the black ceiling resumed its normal flat appearance. The orange/red fissures closed about it, and the blackness faded. I lay in my bed stunned, motionless. I recall hardly breathing. Suddenly I realized that my eyes were *not* open, but closed! I opened them. There was the hotel room, dusky in the early morning light, ivory walls and ceiling, bed, table, lamp, chair . . . all there. The blackness was gone—fading quickly into the dust of dreams. But the voice . . . the voice remained clear and imposing. I stared at the ceiling, felt the bed covers around me, and slowly began to comprehend that I was lying in the same position in which I had gone to sleep the night before—flat on my back, sheets and blankets pulled up to my chin, arms folded over my chest on top of the covers. Wow! What had happened? The irritating snap of the alarm on the electric clock interrupted my thoughts; the music began and so did day two of the exercise. The main difference was that I might have an answer to my question.

I dressed, ate, and hurried to the classroom. I met the early-rising Admiral there who stopped me at the door and with a concerned look on his weathered, careworn, but friendly face asked, "Well, Doug, what's the plan for today?"

"We're going to focus on data base management, Admiral," I replied. "We'll walk each warfare area through their war fighting processes and see which essential war fighting data bases need to interact, highlight those that do not, and see where that leads us."

The Admiral eyed me with surprise. "I did not know you were a data guy."

"I'm not, sir. I really don't know anything about it. I'm just a mud communicator—you know, two wires and a telephone. Data processing is not my area."

"Well, where did you get this idea?" he asked with a searching look.

"I was thinking about it last night, and it sort of—came to me. Anyway, it seems like it might be a good way to get things going. What do you think?"

"Let's give it a try," he replied in a supportive and relieved tone.

We exchanged smiles and moved to the head table to get day two rolling.

Three days later, after many hours of demanding, often stressful and contentious discussion and dialogue, our recommendations led off with the topic "Integration of Essential War Fighting Data Bases" as the most critical investment requirement to ensure future war fighting and defense success. I felt certain then, and believe to this day, that the Hemi-Sync tape *Wake/Know* provided a process that allowed me to know the answer to my question, even though I had no practical experience in that area. Really needing the help surely played a part, but the astounding results were, for me, undeniable.

BEYOND THE UNITED STATES

In recent years the use of Hemi-Sync has spread worldwide. Outreach trainers are resident in 13 countries outside the United States, and individuals from more than 50 countries around the world have attended residential courses in Virginia.

In this chapter, Linda LeBlanc discusses the introduction of Hemi-Sync to Cyprus, in the Eastern Mediteranean, where she organizes about four Outreach workshops a year. The island is divided between Greece and Turkey, with different politics, languages, and religions. Linda lives in Paphos, in the Greek part of the island, and is able to conduct workshops in English, although her participants have represented 13 different nationalities, including Russian.

The first workshop in Poland took place in 1996. All the texts had to be translated into Polish, and a Polish version of TMI's website was created. Pawel Byczuk wrote several articles on Monroe and Hemi-Sync for various journals and himself produced an improved translation and oversaw its printing. Pawel hopes to establish a holistic center in Poland and to encourage TMI trainers to visit and present advanced workshops in the future.

Hemi-Sync was introduced into Slovakia by Peter and Miro Simkovic in 1995. They founded a non-governmental organization called Annwin, which took on Hemi-Sync as one of its interests and makes use of the technology in its various training courses with the tapes presented in both Slovak and English. Annwin is now active in several training programs, and Peter Simkovic is a member of the management board of the European Multicultural Foundation. Both the British and the American embassies have supported Annwin's activities.

In the United Kingdom, the Hemi-Sync center is tucked away in a corner of southwest Scotland where Jill and Ronald Russell moved from Cambridge in 1994. Here they present courses and workshops; they also cooperate with a number of organizations that are interested in integrating Hemi-Sync into their work.

Finally, Jeanne Basteris recounts an incident during a workshop in Puebla in central Mexico. Jeanne presents workshops in Spanish and numbers several doctors and psychologists among the participants.

Hemi-Sync in Cyprus
Linda LeBlanc

Linda LeBlanc is cofounder of Psychognosia, a privately funded not-for-profit center for dissemination of reliable information on anomalous phenomena, based on the Eastern Mediterranean island of Cyprus. She has completed six Monroe residential programs, and as a Gateway Outreach trainer she organizes workshops in Cyprus and other countries.

Cyprus is an island in the Eastern Mediterranean, less than 100 miles from Israel, with a population of about 700,000—the size of a small city. It is often referred to as the crossroads of Europe and the Middle East. Cyprus has a long and rich history with traces of settlements going back more than 10,000 years. It is the mythological birthplace of Venus, goddess of love (Aphrodite as she is known to the Greeks). In recent times, Cyprus has experienced war, invasion, and partial occupation in 1974, which left the island's two ethnic communities of Greek and Turkish Cypriots divided by politics, language, and religion. United Nations peacekeepers have been stationed here for more than 40 years. It is a country faced with difficult choices and centuries-old problems to resolve.

I began introducing Hemi-Sync to Cyprus in 1997. Two years later, I organized the first English-language **Gateway Voyage** on the island, presented by two TMI residential trainers. The program was very well received, and in the following year I began to facilitate Outreach workshops myself.

Culturally there are difficulties here, with little toleration for anything that does not conform to the predominant Orthodox Christianity. Meditation is generally considered heresy and the devil's work, with unreasonable fears about cults and Satan. Language is also a problem, even though many people have some knowledge of English. We have had requests for explanations in Greek, but for Greek speakers I usually recommend Metamusic, which transcends the language and cultural boundaries.

On average, I organize about four Outreach workshops each year. Most participants are complementary therapists or individuals interested in personal growth. In the past three years about a hundred participants, representing 13 nationalities, have attended my workshops, including a Russian who proudly showed me his Russian-language copy of *Journeys Out of the Body*. Feedback has been overwhelmingly positive, although I have had one or two participants suggest that the course is much like programming. Interestingly, before I have a chance to respond, another participant points out that what goes on in daily life out there is the programming—and what we actually do is deprogramming! About a quarter go on to take my other workshops, and several have subsequently traveled to Virginia, where they did two programs back-to-back to save travel costs.

The workshops have been the scene of some unusual happenings. As our first program was ending, two Jehovah's Witnesses (very rare in Cyprus) appeared at the house where it was taking place. Our hostess told them we were just finishing a spiritual retreat. Asked if she had her own religion, she replied that she now had direct-dial! Towards the end of the next workshop one participant noticed a small snake by the front door. We felt it to be a fitting symbol of the power of the transformative weekend we had just experienced. Another time we held a workshop in a former stone quarry cave, which had been beautifully converted into a conference hall. Doing Hemi-Sync in the arms of Mother Earth created a unique atmosphere that seemed to facilitate the unfolding, awakening process of the group.

Some Personal Stories

Barbara Spitzer, a mother of three and an artist, had gone through a near-death experience a few months previously. Since then she had been feeling very isolated, with no one in her family or circle of friends interested in her life-changing experience. After the NDE she had longed to return to "the light." It was a time when she "didn't want to be here." Then, hearing about the Outreach programs, she offered to host a workshop at her home, even though her husband had shown little interest in anything to do with consciousness. The program went so well that Barbara's home is now my favorite workshop location. Her husband has been impressed by the people who come, some even traveling long distances to attend.

During the first program, Barbara had an experience on one exercise that took her back to the joy she had known during her NDE, to the blissful union of cosmic consciousness. This experience was so positive and so "real" that she found it much easier to integrate the aftermath of her NDE, helping her to achieve a balance between spirit and the physical. She said that after using Hemi-Sync she was "able to cope better in a difficult time of life," adding that "my life just worked better." She achieved greater self-confidence and was now able to speak up and express her feelings in group situations. Her husband, who had been gently cajoled into attending the workshop, now thinks differently about many things, realizing that there is far more to the whole experience of life than he had previously imagined. This has led to a deepening of their relationship to the benefit of both. He now avidly reads her books on spiritual subjects!

Dr. Lenia Efthymiou is a dental surgeon, specializing in the replacement of mercury amalgam fillings. Several of her patients have severe long-term health problems, and most of them are nervous, fearful, or anxious when anticipating dental treatment. Lenia plays Metamusic during treatment and finds it to be particularly helpful, leading her patients, especially those with serious health problems, to feel better, more relaxed, more confident, and less nervous. Some don't even require injections, and two actually fell asleep while she was working on them. On return visits, many ask specifically for Metamusic, *Sleeping through the Rain* being the most popular choice.

On a personal level, Lenia says that Hemi-Sync enables her to work better, especially during the more stressful treatments. While she was pregnant she listened to Metamusic for relaxation and introduced it to the gynecological clinic where she gave birth. Her daughter seems to appreciate it also—whenever she hears the music she moves her limbs as if dancing and is a very contented baby. The clinic now plays Metamusic for the newborns.

Marina and Vladimir Hadjidemetriou run a healing Tao center in Cyprus. Every day, between ten and 15 people listen to Metamusic during yoga, tai chi, meditation, and individual treatments. This now often replaces the "regular" music they used to play. Marina teaches yoga to pregnant women and introduces them to the **Opening the Way** series for pregnancy support. Cyprus is a difficult environment for any woman wishing to have a natural birth, as many births here are by Caesarean section. Marina has formed a support group for those who wish for natural births and she uses **Opening the Way** as the common ground to help them connect to each other.

Marina is also a Chi Nei Tsang instructor, using abdominal massage to release residues of emotions. Using *Surf* during treatment sessions, she feels that "the space in the room is transformed by Hemi-Sync," helping both giver and receiver to move into what she calls "that golden space." As a therapist, she feels that she senses more deeply and her clients are able to "surrender and abandon" more easily during treatment. Her favorite selections include *The Visitation, Gaia, Spirit's Journey,* and *Inner Journey* for group meditations. She says, "Hemi-Sync has changed everything—sometimes we don't have to do anything at all."

Judith Worsteling is a relaxation and stress counselor and Reiki practitioner. She reports that Metamusic helps her clients to release traumas more easily and to sink more completely into relaxation. She has found *Gaia* and *Sleeping through the Rain* to be especially helpful and observes that her clients seem to relax automatically as they shift into a state of "body asleep, mind awake." Judith also used the **Positive Immunity** series to help herself in recovery after an emergency operation for an ectopic pregnancy that involved a great deal of pain and emotional release. She listened to the tapes every day for a month following the operation, enabling her to maintain clarity with emotional issues surfacing. Her strength increased day by day.

Anastasia Nicolaou, a British- and South African-trained yoga teacher, uses Metamusic for her students and for herself. It helps her stay more focused and centered, helping her to provide the best training she can while her students are noticeably more relaxed and don't fidget at all. Favorite compositions are *Winds over the World* and *Cloudscapes*. Anastasia has also found *Remembrance* quiets down her three very noisy dogs.

Angela Komatina is the organizing secretary of the Paphos branch of the Cyprus Association of Cancer Patients and Friends. She operates a lending library of Hemi-Sync tapes. Since the mother tongue of most of Cyprus's cancer patients is Greek, Metamusic is the popular choice, with *Transformation* being especially effective in creating a calm atmosphere. The *Pain Control* tape has worked well with English-speaking patients, who are mostly reluctant to return it.

Angela played *Baroque Garden* for her aunt, who was dying of brain cancer; this was the only music to which she responded at all. She also used the **Going Home** series with her father, who listened to it over the three months before he died. In what proved to be his final weeks, she requested a DEC healing for him. The night before he died, he asked her to switch off the light in the room—but there was no light! He was very calm, spoke clearly and lucidly to his family, then said it was time for sleep. He died peacefully the next day. Angela felt that Metamusic and the **Going Home** materials helped to maintain a calming effect in his last days.

Barbara Jones, a teacher with 20 years' experience who has studied learning disabilities, was given leave to use Metamusic in the classroom during a period of substitute teaching. She played *Prisms* every morning before school began, finding that it somehow cleared and crystallized the atmosphere. "The air seemed to sparkle," she said. While the six- and seven-year-olds did their spelling and numeracy tests she played *Baroque Garden* and *Remembrance*. "There was a level of deep concentration and focus during those times," she reported. On one occasion she was playing *Baroque Garden* during a creative writing session when the music, for some reason, stopped. One child, who was borderline ADHD, came up to her frowning and looking quite cross. "I just can't think now the music has stopped," he said. "The others are all distracting me." He found that the music helped him focus directly on his task, instead of the multiple focus that characterized his problem.

Barbara came across one child who had a serious attention problem but, being new to the school, had not been assessed. He was very disruptive in class and had serious difficulties with the boundaries of personal space. After trying a number of different approaches, she gave him *Baroque Garden* with headphones. He was given his own workspace, with defined boundaries, and managed to work on his own fairly well. After Barbara left that school, he was put on Ritalin to control his behavior and was considered to have very poor memory retention. But when Barbara met him some 18 months later, he said, "Miss, remember when I used to listen to the music and work?"

While Barbara cannot say exactly how Metamusic affects the learning process of children, she suspects that each responds in a unique way, as each child has its own way of processing the world and experiences. "I believe the beauty of Hemi-Sync is that it works regardless of the variables. It shifts and moves with the listener, as the waves in the ocean shift and move with the tides," she says. She now uses Hemi-Sync as an integral part of the Programs for Progressive Development, a multidisciplinary approach to all aspects of a child's development to help create physical, mental, and emotional balance and harmony. All the children she works with have access to *Surf* every night. She finds *Flying Free* very accessible for children, with the sounds of the real world helping those who have difficulty visualizing. Many children with ADHD are poor sleepers, often suffering from bad dreams. The positive experience of *Flying Free*, coupled with the deep relaxation it helps to bring about, can have a profound effect on such children. One six-year-old learned to bring the monsters in his nightmares under control. They shrank and shrank until eventually he reported that they made him laugh and even did things to entertain him. "Sometimes they try to be scary, but they don't scare me any more," was his final comment.

Conclusion

In our high-tech, high-stress world, many of us are searching for easy-to-use techniques to help relax both body and mind. In keeping with our modern times, it is appropriate that Hemi-Sync is a high-tech solution to the many problems associated with our fast-paced way of life. But unlike many products of our technically advanced society, this technology benefits several thousands of listeners around the world. Cyprus, owing to its geographic location, finds itself in an even more high-stress situation than most countries. As a microcosm of the planet, with a varied population mix from many different cultures, Cyprus has been a good testing ground for the effectiveness of Hemi-Sync, transcending as it does, especially with Metamusic, the barriers of language and culture. This was again demonstrated when early in 2003 Jill and Ronald Russell from Scotland joined me in presenting two *Going Home* workshops. There was such an enthusiastic response to these courses, which were fully booked, that further *Going Home* workshops are planned. In addition, people from neighboring countries have been travelling to Cyprus to attend Hemi-Sync workshops.

It has been a delightful discovery for me that so many people are open and willing to give this audio technology a chance. With such a small population, word of mouth spreads rapidly, resulting in more and more people coming to know Hemi-Sync. We have seen excellent results in many areas: stress management, teaching, dentistry, cancer, pregnancy, yoga, and personal growth.

Introducing Hemi-Sync here has been both stimulating and gratifying for me personally. My goal is to help others so they can help themselves. It's about self-empowerment, helping people to tap into their greater potential. My experience in Cyprus demonstrates the effectiveness of Hemi-Sync as a universal tool for self-help and self-discovery.

Hemi-Sync in Poland
Pawel Byczuk

Pawel Byczuk has an M.S. in biomedical engineering and currently works as a software developer. He has been involved with Hemi-Sync since 1995 and is responsible for all the technical elements in presenting workshops. He manages a website and edits printed materials for a variety of activities. In a country with severe economic problems, Pawel is greatly concerned with securing the future for himself and his wife. As he says, promoting products such as Hemi-Sync cannot guarantee an acceptable level of living.

It was in the early 1990s when Robert Monroe's *Journeys Out of the Body* was officially published in Poland for the first time. But you can't say it wasn't known about before—just the opposite. Even before the fall of the Berlin Wall, one could get a poor-quality duplicated copy from some underground printing firm. In those days behind the Iron Curtain, people in Poland lived in quite a different way. The years of communism developed specific needs, aims, and values far different from those prevailing in the West, and usually beyond the West's understanding. Spiritual searching, although sometimes producing valuable or even outstanding results, grew on a poor base from the literature that was obtainable, with some slight influence from Eastern and Western achievements in the exploration of human consciousness. A good "paranormal" library in those days consisted of a collection of books and pamphlets occupying one short shelf. It was much the same with audio recordings or advanced electronic devices. But the changes in Russia and Central Europe at the turn of the 1990s brought radical improvement. Poland and neighboring countries opened themselves to the new technologies and ideas.

Soon after the first volume of Monroe's trilogy was published in Poland, one of our friends, Dana Torriente, much affected by his experiences, came into contact with the Institute. After a while, once we had overcome the financial and customs barriers, we could enjoy our first Hemi-Sync tapes, but these were not the only barriers to be conquered. The last and seemingly most serious was the language. In the countries behind the Iron Curtain, the education systems provided Russian as the only foreign language. Only a very few people managed to learn some of the Western languages through their own efforts. In our interest group just a few individuals here and there had a good command of English. Still, as we were willing to make full use of Hemi-Sync we had to understand the verbal guidance, and the only way to do that was to translate the texts of the tapes. Then the listener having both the original and the translated text could follow the exercises, learning the sequence of instructions and picking out keywords such as "Focus 10," "Access Channel," and so on. This worked well in practice. It required additional work from the listener but brought good results. Translating proved a major challenge for those who undertook it. It was a very absorbing process, especially as transcribing the verbal guidance onto paper was made more difficult by the relaxing Hemi-Sync sounds that detracted from peak, fully conscious performance! Copies also had to be made. Later we could use original transcripts that TMI made available, but the beginning was tough.

In spring 1995, being greatly impressed by this extraordinary sound technology and now with some experience of it, some of us joined the Professional Division or became Sustaining Members. This was a crucial time for the future of Hemi-Sync in Poland.

The first few years of political change in our country provided a very good base for making use of new, valuable, or unusual technologies and practices. The market was lively, with a large number of New Age festivals and fairs being held almost every weekend. This gave us many opportunities of presenting Hemi-Sync to a wider audience. The first serious presentation of TMI's sound technology took place during the Second Pomeranian Esoteric Meeting in Szczecin in November 1995. That event was prepared by Grazyna Byczukowa (like myself, a professional member) with considerable help from our whole family and was reported in *Focus,* Summer 1996. It was intended to provide valuable knowledge, and it presented interesting ideas through lectures and seminars by experts in various disciplines. It worked very well and resulted in a growing interest, countrywide, in many of these new ideas, especially in Hemi-Sync. From then on, opportunities greatly increased. I contributed several articles on Monroe's research and its results and on the basics of Hemi-Sync to most of the popular New Age journals in Poland. Also Grazyna and I were interviewed on radio and television. All this increased interest in TMI and its products, so to meet the needs we obtained Hemi-Sync dealer status. About this time, the Polish version of TMI's website appeared, increasing the amount of information available.

We now had to become more professional and to provide better-quality translations and informational materials. I created an entirely new edition right through from translation to final printing. Language was not the only barrier; in a country where the average salary was about $150 a month, $15 for a single tape was a great sacrifice. But many of our increasing group of Hemi-Sync users dreamed of more exciting adventures and wanted the whole **Gateway Experience.** Amazingly, this whole program, especially **Wave 1** *Discovery*, is among our bestsellers!

However, tapes and printed materials were not enough. The logical consequence was to introduce Hemi-Sync workshops. The first workshop was held in May 1996 in Rzeszow, led by Julie Mazo, at that time TMI's Director of Projects. It was a great event, attended by about 30 people from all over Poland. It was held in a primary school gym during the holidays and must have resembled TMI's touring workshops in the early years. However, that workshop was only a short-term solution as it could not be repeated in the same format.

We had to make the next move, and in 1997 we obtained Workshop Presenter status. Grazyna and I set up a first workshop in March in a small boarding house on the edge of a forest on the slopes of the Karkonosze Mountains in the south. Conditions are perfect:

calm and quiet, close to nature, and with the good vibrations of the mountains. The room takes ten persons lying on mattresses, ideal for a two-day workshop. Our workshop program is designed on a number of levels. The first level is mainly based on *H-PLUS* exercises, with lectures and social games. The second level deals mainly with the exploration of expanded awareness, involving both mental and spiritual work. The third level is intended to create a baseline for coordinated action for healing and for encouraging consciousness development. We decided not to use headphones but to continue with speakers on both sides of the room so that everyone could experience a unique resonance of the whole body with the sound. It is an ideal acoustic environment where the whole room resonates with Hemi-Sync. We have had more than 200 participants in these courses so far.

The tapes most in demand include *De-Hab, Let Go, Mobius West,* and *Eight Great.* Also among the bestsellers are *Moment of Revelation, Concentration,* and *Remembrance.* There is interest in Metamusic and in CDs, but our countrymen lack funds to invest in Hemi-Sync with music only.

At the present time things have rather slowed as other practices have attracted attention, but the number of Hemi-Sync users continues to grow, though more slowly than before. The Internet does help us to reach a larger audience. We have met several people who have had experiences with extraordinary states of consciousness, healing, dowsing, and meditation. Some of our original workshop presenters hold workshops elsewhere in Poland, mostly using the **Gateway Experience** program.

We can record considerable success—Hemi-Sync does flourish in Poland, but there are still further goals to achieve, including establishing a holistic center and offering advanced workshops led by accredited TMI trainers. With the continuing changes in our country and in the consciousness of Poles, our plans may well be realized.

Hemi-Sync in Slovakia
Peter Simkovic

Peter Simkovic, cofounder of Annwin, based in Banska Bystrica, is a project manager and trainer. He has attended several training courses on working with individuals and groups and mainly focuses on the personal growth of individuals by conducting shamanic and Hemi-Sync workshops. Since its foundation, Annwin has concentrated on personal growth and the transformation of Slovakian society. It is active in several programs, including democracy and human rights; social area programs; NGO programs; and health, private sector support, and spiritual programs. In all programs the trainers combine the techniques of Process-Oriented Psychology, Hemi-Sync, and shamanism. In October 2002 Peter was invited to join the board of management of the European Multicultural Foundation.

First Touch in Scotland

It was late summer in 1995, a few days after our first shamanic experience, when my brother Miro and I were sitting in a plane on our way to London. We landed at Heathrow and made our way by train to Scotland, where we met our trainers and our friends Jill and Ronald Russell. We stayed with them for a week while we experienced Hemi-Sync for the first time. Our stay there was like visiting grandparents at a beautiful house full of little miracles. While we were experiencing many Hemi-Sync tapes, Jill was preparing very tasty food for lunch and dinner. She took great care of our comfort, and the atmosphere was very special.

During one tape experience I took a journey to a cave in a place without time. There I met my power animal, which I had contacted for the first time only a few days before. It was a wonderful journey, full of colors and pictures from different places and cultures. I went through a gate where everything was full of light, accompanied by a wonderful sound. This was not music, just a gentle sound. It seemed that my body was full of that sound.

My English then was poor, so my brother, who had been studying English for many years, interpreted for me the important parts of our discussions with the Russells, but I had no problem understanding Bob Monroe's instructions on the tapes. I felt that his voice was leading me into the 10 and 12 states. A year later, my English had greatly improved.

First Course in Slovakia

I established Annwin (www.annwin.sk) along with my brother and my wife, Vierka, in 1995. Annwin is a nonprofit educational organization, with the goal of organizing seminars, courses, and workshops designed to support the individual's growth. There was a vision of supporting people to become more free, responsible, and mature, after the climate of our society had changed, and to make spirituality part of their everyday lives. Making important spiritual techniques accessible to people was critical because there were many schools and techniques appearing with no apparent quality and without any scientific background. Later, we also learned how to bring spirituality into our everyday work as trainers and to apply it in techniques and training, for example, in communication or conflict resolution.

A few weeks after our first Hemi-Sync experience in Scotland, Annwin organized in cooperation with the Russells the first Hemi-Sync course in Slovakia. This held a special atmosphere for me, as I had been married only a week before and it was a wonderful way to spend a honeymoon. The course was prepared with great help from the Department of Culture of the Zvolen City Authority, especially by Ms. Katarine Hrckova. She helped us by copying and distributing the course leaflets, and she found a way to arrange for the Russells' accommodation at Zvolen City Castle, a property of the Ministry of Culture of the Slovak Republic.

The course itself took place in the Hotel Kralova, in the mountains near Zvolen. The atmosphere of late autumn with its colors contributed to the feeling of comfort and calmness. The 26 participants, who came from various educational, professional, or spiritual backgrounds, were active during discussions following the Hemi-Sync tapes. The Monroe Institute and members of the Professional Division were very helpful in providing a supply of tapes. This training, as well as making personal contact with Jill and Russ, was a life-changing experience for many of the participants. They obtained skills for dealing with spiritual experiences that were larger than themselves—helping to end the war in Croatia was the task for one of the participants. A group of middle-aged men had common catastrophic visions, probably connected to experiences of their generation, especially during 1968 when the Soviet army stopped the nascent freedom in our country by invasion. Thanks to new skills learned and the help of their inner teachers, as well as the support of our trainers, they were able to deal with those visions and transform the energy into creative matter.

Two years later we organized a course presented by the Russells and ourselves in Plzen, in the Czech Republic. This took place in the meeting room of a large mental hospital. The participants, including two senior doctors, came from different departments in the hospital. Like Slovakia, the Czech Republic was still suffering from the aftereffects of the occupation. The course itself was enjoyed by the participants, who were also impressed by the fact that the wards above the meeting room were exceptionally quiet while the course was being held. In 2003 we returned to the Czech Republic to present introductory courses in the university city of Oloumoc and in the capital, Prague, which were well received and attracted more men than women. We expect increased interest with the recent translation of Robert Monroe's *Far Journeys* into Czech and the translation of *Ultimate Journey* in the near future.

Daily Use

Hemi-Sync provides some powerful tools that are very simple to use, for example: the REBAL (Resonant Energy Balloon), **H-PLUS** function commands, and a simple way of entering the Focus 10 state. I found especially that REBAL in everyday use is an effective tool for conflict and problem resolution or prevention. Let me illustrate this. Slovakia as a former communist country has well-developed public transportation. This is mainly because of the shortage of private cars, as they were too expensive for the average family. Every big city has a transportation system with buses, trams, or trolley buses. As a young man I used public transport. Sometimes when I was traveling home from far away outside the city where I lived, I would be in a stressful situation worrying if I might catch my bus, as there were only a few minutes to spare. I used my REBAL so that there was a green light at every crossroads, and finally I caught my bus. The REBAL is also very useful in personal contact with officials, colleagues, or bosses. Each time we meet a new group at training we use the REBAL to reduce the tension in the group. Our graduates also use this technique frequently.

Good Response

Among our earlier undertakings were weekend training seminars using a psychological approach based on the work of Arnold Mindell. Process-Oriented Psychology (POP) offers very useful skills for transforming disturbing experiences such as physical symptoms, relationship conflicts, chronic diseases, dreams, and group problems into positive experiences for growth and development. Combining the work of Jung, Neuro Linguistic Programming, Taoism, and shamanism in a specific and creative way, Mindell has developed methods helpful in personal, small group, and community development.

We used Hemi-Sync as an effective tool for creating a comfortable, relaxed, and open atmosphere. During one of these training seminars when people openly talked about their views on spirituality, I decided to introduce Hemi-Sync in the evening, although it was not actually on the schedule. We listened to *Deep 10 Relaxation* and then *The Visit.* When the participants returned to everyday consciousness, one of them began to cry. After a while she openly explained to the group that she had met her father, whom she had never known because he had died a few months before she was born. She was very happy to have met him, and this experience had a positive impact on the following group processes.

In 1996 there was a survey of public health matters in Banska Bystrica. One of the factors that were found to influence health negatively is stress. We offered a new "Hemi-Sync: Anti-Stress" evening program based on Hemi-Sync technology. Our target group was women living in the city and its surroundings. Through grants in 1996 and 1997 from the Healthy City Community Foundation, we were able to offer participation to women from poorer areas who could not afford to come. The full program consisted of six evening sessions, with participants experiencing two tapes each evening. We found that a main benefit from this kind of program was the continuous feedback from participants, as they had a week to use the tools they had learned. The feedback was very positive, and many of the participants wanted to attend the program again.

One participant in this program was a neurologist who had been using yoga for many years. She reacted strongly after hearing *Deep 10 Relaxation*, saying she had never experienced such a deeply relaxed state of mind. She was so excited that she sent us some of her friends from the yoga group she belonged to. Another participant lived in a rough and dangerous neighborhood and was constantly under tension. I was very surprised when I met her a few months after she attended the course. She thanked me very much for helping her. She was, she said, a new person. She had found the inner power to keep her family and herself safe and secure.

Death and Dying

Vierka and I attended the advanced shamanic training course in the Austrian Alps, led by Michael Harner of the Foundation for Shamanic Stidies. During that training I traveled for the first time to the "land of death." I had an interesting experience on that journey—I met Bob Monroe, who guided me. I never met him during his life, although I knew his face from photographs and his voice from the tapes. This was a most exciting experience—and I can say I know Bob Monroe a little bit more!

A year later Vierka, Miro, and I went to Scotland again. We spent a week at the Findhorn Foundation and then visited the Russells, where we went through the ***Going Home*** series. It took two years to prepare and organize a ***Going Home*** workshop in Slovakia. This took place in a small hotel in the mountains, and the British Embassy in Bratislava financially supported the project. We conducted a preliminary weekend workshop ourselves, during which I talked about The Monroe Institute, Hemi-Sync, and Bob Monroe and introduced the participants to exercises in Focus 10 and 12. Jill and Ronald Russell came over to present the *Going Home* workshop and attended a press conference in our office. The participants who attended this program included professionals working with older persons, people with cancer, the chief of the regional Red Cross office, the head of a mental hospital, a doctor who traveled from Poland, and people interested in death and dying issues. Discussions during the workshop were full of personal experiences of participants who met relatives and others who were no longer physically alive. For many this proved a valuable therapeutic process.

The youngest participant in this course was our son Patrik, just ten weeks old. He slept soundly through all the tapes, sharing his deep state with the rest of the group. He woke up immediately at the instruction, "one . . . wake up. . . ." He continued to sleep during discussions and the break.

A year-long, follow-up networking program was conducted to support the work of our graduates, and we offered *Going Home* training to two new groups.

Other Activities and Hemi-Sync

In 1997 and 1998 Vierka worked as a part-time psychologist at a social house for mentally and physically disabled persons. As she has a disabled sister herself, she always dreamed of sharing POP techniques with personnel working in those institutions. With her experience and her three-year POP training, we prepared a new program for those working with the disabled. This program included teaching the basic skills of using special nonverbal (minimal) signals, drawn from POP techniques, for better communication with disabled persons, as well as using Hemi-Sync tapes during their daily work. Aware of the burden of their work, we offered them the Hemi-Sync Anti-Stress course. Several positive experiences have been reported, especially in making better contact with autistic children. While listening to Hemi-Sync, eye contact becomes longer, and the child is more open to communication and playing.

In 1999, the Mayor of Zvolen asked us for help in the organizational development of the Zvolen City Authority. This work had two levels. We worked with some members of senior management using psychological tests, then prepared an educational training project for all management levels, financed by the Westminster Foundation for Democracy, London. The main purpose of this work is to help officials to work better, cooperate, and communicate both within the municipality and with citizens. Our work with municipal education continues this year with another project including the Hemi-Sync Anti-Stress workshop and advanced training in communication.

A Personal Note

A couple of years ago there was a fire in our flat. A hectic time followed, and it took a lot of energy to repair the damage, to care for Vierka and little Patrik, and to continue with work. I began to feel extremely tired, and never felt I had enough sleep.

Then I discovered my blood pressure was very high, about 155/90 for several months. I have a digital blood pressure monitor, so I could keep observing what was happening. Then when I was organizing material for a Hemi-Sync course, I found the **H-PLUS** tape *Hypertension* in our library. I listened to it and let it work for a few days. When I checked my blood pressure for the first time after using the function command, I found it was 132/85.

I decided to try an experiment. I took my BP (140/87), used the function command, and monitored my BP immediately afterwards. The result was 119/80! I repeated it after a while with the same result. As my blood pressure continues to fluctuate during the day, I am now using **H-PLUS** *Heart: Repair and Maintenance* at night, hoping that the two function commands will work together to stabilize it.

Our Current Project

Annwin is now well established with offices and a meeting room in the center of Banska Bystrica. Miro has left us to pursue his own career, and we now have others working with us. We are very busy with workshops for people working in the social area, and we are planning another *Going Home* course. Just now we are involved with a three-year project to create forums for working with national, ethnic, and racial tensions in cooperation with CFOR (London). The first-year funding is by Allavida (Charity Know How) London and the Westminster Foundation for Democracy. For future funding we apply to the European Union.

With a Scottish Accent
Ronald Russell, M.A., and
Jill Russell, LCSP(Phys.), M.F.Phys.

Ronald Russell is a graduate of Oxford University and an author and lecturer with several books to his credit, the most recent being *The Vast Enquiring Soul*. In 1993 he edited *Using the Whole Brain*, the predecessor to the present volume. He lectures from time to time for Glasgow University on issues concerning human consciousness.

Jill Russell was a departmental librarian at Cambridge University until she changed direction and qualified in 1980 as a remedial massage therapist. She employs craniosacral techniques and is also trained in remedial yoga. Jill is a long-distance swimmer, now approaching 4,000 miles raising money for various charities. She holds the record for the greatest number of Amateur Swimming Association Supreme awards gained by a woman. The Russells are members of the TMI Board of Advisors.

New Galloway is Scotland's smallest Royal Burgh. Its population is about 340, much as it was shortly after it was founded in 1631. It has a post office, one shop, a nine-hole golf course, and is set amidst fields, forests, lochs, moorland, and hills with the River Ken within sight. Since 1994 it has been the only Hemi-Sync center in the United Kingdom.

For seven years we had been presenting courses and workshops in Cambridge, a university city with a lively population of inquiring minds eager to investigate new technologies and to find new ways of self-improvement. New Galloway is, well, different. How would the good folk of southwest Scotland respond to this weird stuff?

Strangely, they did not find it weird at all. Most of those who came to use Hemi-Sync were introduced to it through Metamusic, which helped them to relax physically while keeping them mentally awake and alert during their time on Jill's massage table. Many asked questions about what they had been listening to and then went on to buy or borrow a tape or CD, usually *Inner Journey* or *Sleeping through the Rain*, or, if it seemed appropriate, *Remembrance*. *Higher* is another composition that often helped to achieve emotional release, sometimes freeing up "past-life memories" or recollections of traumatic events. Patients might also be introduced to *Deep 10 Relaxation* or *Energy Walk*, depending on their needs. Some went further, investigating the home **Gateway** series or selected **H-PLUS** exercises. There have been no negative reactions.

We have two attic bedrooms that are wired for headphones with the audio equipment housed in a cupboard between the rooms. Up to seven people can be accommodated. For several years we presented weekend courses, with participants coming from nearby villages or from as far away as Dover and South Wales, both more than 400 miles distant. A group from Newcastle-upon-Tyne, 150 miles away, completed three of these weekend courses and undertook to come again any time we had something new to offer. The longest journey, however, was that of the Simkovic brothers, founders of the Annwin centre, who came from Banska Bystrica in Slovakia to be introduced to Hemi-Sync (for their story, see their article in this chapter). In return, we traveled twice to Slovakia to present introductory workshops, and, two years later, we ran the first **Going Home** workshop undertaken outside the United States. We also cooperated with the Simkovic brothers in organizing an introductory workshop for the staff of a mental hospital in Pilzen in the Czech Republic.

Presenting two- or three-day courses in one's own home is not easy when it involves providing overnight accommodation and full catering. It was a relief when in 2002 we were invited to present an Excursion workshop on the well-equipped premises of the Upledger Centre in Perth, Scotland. John Page and Carol Houston, who run the Centre and spearhead its work in the United Kingdom and much of Europe, have themselves attended two courses in Virginia and are eager to integrate Hemi-Sync into their work. We hope to organize more workshops in Perth in the near future.

Since moving to Scotland, we have accumulated a large number of contacts—people who phone with inquiries or to order tapes or CDs, who have come across the Monroe website and want more information, or have had unusual experiences and somehow have discovered our phone number or e-mail addresses. One such was Angela, from Glasgow, who phoned to ask if we had ever heard of such a thing as an out-of-body experience. In our conversation she revealed that for the past 12 years she had been subject to a strange feeling that she was being pulled out of her body as she lay in bed—and she was terrified lest she fail to get back into it. This might happen four or five times a night. She saw doctors, who sent her to psychiatrists. She was physically examined and brain-mapped. She visited the Parapsychology Department at Edinburgh University, which failed to help her, and consulted a psychic healer who told her the Devil was after her soul. Eventually she called at the Mitchell Library in Glasgow, one of the largest public libraries in the United Kingdom. Somewhere in her inquires she had come across the phrase "astral travel," so she asked the librarian if there were any books on that subject. The librarian, more than surprised by this question, which had never been put to her before, checked the records and came up with a first edition of *Journeys Out of the Body.* Angela sat down, opened the book at random, and found herself reading a description of her own experience. She finished the book, spent much time and money trying to contact The Monroe Institute by telephone (the contact number in the book was of the Whistlefield address!), and after a long struggle with the overseas operator was connected to the wonderful Helen Warring, who gave her our number.

Since then, Angela has visited us several times and worked with several Hemi-Sync tapes. She has learned to overcome her fear and to control the out-of-body experience, and she has also taken part in a research project on the OBE. She is just one of the many interesting and resourceful people we have met through our work with Hemi-Sync.

In the last two or three years we have turned to working with various organizations which find Hemi-Sync helpful in their own programs. Members of the local cancer support group are very interested in the *Chemotherapy Companion,* and we have had encouraging and positive reports from everyone who has used it. Currently we are cooperating with Cancer Bridge, a new cancer support center in Northumberland, opened by Prince Charles. Recently we introduced some of their staff to the **Going Home** series on a weekend course. We are drawing up a program for an organization dealing with dysfunctional youngsters and their families and hope to have Hemi-Sync installed in a music room they are designing. One other organization we have cooperated with is the South-West Scotland Rape Crisis Centre. Having found that playing *Inner Journey* in the background during interviews enabled sensible conversation to get under way very quickly, the Centre organizer went on to purchase a further 17 CDs and also introduced Hemi-Sync to patients in the local hospital.

Our work with individuals carries on all the time. In this regard, we are delighted with the new Metamusic releases, especially with *Indigo for Quantum Focus* and *The Seasons at Roberts Mountain,* which make effective alternatives to *Remembrance.* Jill has also had an excellent response from patients when playing *Deep Journeys* during treatment.

Another new departure came as a result of discovering that research is being undertaken on the effects of cat's purring on bone and tissue repair. Cats' injuries heal remarkably quickly, and it appears that the 25 Hz frequency at which cats purr is effective in aiding this healing process. The thought occurred that this might be good for humans as well. However, as cats cannot be guaranteed to remain purring continuously in the proximity of an injured limb, the Monroe laboratory has produced a Hemi-Cat—a CD of purring with a 25 Hz signal embedded. We have used this with a suspected case of osteoporosis that on later investigation was found no longer to exist! This points in a direction that we hope will be followed with further research.

One of the most fascinating things about Hemi-Sync is that there seems to be no end to the uses to which it can be put.

Hemi-Sync in a Mexican Thunderstorm
Jeanne Basteris

Jeanne Basteris is a Monroe Outreach Trainer who lives and works in Mexico, presenting the Gateway Excursion and other workshops in Spanish. Jeanne is a member of the Professional Division and the Dolphin Energy Club and has made Hemi-Sync programs her full-time activity. She was born in Toronto, Canada, and went as a small child to live in England. Educated there, she later returned to Canada, where her varied interests led her through a career in the fashion industry, a small family homestead farm, and later to veterinary work on a cattle ranch in Alberta. At a family occasion in 1985 she met Luis Basteris, a Mexican businessman, who invited her to "come know Mexico." A year later they were married.

When I am preparing a group of workshop participants for their pending changes in consciousness, I always make a point of including some suggestions for them to deal with distractions during the process. Mexico is a very busy country with lots of people going about their daily activities. To find an isolated, quiet place that has the required amenities for presenting a Hemi-Sync event is not always possible. I often have to settle for a location right in the midst of a bustling town or city. That was just the case when I went to present the first Monroe Excursion Workshop in the city of Puebla, about two hours southeast of Mexico City.

I was rather nervous about the event during the days before I went to set things up. I had been told by the lady who was sponsoring the workshop that she had several doctors registered as participants. I thought, "Oh heck, they're going to be a really skeptical bunch, refuting and challenging the technology." It was also one of the first workshops that was wholly in Spanish. Previously, I had been presenting English programs in the United States, but in Mexico only to participants who had good levels of English, until the workshop tapes became available in Spanish. I wondered if my level of Spanish at the time could handle technical discussions with skeptics. I was on my own.

Somebody must have been smiling down benevolently on me, because I was lucky enough to find myself with a group of medical practitioners who employ holistic and alternative treatments together with "conventional" medicine for their patients. Most were specialists of one kind or another, as well as being general practitioners. All were strong proponents of the power of mind and body working together in the healing process. Great!

The group had 18 participants: seven doctors, three psychologists, two civil engineers, two university students, one university professor, and three homemakers. It was May, the beginning of the rainy season in central Mexico. From May to the end of September, usually in the late afternoon, we get very sudden storm cells which move in and dump torrents of rain, along with intense electrical activity—big claps of thunder and lots of lightning flashes touching down. The storms rarely last more than an hour, but they are very dramatic. They stop as suddenly as they begin, and out comes the sun as if nothing has happened! They're impressive displays of the forces of nature's energy that we live with. Power failures are common, due to the frequent lightning strikes, so trying to finish the workshop before the storms arrive is another consideration. The electronic equipment that delivers the sound evenly to multiple headphones does not run on batteries!

It was on the second day of the workshop, and the group was about to explore the exercise *Problem-Solving in Focus 12*. The two adjoining office rooms where we held the event had large picture windows along two sides. I had darkened them with big sheets of construction paper to about three-quarters of their height, and the sky was still clearly visible in the upper areas. The horizon became really black, and something told me that I had better give the participants a suggestion of how to manage a thunderclap, because the ominous cloud cell was going to arrive during the upcoming exercise.

During the opening discussions on the first morning of the workshop I had offered the group ways of dealing with distractions—noises like dogs barking, people shouting in the street, or invasive traffic. However, everything in me pressed me to think fast about how they might deal with thunder. So I suggested that they use any sudden flashes of energy as if they were the booster rockets of the space shuttle leaving the atmosphere. They might consider that the energy represented a powerful launchpad to accelerate themselves to where they were headed. This was not exactly the quiet, relaxed drift up to Focus 12 that they get from the tape. However, it was better than having their whole exercise ruined by the shock and surprise of an electrical discharge whacking them back into the material world!

About ten minutes into the exercise, a lightning strike occurred so close to the building that the crack shook the window and made me jump off my chair. I quickly scanned from my adjoining doorway seat the two rooms of participants laid out in their "nests" of foam pads, sleeping bags, and cushions. To my amazement, every one of the 18 reposed quietly, breathing deeply. Just one person opened her eyes briefly, then went off again. I was so proud of them, serenely continuing their exercise while their trainer was bounced off her seat!

Afterward, while we were in a sharing circle of discussions, one of the doctors told us how he had seen a bright red flash, and that he had used it to catapult himself to a level of awareness that he had never experienced before. He had embraced it and incorporated it into his experience. The group all agreed that they had either ignored the passing storm or had used it in their progression to the expanded energy state of Focus 12. Only one lady, the one who briefly peeked out at the room, said that she felt a little scared by the strike, but that when she saw all was well she embraced it happily!

Of course Hemi-Sync didn't do that! It merely provided the opportunity for the participants to use their own innate abilities in dealing with the surprise. This is the aspect that fascinates me so much—that with the aid of Hemi-Sync, any average person can so easily and quickly access areas of his own psyche and encounter such abundance and wisdom. For me personally the most useful application of Hemi-Sync is in the medical arena. The more accepting our medical community becomes of the reality and the usefulness of the "mind and body" connection, the closer we get to opening science and research to move onward in exploring and furthering the use of this marvelous capability that we all possess.

ANIMALS

If you accept that animals possess consciousness (and surely that is undeniable), then there is no reason why they should not be affected by listening to Hemi-Sync. More research in this area would be very welcome, and it would also be interesting to see what differences it would make if Metamusic were played in veterinary surgeries. So far, all we have is anecdotal evidence—as included in this chapter—apart from the experiments with Some Match and Kerry Mist reported by Helene Guttman in *Using the Whole Brain*.

In the meantime, the reports in this chapter suggest various ways in which Hemi-Sync can benefit dogs, cats, and horses, and readers may be encouraged to attempt their own experiments. Goldfish and pigs should make interesting subjects for study. What about placing a tape player on the bird table? *Midsummer Night* should be an appropriate tape to play.

Metamusic to Enhance Physical and Emotional Comfort in Animals
Suzanne Morris, et al.

Suzanne Morris's Pets

For more than 20 years I have used Hemi-Sync to support my personal well-being and to enhance the comfort level and learning abilities of infants and young children with special needs. Through these personal experiences with humans, I began to consider whether an animal in distress could become more at ease with the support of Metamusic. This is the story of three animal members of my family who taught me what a powerful contribution Metamusic could make to their lives.

Salem

Salem sat with his lovely auburn back in the straight, regal posture known to every Abyssinian cat. His world revolved around our family, and his purr could be heard whenever he crawled up into a lap for his special caresses. Salem's world was turned upside down when we moved from Wisconsin to Virginia. His perceptions were heightened the day the moving vans arrived, and he expressed his fear by escaping and hiding in a corner of our roof deck. Eventually he was recaptured and endured a three-day cross-country trip to his new home. His distress continued. For weeks after the move, he expressed anger and fear in his body movements. He was frightened of being outside, yet was unhappy being in the house all day. He did not want to be held and seemed agitated when we stroked his back.

Salem had been a very clean and fastidious cat who used his litter box and kept his coat clean and shining. Gradually he began to urinate on the furniture and have bowel movements on the rug. He refused to use his box. I tried every strategy I could think of to calm him down and to deal with the increasing number of messes in our house. Nothing worked. I became desperate and found myself expressing anger at the situation by rubbing Salem's nose in a pile of cat poop and throwing him outside. I was appalled that I had reached this level of response. In order to calm myself, I sat down with my headphones and a Metamusic tape. As I got more in touch with what I wanted and what I didn't want in this situation, I thought about the possibility of using Hemi-Sync with Salem.

I had just completed a pilot study that looked at the responses of 20 young children with developmental disabilities when music containing Hemi-Sync was used during therapy. At that time I knew that Hemi-Sync affected the way in which I personally responded to the world; however, although I saw initial positive responses with the children, I was very skeptical. I had also seen positive responses when other types of music were used in therapy and initially thought that the children were responding positively to the music alone. Over a five-year period I systematically observed the children who came weekly for therapy. I charted their responses to sessions in which no background music was used. I observed their reactions to similar sessions in which a specific calming musical selection was played. Finally, I observed and charted their responses when Hemi-Sync signals were added to this basic musical selection. Seventy-five percent of the children showed positive responses to the Hemi-Sync sessions that were substantially greater than to sessions using only the music.

As I sat and considered the predicament that Salem and I shared, I contemplated the similarities between his responses and those I had seen in children who had difficulty processing and integrating sensory information. I was intrigued but realized that I didn't want to rush in and use Hemi-Sync as a Band-Aid. I was upset and angry and knew that this would be communicated to Salem. I also had no idea how I would offer Hemi-Sync to an animal that was in constant nervous movement. He was totally uninterested in music coming from stereo speakers when it was playing in the room. I decided to approach Salem as I had the children in my study. I wanted to know whether it could really make a difference, not just in getting him to resume use of his litter box, but in easing the overall distress that was clearly guiding his behavior.

I began to use a Metamusic tape daily for my own personal calming. I systematically cleaned up Salem's messes without anger and without punishing each transgression. The messes continued at the same rate as before, approximately three "accidents" per day. I also kept track of the length of time that Salem would let me touch and stroke him. He initially accepted my handling, but within 30 seconds he seemed uncomfortable and would jump off my lap. I recorded baseline data, and at the end of the week the chart showed 35 messes in the house. He still was not using his litter box.

During the second week I decided to use a modification of headphones rather than a stereo presentation of music. I purchased an inexpensive set of headphones for a Walkman-type stereo player, cut the metal headband, and taped the pieces together so that it was slightly wider than the cat's head. At the end of the first week I introduced Salem to the headphones without music. He sniffed them and was curious but soon lost interest. I then began to play a tape with rhythmic, calming music through the headphones. I held them at ear level and engaged Salem's curiosity in the sounds that he could hear. He was quite interested but withdrew if the headphones approached his ears. For the next two days I enticed him with the music three or four times a day. Gradually he accepted the headphones held gently against his ears. He sat in my lap and listened for a minute or two several times a day. I also used a splitter that enabled me to listen simultaneously to the music through my own headphones. During that week his messes decreased by 20 percent. I felt encouraged and knew that Salem was feeling more comfortable.

In the third week I changed to *Midsummer Night*. Salem's transformation began almost immediately. During the first session, Salem sat on my lap and listened to the music for five minutes. In the previous week his longest listening session had been two minutes. His body became very heavy, as though he were very deeply relaxed. During his second session with Metamusic I tried to communicate with him mentally. He was deeply asleep and purring. I created a guided imagery, which I communicated to him through images in my own mind. I envisioned Salem, asleep on my lap. In the picture story, Salem felt fullness in his abdomen, woke up, went downstairs, and relieved himself in the litter box. Within a minute of this communicated imagery, I felt Salem's abdomen get firmer; he woke up, stretched, and went downstairs and used the litter box! He had definitely received and responded to my communicated request that he use his box again. After that session Salem had a few more accidents in the house but began to use his litter box regularly. I continued to do Metamusic sessions with him daily. He loved them and often slept deeply with the music for up to 40 minutes. One day he came to me and meowed and led me to the table where I had placed the Walkman. He leapt up on the table and began to bat the headphones. He had recognized his own need for listening to Metamusic. Salem continued to be entranced by the listening sessions for several more weeks. During this period he returned to his former level of happiness and comfort. He loved to explore outside and loved to be held and stroked.

I have always used the guideline in therapy that children know what they need and are drawn toward it. A child often engages in an activity that supports comfort or learning and then discards it when it is no longer needed or helpful. I saw the same pattern with Salem. Once he discovered Hemi-Sync he wanted to listen and spend time with the music. However, as he internalized the benefits from Hemi-Sync and his sensory and emotional systems returned to a state of balance, he no longer needed the listening sessions and gradually lost interest.

Galadriel

After moving from the city to the country, my 11-year-old son was excited about adopting his first dog. As soon as we approached the litter of golden retriever puppies, Galadriel rushed toward David with ecstatic enthusiasm. She was a mass of puppy wiggles who delighted in everything, almost to the point of hyperactivity. We had decided to raise Galadriel as an outside dog who had inside privileges. She had a small doghouse and fenced area adjacent to the house. David spent most of his summer hours with her and they became inseparable friends. It was his responsibility to help her learn appropriate behavior when she was in the house. This proved to be an immense task. Galadriel became so excited when she came inside that she was almost uncontrollable. She ran and jumped and barked and careened into furniture. David showed patience with her and tried to help her learn to calm down. However, once she became overly excited about being inside, it was impossible to help her learn to be calm.

David had observed the changes in our cat, Salem, when I used Hemi-Sync. One day he asked if he could try it with Galadriel. He had the idea that if she could be calm when she initially came into the house, it would be easier for her to learn. I created a dog-size set of headphones for him and gave him the tape player and a Metamusic tape. He and Galadriel sat on the front porch with the headphones and music. Galadriel sat on his lap and listened briefly. David stroked her and told her how nice it was when she sat quietly and calmed down. As her moments of calm behavior became more frequent, David moved closer to the front door. During the week, he and Galadriel gradually moved inside the house for their listening sessions. Galadriel was quite calm when the headphones were removed and maintained her ability to control her exuberant behavior for longer periods. Hemi-Sync helped her learn what it felt like to be happy and calm when she was in the house.

Six months after Galadriel joined our family she began to chase cars. One afternoon a slowly moving car hit her. She was badly frightened and bruised. We used her headphones and Metamusic to help her remain calm in the car on the trip to the veterinary hospital. Our veterinarian was surprised that she had no physical symptoms of shock after this accident. He said that she should remain in the house for several days in order to rest and recover. Galadriel was uncomfortable and in some pain, even with medications. During this period she was greatly comforted by intermittent sessions of listening to Metamusic with her headphones.

Finn

Finn participated in the life of our family for nearly 13 years. He was a relatively calm and quiet golden retriever who seemed to take everything in his stride. He loved life and running in the beautiful fields and woods around our home. Thunderstorms, however, turned him into a quaking mass of fear. He typically sensed a storm's arrival 30 to 45 minutes before the skies blackened and the lightning began. He would begin to quiver, and eventually his whole body was overcome with small tremors. He drooled and whined and hid under furniture. He was most comfortable taking refuge in a small bathroom that had no window, but he did not return to his normal state until nearly an hour after the storm had passed.

For years I dealt with Finn's fear of thunder in standard ways. I spent time with him during storms, stroking him and talking with him. I gave him homeopathic and herbal remedies. Our veterinarian even prescribed a prescription medication. In time I simply learned to live with Finn's fears, thinking that there was nothing left to explore.

For eight years he lived his life in fear of these noisy storms, and I adapted my life to try to make it easier for him to bear. Despite my continued use of Metamusic in my personal and professional life, it never occurred to me to try it with Finn. Then during one particularly noisy storm, I noticed that my boombox was sitting on the living room floor near the table under which Finn was cowering. Without thinking, I turned it on, placed it right in front of his nose, and played *Inner Journey*. Within five minutes his tremors had stopped. The wild look in his eyes began to recede. He placed his head down on his paws and appeared to be listening to the music. Within ten minutes his eyes closed, and he slept through the remainder of the storm. At that moment thunderstorms ceased their power over Finn's life, although he continued to be uneasy when he anticipated the approach of a storm. However, he now had a special boombox, which I placed on the floor of the downstairs bathroom, his storm retreat room. When he came into the house, he immediately headed for the bathroom and lay down with his nose against the boombox. He calmed as the Metamusic filled his ears. He usually slept during the storm itself and emerged as soon as it was over.

Salem, Galadriel, and Finn expanded my perceptions about Metamusic and its impact on physical and emotional well-being. They have taught me that the effect of sound and music on the nervous system is not exclusive to human beings. Animal companions can find comfort and healing in an environment of binaural beat sound technology.

Carol Hanson's Brandy

(Adapted from an article by Carol Hanson in *Focus*, vol. XXIII, no. 4, Fall 2001.)

Carol's elderly dog, Brandy, was becoming more and more "hyper" (as she described it) as the years passed. At 14, her nervous behavior was disruptive, especially during thunderstorms. Sedative drugs did little to help the situation. Brandy would fuss to the point that Carol had to change her own sleeping habits in order to accommodate her dog's need to feel close and secure.

Wondering what she could do to calm Brandy's behavior, Carol recalled the calming effects of the Hemi-Sync CD *Surf*. As all else had failed, she thought she might as well try it, although, as Brandy was nearly deaf, she was not very optimistic. However, Brandy responded well and in time became so attached to the relaxing sounds that she would "ask" for it by standing in her bed facing the CD player. There she would wait, remaining standing, until Carol put the recording on. Brandy would then lie down, settle herself, and enjoy!

Brandy became accustomed to Carol's own use of Hemi-Sync also. This was shown one day when Carol was reclining and listening through headphones to *Energy Walk*. Instead of climbing up on her, as she usually did when Carol was lying down, Brandy just sat quietly in front of her. When the tape ended, Brandy moved across to her bed and lay down, totally relaxed.

The Russells' Suki

Over the years we have had several queries about using Hemi-Sync with animals. The most bizarre was from a farmer in Northern Ireland whose cattle were continually disturbed by low-flying helicopters, to the extent that they charged around the field in a state of panic. Would Hemi-Sync help to pacify them, he asked. We explained that he would need to install at least two and preferably four or more loudspeakers in the field, and provided he could achieve sufficient volume there was no reason why it would not help. We sent him a couple of tapes and are still awaiting his report.

More practically, we were told that there was often a problem with horses being taken to competitive shows. Before leaving the stable yard they were measured to ensure that they came within the limits of the class in which they were entered. On arrival at the showground, however, when they were re-measured by the judges it was sometimes found that one or two of them now exceeded that limit—if only by a millimeter or two, but enough to disqualify them. This tended to happen with younger, less experienced horses who apparently tensed up during the journey by horsebox, adding those critical millimeters to their withers. The larger horseboxes were wired for music, mainly for the entertainment of the driver and grooms on long journeys. By including Metamusic in the repertoire, the horses noticeably relaxed and the problem of anomalous measurements disappeared.

Lastly there's the story of Suki. Suki was a calico cat of distinctive character and great beauty. In her earlier years there were occasions when her hunting instincts came to the fore, and she would bring in a small bird or mouse that she had killed. When this happened, she would be shut into a room with Metamusic playing, usually *Midsummer Night*, in the hope that this might not only relax her but also provide her with, in Bob Monroe's words, a different overview. It appeared to work, in that gradually she ceased to kill her prey on the spot but would bring the bird or mouse into the house, release it, and observe it until one of us was able to rescue it and return it to the garden.

Suki remained fit and well until she reached the age of 18. Then her health deteriorated, and eventually she needed vitamin injections every two or three months to keep her in a reasonable state. But the time came when it was clear that she could not continue like this. A local vet, John, had looked after her for some months, and she appeared to like him. We called him, and he agreed to look in after he had dealt with the bullocks on a nearby farm.

That morning, Jill was ironing in the bedroom. Suki lay on the bed. Metamusic was playing, *Inner Journey* and *Sleeping through the Rain,* and Jill invited Suki to make her transition there and then, should she so desire. Suki just yawned and stretched out on the bed. When Jill finished ironing and went downstairs, Suki followed. It was a warm, sunny day. We sat in the garden waiting for the vet to arrive, and Suki curled up beneath the garden table.

John is an experienced country vet, mainly concerned with farm animals, a down-to-earth, practical person. He had phoned to say he would be late—some of the bullocks had not been cooperative—and when he arrived he sat down with us and we chatted for a while. Then he examined Suki, very gently, and declared that yes, it was time, and it would only take a moment. There was a gentle breeze blowing, and our chimes were sounding melodiously.

John took out his syringe, picked up Suki very carefully, and in a couple of seconds it was over. He laid her down on the grass, curled up as she had been a few moments before. Jill went to fetch a wicker basket made in her village many years before and lined it with a towel that had been used over time by all the family. She asked John if he would place Suki in the basket. He knelt down, lifted her very gently, and lowered her into the basket. Then he rocked back on his heels and shook his head. We asked him what was wrong.

"I don't . . . I don't understand . . . " he said. "Something happened . . . I don't understand. . . . "

"Can you tell us?"

"Well . . . as I picked Suki up the wind dropped, but I could still hear your chimes. Then . . . as I put her in the basket, she sat up . . . in a circle of golden light . . . "

Neither of us had seen or heard anything at all out of the ordinary—but John was clearly shaken. We gave him a cold drink, and he sat and talked quietly with us for a while, every now and then shaking his head.

Eventually he composed himself and prepared to leave. He took up the basket and placed it carefully on the front seat of his car. As he turned to go, he suddenly said, "I'll recognize her when she returns, and I'll bring her back to you." Then he drove away.

Several days later there was a knock at the door. John stood there with a small wooden casket in his hands.

"I still don't understand what happened," he said. "I've never experienced anything like that before. And . . . I can't tell anyone about it. They'll think . . . ." He left the rest unsaid.

He handed us the casket, neatly labeled with Suki's name and accompanied by a card signed by the person who had witnessed her cremation, and a small bunch of dried flowers.

As he turned to leave we reminded him of what he had said about recognizing her and bringing her back to us. He looked amazed.

"Did I say that?" he exclaimed. "I remember everything else—but I don't remember saying that!"

But he had said it, and, one way or another, it will happen.

SCIENTIFIC AND TECHNICAL

Since *Using the Whole Brain* was published in 1993, research into the Hemi-Sync process and its effects on states of consciousness has steadily progressed. As F. H. "Skip" Atwater says, we have to step back from "the limited concepts of binaural beat entrainment" if we are to understand more precisely how Hemi-Sync influences consciousness.

Three papers in this chapter, by James Lane, Skip Atwater, and Jonathan Holt, demonstrate the sort of intensive research now being undertaken by experts in their field. Research of this nature is essential if the value of this audio technology is to be more widely accepted in the scientific community, and hence more widely used to the best effect.

In contrast, but also highly relevant, is Stephen Graf's analysis of the impact of Robert Monroe and the Institute on consciousness literature. His findings speak for themselves and stand as a remarkable testimony to the influence of Monroe's discovery and writings.

Research on the Effects
of Binaural Beats
James D. Lane, Ph.D.

James D. Lane, Ph.D., is an associate research professor of medical psychology and behavioral medicine in the Department of Psychiatry and Behavioral Sciences, Duke University Medical Center, Durham, North Carolina.

Since the beginning, much of what has been learned about binaural beats and the effects of Hemi-Sync has been learned though individual exploration. More knowledge has been gained though the trial-and-error testing of volunteers and the careful observation of the therapeutic effects of Hemi-Sync programs on clients and patients. However, through the years there have been very few scientific studies of Hemi-Sync or the effects of simple auditory binaural beat stimuli.

This approach may have resulted from Robert Monroe's emphasis on the importance of individual experience, converting personal beliefs into "knowns" through direct participation. Although the ongoing accumulation of anecdotal information has generated a significant body of shared knowledge, the focus on personal experience may have had unintended consequences that limit the use of Hemi-Sync in clinical and educational settings. For someone with personal experience of the effects of Hemi-Sync, anecdotal reports from others are sufficient to confirm what is already "known." However, anecdotal evidence

263

alone will not persuade the larger, more skeptical, audience of health-care and educational professionals. Establishing a more public truth for those without direct experience requires the gathering of objective evidence. Scientific research provides rigorous methods for accomplishing this task. The objective, public evidence that scientific studies can provide may help the professional community and the public at large to recognize the potential benefits of Hemi-Sync and may foster greater acceptance of Hemi-Sync programs and treatments.

This chapter describes an experimental study, among the first to be published for scientific audiences in a peer-reviewed journal, that begins what I hope is a continuing program of research on the effects of binaural beats and Hemi-Sync. Although the original paper can be found elsewhere, the intent of this chapter is to describe the thinking processes behind the study. I hope that this might encourage, stimulate, and guide others who would contribute to this scientific effort with their own research.

The Ideas behind the Study

Hemi-Sync programs elicit their effects through the complex interplay of several active components, not just though the presentation of auditory binaural beats. Verbal instructions are combined with music, sound effects, and binaural beats to support the expectations and intentions of the listener and produce the desired change in consciousness or other mind/body/spirit functions. Although we recognized that Hemi-Sync is much more than binaural beats, we chose to focus our initial research on them for several reasons.

First, the use of binaural beats (BBs) is a common feature of Hemi-Sync that distinguishes it from other kinds of mind/body/spirit programs. Second, it is this unique feature that is most difficult for the skeptical audience to accept. The scientific literature offers little evidence that simple presentations of auditory signals could have profound effects on consciousness. The apparent implausibility of binaural beat effects would easily lead skeptics to reject any claims of benefit from Hemi-Sync. Finally, it is easier to study the specific effects of binaural beats with rigorous scientific methods than it would be to study the complex effects of the application of Hemi-Sync programs. Successful laboratory studies would set the stage and justify larger, more complex tests of the health and personal development applications of Hemi-Sync. We decided that the best place to start was to gather scientifically rigorous evidence that BB stimulation could influence consciousness and cognitive processing. If we could establish this core effect, the evidence of a possible mechanism for beneficial effects would encourage others to study the beneficial effects of Hemi-Sync applications.

A second decision was made to study the effects of BBs on attention, mental alertness, and concentration. Enhancement of attention has been a popular application of Hemi-Sync both for the treatment of attention-deficit and other disorders and for improved performance in educational and business settings. On the other hand, Hemi-Sync programs have also been developed to decrease arousal and induce sleep. The BB patterns that are effective in these applications are well known and could be tested in isolation from other Hemi-Sync components. Furthermore, we could contrast these two patterns in a single study, to enhance and to impair alertness and concentration. This would create a larger difference between our experimental conditions and increase the likelihood that BB effects would be observed in our first attempt to study them.

The Binaural Beats

We selected a pattern of binaural beats that we thought would enhance attention and concentration and another that we thought would impair these functions by inducing drowsiness. The first pattern included two binaural beats in the EEG beta frequency range, one at 16 Hz and another at 24 Hz, which we designated as the "beta" condition in our study. Beta EEG frequencies are commonly associated with alert mental activity, and these frequencies have been commonly used in Hemi-Sync applications designed to enhance attention and concentration. The second pattern included BBs in the EEG "theta" and "delta" ranges, at 4 Hz and 1.5 Hz, respectively. The EEG theta and delta ranges are commonly associated with drowsiness and sleep, and these specific frequencies have been used in Hemi-Sync programs to induce these states. This second pattern was designated as the "theta/delta" condition in our study.

We did not want subjects to know that they were listening to special auditory stimuli in the study, or be able to tell one binaural beat pattern from the other. The two binaural beat patterns were presented with the same background of pink noise, a uniform mix of low frequencies that sounds like rushing water. Several different carrier frequencies (tones) were used to present the different binaural beats, but all of the carrier frequencies were included in the final mix of sounds for each pattern. The beta and theta/delta stimuli were recorded on separate cassette tapes. A third tape was also created for use during the task training sessions. This contained all of the same background and carrier tones, but none of the binaural beats. With these precautions, all three tapes sounded the same.

The Vigilance Task

We chose a type of experimental test known as a "vigilance task" to provide a controlled, standardized setting that would enhance our detection of BB effects. The vigilance task has a long history in research on alertness and attention, dating back to World War II and studies of radar monitoring performance. It is a well-accepted procedure, with many variations, used to test an individual's ability to sustain attention and keep concentration focused under monotonous conditions. We thought that this task would offer a good opportunity to study the effects of our two BB stimuli.

For our study, the subject sat in a quiet, darkened room and viewed a computer video screen. A series of block capital letters was presented one at a time. A new letter appeared every second, and each was displayed only 0.1 seconds. The subject watched for "targets," when the same letter was repeated twice in a row, and responded by pressing a key as quickly as possible. Targets were relatively infrequent, presented only six times each minute, and subjects had to pay close attention constantly to the display to avoid missing one. The task ran continuously for 30 minutes, without breaks. The subject had to maintain concentration to perform well and resist the tendency to let attention drift under these monotonous conditions.

Vigilance performance was scored by counting the number of targets correctly detected ("hits") and the number of times that subjects mistakenly responded when a target was not presented ("false alarms"). In a typical vigilance task, the ability to detect targets diminishes over time as attention wanes. Subjects miss more targets and make more false alarm responses. We expected that exposure to the beta frequency BBs during the task would help subjects keep their attention focused on the task and improve their performance. In contrast, exposure to theta/delta BBs would tend to make subjects drowsy and lose concentration, which would impair performance.

How the Study Was Conducted

We recruited 32 young-adult and middle-aged male and female volunteers to take part in the study. All of them reported normal hearing in both ears. Our subjects were students or worked at Duke University or in the surrounding neighborhood. Each subject completed three test sessions, a training session with no BBs, as well as both the beta and theta/delta test conditions. This kind of study design, where each subject experiences all of the experimental conditions, is often superior to a design in which subjects in different groups experience only one condition. However, repeated testing of the same subject can create problems that could invalidate a study. We took appropriate precautions.

All three test sessions were conducted following the same protocol, but the first test session was in reality a training session, to provide each subject with the opportunity to develop a stable level of performance and to overcome any uncertainties or confusions related to the novelty of the vigilance task. No BB stimuli were presented during training. The beta and theta/delta BB conditions were presented in the second and third sessions, but we alternated randomly which condition was presented first. These procedures ensured that any systematic changes in performance from day to day, either continued improvements with practice or decrements due to the development of boredom with repeated testing, could not bias our comparisons of the two BB conditions and invalidate our results.

We did not tell subjects about the presence of BB stimuli, or our experimental hypotheses, because we wanted them to be unaware of the presence of BB stimuli. We did not want anyone to try to discern the presence of BBs, because that would take attention away from the vigilance task and might keep them more aroused and alert. As a cover story, we told subjects that the purpose of the study was only to evaluate how performance on the vigilance task changed from day to day. They were told that they would perform the task under exactly the same conditions on each day. They were also told that the sounds on the cassette tapes were used only to provide a constant sound background and mask any noises from outside the testing room. This deception was considered necessary to the study, and its use was approved by the local human subject protection committee. Subjects were told the full story at the end of the study.

We wanted to ensure that the experimenter could not influence the behavior of a subject in order to produce favorable results. The beta and theta/delta cassette tapes played during the sessions were labeled only with code numbers. As a result, no one knew whether a subject was hearing the beta or the theta/delta stimulus during a test session. This prevented the possibility of conscious or unconscious manipulation of the subject during the test.

All test sessions were conducted in the early afternoon, scheduled to start between 1 and 3 P.M. At this time of day, circadian rhythms produce a reliable state of low alertness and arousal in most people, which we thought would be conducive to the observation of BB effects. All three sessions for an individual subject were conducted at exactly the same time of day, so that time-related variations in alertness could not obscure the experimental effects.

In the training session, we gave the subjects instructions for the vigilance task and supervised a brief practice period that continued until the subject could perform the task without error or confusion. Then the subject performed the vigilance task for 30 minutes while listening to the cassette tape that contained no binaural beats, but only the background noise and carrier tones.

In the two subsequent test sessions, each subject was exposed to the beta or theta/delta stimulus during the entire 30 minutes of vigilance performance. Half of the subjects were tested first in the beta condition, and the other half were started with the theta/delta condition.

Before and after the vigilance task, we asked subjects to complete a standard questionnaire that assessed their mood at that moment. The Profile of Mood States (POMS) provides 65 mood-descriptive adjectives (e.g., friendly, tense, grouchy, etc.) that a subject rates, using a five-point scale, to describe his or her current state of mind. Responses on the 65 test items were used to create scores for six different moods: anger/hostility, confusion/bewilderment, depression/dejection, fatigue/inertia, tension/anxiety, and vigor/activity. We expected that BB stimuli might affect mood as well as vigilance performance, especially with respect to the measures of confusion and fatigue.

Of the 32 subjects who began the study, 29 completed the protocol. Each received $30 for their participation. When interviewed after the study, none of the subjects reported noticing anything unusual about the sounds on the cassette tapes or detecting any differences in the sounds from day to day.

The Observed Effects of Binaural Beats

Vigilance performance was scored as the number of targets correctly detected (hits) and the number of times a response was made incorrectly when no target was presented (false alarms). We summarized performance for the entire 30-minute task and for each five-minute segment of the task, which provided a glimpse at changes in performance over time. These scores are shown in the accompanying figures. Statistical comparisons revealed that subjects did detect more targets and had fewer false alarms while listening to beta BBs than they did in the theta/delta condition. The difference amounted to six more hits for the 180 targets presented. Subjects also had fewer false alarms in the beta condition, with an average of 6.6 in 30 minutes compared to 8.7 false alarms in the theta/delta condition.

We did see the expected deterioration of performance from the beginning to the end of the task (vigilance decrement). Although the

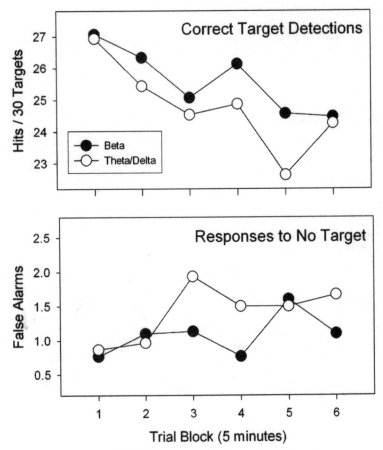

Figures 1 and 2. Vigilance task performance during the presentation of EEG beta and theta/delta binaural beats.

figures suggest that the vigilance decrement was faster and larger in the theta/delta condition, we could not confirm this statistically. Tests did confirm that differences between the beta and theta/delta conditions did not emerge until more than five minutes of the task had passed. Apparently, subjects do not respond immediately to BB stimulation of this kind.

The effects of BB condition on mood were explored by comparing the observed changes in POMS mood scores from the start to the end of the vigilance task. Performing this vigilance task for 30 minutes was associated with significant increases in scores for confusion/bewilderment, fatigue/inertia, and depression/dejection in both BB conditions. However, the increases were significantly larger in the theta/delta condition, indicating that the two BB patterns had different effects on state of mind as well as performance. The beta condition appeared to keep subjects more alert, positive, and clear thinking during this monotonous task.

The Contributions of This Study

The study was successful in demonstrating that binaural beat stimulation, the unique component of Hemi-Sync, can produce changes in cognitive performance and mood. These effects were consistent with our predictions about the differences between these two contrasting patterns of binaural beats. Listening to EEG beta frequency BBs produced better vigilance performance and a more alert mood than was observed with theta/delta frequency BBs. What is especially remarkable is that these effects were observed even though the subjects were completely unaware of the presence of anything special in the sounds they heard. This aspect of the results suggests that BB patterns may have a powerful influence on behavior and mood that may take place totally outside of the individual's awareness.

The study was designed to maximize the experimental difference by comparing two contrasting patterns of BBs that were expected to have opposite effects on performance and mood. Such a design does not provide the opportunity to determine whether beta BB patterns produce vigilance performance and mood that is better than that observed with no stimulation. Although the cassette tape for the training session included no BBs, this training condition was always presented first and cannot be compared to the beta and theta/delta conditions that were presented later in counterbalanced order. However, this kind of comparison can easily be included in future studies if a fourth test session without any BBs is included in the protocol.

The most important contribution of this study is that the use of rigorous experimental controls rules out most, if not all, alternative explanations for the differences between the beta and theta/delta conditions.

These observed differences could not be due to the subjects' expectations of an effect, because subjects were unaware that stimulation was present and that it differed from day to day. Differences could not have been produced by the conscious or unconscious actions of the experimenter, because all project staff were kept blind to the kind of BB presented on any day. The effects could not be due to practice effects or other temporal changes, or to differences in the time of testing. The only alternative explanation that a skeptic could suggest is that these results were a complete fluke, produced only by the unfortunate confluence of random events and not likely to be seen again. This possibility arises for any new scientific discovery. The only way to rule it out is to replicate the observation in more studies. However, at the present moment the most plausible explanation for the observed differences in vigilance performance and mood is that they were caused by the different BB patterns.

We recognize that this and other studies of binaural beats do not speak directly about the effectiveness of Hemi-Sync programs. However, studies like this one do make important contributions. Rigorous experimental trials of specific Hemi-Sync programs are necessary to generate the kind of systematic evidence that will convince the professional community and the public of the therapeutic benefits of Hemi-Sync. The scientific evidence collected in this BB study, which demonstrates that this unique component of Hemi-Sync can indeed affect mind and body, helps to justify the commitment of time and effort required for such trials by showing how the therapeutic effects are possible, and perhaps even likely. In this way, basic research should help to foster explorations of the potential applications of Hemi-Sync programs in educational, healthcare, and personal development settings.

Author Note

The original published version of the scientific paper described in this chapter (J. D. Lane et al. "Binaural beats affect vigilance performance and mood," *Physiology & Behavior*, 63 (1998): 249–252) is available from the author. Please e-mail him at the following address: jdlane@duke.edu, to request an electronic copy via return e-mail.

Consciousness, Hemi-Sync, and the Brain
F. Holmes Atwater

In 1988, shortly after he had retired from the army, where he had served as operations and training officer for the remote-viewing unit at Fort Meade, Skip Atwater (as he is universally known) accepted the post of Research Director at The Monroe Institute. At that time, while there was ample anecdotal evidence that the Hemi-Sync process could effect changes in states of consciousness, little research of the type that would be acceptable in scientific circles had been undertaken into how this actually happened. This did not prevent professionals in the areas of health, education, psychology, child development, and so on from conducting their own research and experiments and publishing the results. Hence it became clear that Hemi-Sync could be associated with improved sleep patterns, enriched learning environments, enhanced memory, pain management, stress reduction, and other benefits. Skip, however, felt that the only way he would know for sure how Hemi-Sync worked was to find out for himself.

The following account of two studies designed to investigate whether changes in cortical arousal occurred in response to Hemi-Sync is reprinted, with minor omissions, from *Captain of My Ship, Master of My Soul*, by F. Holmes Atwater (Hampton Roads Publishing Co., 2001).

Altering Consciousness with Hemi-Sync

Our state of consciousness can be described as a balance of cortical arousal level and subjective content. The reticular activating system in the brainstem is responsible for maintaining appropriate levels of arousal in the cortex as well as other specialized areas of the brain. And the subjective content (presumably, intracortical intercourse) of our experiences is dependent upon an individual's experience level, one's social-psychological conditioning, cognitive skills, and neurological development.

The Hemi-Sync sound technology engenders the auditory sensation of binaural beating, and this rhythmic waveform can be objectively measured as a frequency-following response, providing evidence that it manifests within the brain.

Since this waveform is neurologically routed to the reticular formation and since the reticular activating system governs cortical brainwave amplitudes, Hemi-Sync binaural beats (through the mechanism of the reticular) thereby induce alterations in brain-wave amplitudes or the arousal side of the consciousness equation. From this understanding, Hemi-Sync focus levels (Focus 10, Focus 12, etc.) become levels of brain-wave arousal.

I have read numerous anecdotal reports of state changes (alterations in consciousness) encouraged by various low-frequency binaural beats. Listening to selected binaural beats seems to promote propitious states of consciousness in a variety of applications. It has been reported that binaural beating has different effects depending on the frequency of the binaural-beat stimulation.

I read that binaural beats in the delta (1 to 4 Hz) and theta (4 to 8 Hz) ranges are associated with reports of creativity, sensory integration, relaxed or meditative states, or as an aid to falling asleep. Binaural beats in the beta frequencies (typically 16 to 24 Hz) are associated with reports of increased concentration or alertness and enhanced memory function.

Independent research has associated Hemi-Sync with changes in arousal leading to sensory integration, alpha biofeedback, relaxation, meditation, stress reduction, and pain management. I have read research reports linking Hemi-Sync with improved sleep, healthcare, enriched learning environments, enhanced memory, creativity, treatment of children with developmental disabilities, the facilitation of attention, and so-called peak experiences.

Further research validates Hemi-Sync's use in the enhancement of hypnotizability, treatment of alcoholic depression, the promotion of vigilance, performance, and mood, increased intuition, improved reliability in remote viewing, telepathy, and out-of-body experience.

I found several free-running EEG studies that suggest that binaural beats may induce alterations in cortical arousal (ongoing brainwaves) and consiousness states. But I needed to do my own research. The only way I would know for sure how Hemi-Sync works was to find out for myself—something Bob Monroe had insisted on years ago.

Hemi-Sync and Brain-Wave Arousal

I decided to do two free-running EEG studies. In the first study, I measured the neural accommodation (changes in ongoing or overall brain-wave activity) associated with complex binaural-beat stimuli. In the second study, based on the same protocol, I measured changes in ongoing brain-wave activity associated with placebo stimuli. By comparing the results of these two studies, I hoped to be able to validate the power of Hemi-Sync to alter consciousness.

The hypothesis in the first study was that listening to Hemi-Sync for several minutes would modify ongoing brain-wave activity in the direction of the binaural beat stimuli. That is, increasing the amplitude of delta-frequency binaural-beat stimuli while decreasing the amplitude of alpha-frequency binaural-beat stimuli would result in comparable changes in arousal as measured by free-running EEG.

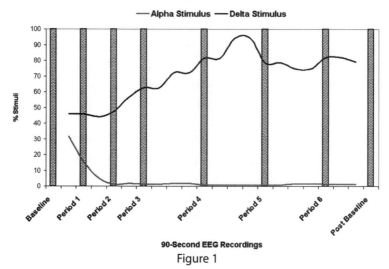

Figure 1

275

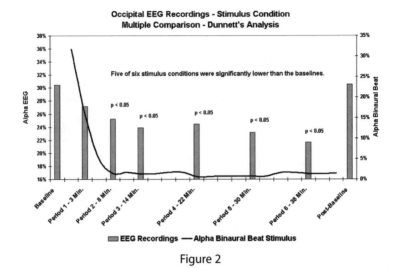

Figure 2

I wanted to mimic existing, commercially available Hemi-Sync recordings, so the experimental binaural-beat stimuli consisted of mixed sinusoidal tones producing complex frequency patterns (waveforms) changing over a period of 45 minutes. I first recorded brain waves during a no-stimulus baseline condition. Next, I recorded brain waves for each subject during six periods for the 45-minute sequence of changing binaural beats condition. Finally, I made an EEG recording during a no-stimulus post-baseline condition (figure 1).

I rejected the data from two of the subjects due to excessive movement artifact and used the remaining 18 subjects' records for analysis. To determine statistical validity of the data, I conducted a multiple comparison procedure following a one-way analysis of variance (ANOVA), Dunnett's Test, which compared the combined baselines (before and after) as a control mean with the binaural-beat stimulus periods. This analysis showed the reductions in the percentages of occipital alpha during stimuli conditions were significant (individually, $p < .05$, and together, $p < .001$) during five of six stimulus periods compared to baselines (figure 2).

Statistical analysis of the data also showed the increases in the percentages of central delta during stimuli conditions were significant (individually, $p < .05$, and together, $p < .001$) during four of six stimulus periods compared to baselines (figure 3).

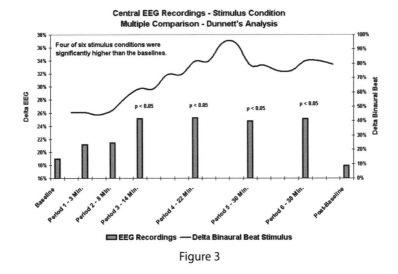

Figure 3

So, the results of this first study showed changes in brain-wave activity during the stimulus periods when compared to the baseline recordings both with increased central delta and decreased occipital alpha. These decreases in alpha amplitudes, coupled with increasing delta activity, indicated reduced cortical arousal. The mounting changes over the time of the test and the course of the stimuli suggest a deepening trend of progressive relaxation and falling asleep.

A basic question raised by this first study was the role of Hemi-Sync stimulation in solely or directly causing the brain-wave changes observed. Several of the subjects had had considerable previous experience with Hemi-Sync. Could it be that these subjects were naturally adept at altering levels of arousal or had acquired this ability through repeated Hemi-Sync practice? The deepening trend over time also suggests the need to take into consideration naturally occurring, progressive state changes associated with falling asleep. I designed a second study to address these concerns.

The hypothesis of the second study was that listening to monotonous tones (a placebo stimuli without binaural beats) for several minutes would result in habituation of the stimuli, a slowing of ongoing brain-wave activity, and a progressive state of relaxation.

The placebo stimuli consisted of the same sinusoidal tones used in

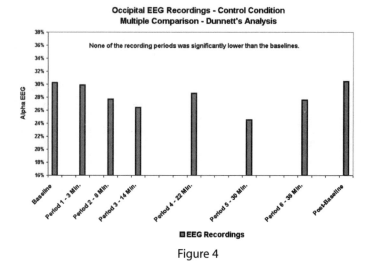

Figure 4

the first study, except that they did not produce binaural beating. As in the first study, the volunteer subjects experienced a no-stimulus baseline condition during which a 90-second EEG recording was taken. Next, each one listened to the same 45-minute sequence of changing tones during which six 90-second EEG recordings were taken at regular intervals. To reduce the influence of expectation, subjects were again blind as to the character of the tones. Finally, during a no-stimulus post-baseline condition, a 90-second EEG recording was made.

A multiple comparison procedure following a one-way ANOVA (Dunnett's Test) comparing the combined baselines as a control mean with the placebo stimuli periods showed nonsignificant reductions in the percentages of occipital alpha during stimuli conditions compared to baselines (figure 4).

Statistical analysis showed the nonsignificant increases in the percentages of central delta during stimuli conditions compared to baselines (figure 5). The results of this second study, unlike the first, did not significantly distinguish occipital alpha and central delta brainwave activity during the placebo stimulus periods from the baselines.

The hypothesis of this placebo study expected observed decreases in alpha amplitudes coupled with increasing delta activity as a reaction to listening to monotonous tones. These changes, however, were not sta-

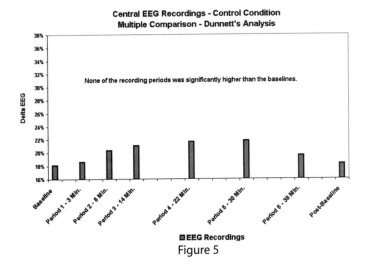

Figure 5

tistically significant, meaning that they could be expected to have happened by chance alone.

Meaningful Results

Together, these studies demonstrate that Hemi-Sync has a direct effect on brain-wave activity, involving the interaction of binaural-beat stimulation with the basic rest-activity cycle, other sensory stimulation, and higher-order memory or attentional processes under the scrutiny of the reticular formation. All of these systems cooperate to maintain our homeostasis and optimal performance.

Our natural state-changing mechanisms, ultradian rhythms, individual differences, prior experience, and beliefs all contribute to the effects of and response to Hemi-Sync. But for me the bottom line, so to speak, was that these two studies provided statistical observations demonstrating changes in cortical arousal in response to Hemi-Sync. I had my proof.

These studies showed me that the power of Hemi-Sync to provide an environment conducive to personal explorations beyond our physical senses was real, not snake oil, or self-fulfilling prophecy, or just wishful thinking, but real—real, that is, at least in terms of modern neurology.

But did this mean that the binaural beats of the Hemi-Sync process constituted an irresistible force that could really put the *whammy* on you, so to speak? No! And I think Bob Monroe explained it best:

> Hemi-Sync is like music. Imagine yourself out for an evening for dinner and dance. There you are, sitting at your table, having a cocktail, when the band strikes up a tune. Observing the couples around you, you see that some are getting up to dance, while others remain engrossed in their intimate conversations.
>
> You notice that you are tapping your foot to the beat of the music and your companion has stopped talking and is listening intently to the familiar tune. The waiter suddenly appears, and your attention and response to the music fall away as you focus your attention on savory menu items.
>
> What this all means is that music, like Hemi-Sync, only provides an inviting environment conducive to shifting your experience. The band music did not force or compel couples to dance. And Hemi-Sync cannot force or compel you in any way. Only you can change you. Your response to Hemi-Sync depends on you. If you willingly participate with the music, your experiences will be limited only by your own skill, expectations, and beliefs.

Notes

Copies of two technical papers, *Binaural Beats and the Frequency-Following Response* and *Binaural Beats and the Regulation of Arousal Levels*, by F. Holmes Atwater may be obtained from The Monroe Institute, 62 Roberts Mountain Road, Faber, VA 22938.

Captain of My Ship, Master of My Soul may be obtained from bookstores or from the publisher, Hampton Roads Publishing Co., Inc., 1125 Stoney Ridge Road, Charlottesville, VA 22902.

Pilot Exploration of CNS Electro-physiology of Hemi-Sync and Related Altered States of Consciousness

Jonathan H. Holt, M.D.

While working at the Albany V.A. Medical Center in the 1990s as director of consultation—liaison psychiatry (psychiatry of the medically ill), I received funding to obtain an EEG biofeedback and spectroscopy machine (CAPSCAN from American Biologic Co.). This allowed me to get clinical and pilot data on brain-wave frequencies during various altered states of consciousness and treatments, including the use of Hemi-Sync. While the data I obtained does not constitute statistically based confirmation, it is suggestive of underlying processes and may indicate directions for further study.

The machinery was capable of producing three processes related to the neuroelectrophysiology of patients listening to Hemi-Sync. The equipment could give second-by-second spectrographs of EEG data measured from a single location on the scalp (generally the middle of the skull, top of the head). Secondly, it could provide brain-wave training protocols both from a single point and from four points, on each side of the head. Thirdly, it could give information on interhemisphere synchrony, or how in-phase or out-of-phase the EEG waveforms were, comparing one hemisphere to the other. Research before and after this pilot data was obtained indicated that Hemi-Sync and some other methods of sensory stimulation (e.g., flashing lights, repetitive sounds like drumming) could affect brain-wave frequency and interhemisphere synchrony. This process is termed entrainment. The equipment in the electrophysiological lab provided vivid demonstrations of how Hemi-Sync and some other related therapeutic interventions have similar or comparable electrophysiological effects.

The first demonstrations of Hemi-Sync effects came from using the brain-wave training protocols with and without Hemi-Sync. Beta training—brain-wave frequencies between 16 and 30 cycles per second (Hz or cps)—was tried on several subjects first without entrainment and then using the Hemi-Sync tape *Concentration*. The brain-wave training goals were reached significantly faster when the tapes were played. A comparable result was obtained with alpha-theta brain-wave training (slower frequency groups) using Hemi-Sync tapes with slower frequencies (e.g., *Surf* and various Metamusic tapes). Similar results were also found using a binaural beat generator. Use of the "wrong" frequency tape did not enhance brain-wave training performance. Use of Hemi-Sync tapes also increased the speed of reaching performance goals in training interhemisphere synchrony.

The second application used the single-site spectrograph (CZ placement) to do spectrographic analysis at key or representative moments in time during various procedures and processes. The computer was programmed to "freeze frame" at the push of a keyboard key amidst the ongoing EEG analysis. The spectrograph shows frequency increasing from left to right, with each vertical section line indicating four cycles per second. As with a prism refraction of regular light, the spectrograph of one time unit of a "raw" or regular EEG actually contains variable amounts of electrical energy of different frequencies. EEG, biofeedback, and entrainment data indicate that in different states of consciousness, with attention focused outwards, beta frequencies (12 or 14–30 cps) are at their highest amplitudes. However, they are not necessarily higher in amplitude than the alpha (8–12 cps), theta (4–8 cps), or delta (0.5–4 cps).

EEG spectrographs taken during various phases of a standard hypnotic session begin with the subject, without known neuropathology, in an awake state. The start of the induction phase shows the subject receiving instructions, and then their attention is focused, coned down onto one object of attention. Beta activity may increase as initial instructions are given and processed. However, as focusing increases, alpha frequencies become more predominant. In the deepening phase, there is continued focusing (as in counting up or down), but imagery processing is added (as in imagining a descent or an ascent). Here the spectrograph shows decreased beta and increased alpha and theta. In the utilization phase the subject is asked to imagine a scene (or imagine carrying out an action, which amounts to the same thing). Focusing on a singular object of attention has stopped. This produces a theta ridge without the same amount of alpha seen previously. In the termination phase, one can see a return of alpha and theta, but often with residual theta (and perhaps some delta) which can persist for some time into the reorientation.

The previous demonstration of brain-wave frequencies and changes in attention and consciousness were borne out in the serial spectrographs of an expert in Vipassana, or awareness meditation. In this form of meditation, attention is switched from the ordinary pattern, sometimes described as "catch, grab, and process," to an "awareness" pattern. In this, attention registers anything in the sensory field and then lets go without processing or thinking. The alpha region is increased markedly with somewhat less beta activity. This same pattern was borne out in the spectrographs of other Vipassana meditators. There was no period during these meditations when imaginative thinking was encouraged as in the utilization phase of hypnosis, and a separate theta ridge is not observed.

The interrelationships of EEG frequencies, Hemi-Sync, and altered states of consciousness were further demonstrated in the investigation of serial spectrographs of a subject listening to and experiencing the Hemi-Sync tape *Moment of Revelation*. This tape is a guided meditation tape or a hypnotic imagery tape, but with Hemi-Sync tones designed to support and expand the experience. The listener is instructed to imagine climbing a multicolored stairway into the sky, through and beyond the clouds. Then one is instructed to experience some inspiration or to receive an inspired communication (content unspecified). Much time is given to this section with Hemi-Sync tones and music, but no words or instructions. Instructions are then given to descend the staircase and to return to normal consciousness. The subject listening to the instructions shows beta activation but also some alpha. Experiencing the "climbing the staircase" section corresponds to the deepening phase of the hypnosis process—attention is focused but there is also imagery. Comparison of the spectrographs of this phase and the hypnotic deepening spectrograph shows (a) similar profiles and (b) markedly higher amplitudes of brain activity at those frequencies. In the section of the tape "above the clouds," counting has stopped and there is more theta activity. Further into the inspiration section, one sees a marked theta ridge with some delta activity, perhaps relating to the breakthrough of deeper or higher consciousness material. The key difference between hypnosis and Hemi-Sync guided imagery seems to be markedly increased amplitudes of the frequency changes.

Because of limitations in the equipment, it was not possible to get information about interhemisphere synchrony at the same time as getting spectrographic pictures of the frequency-following response, as had been done in the previous investigations. A separate setup was used to measure (and train for) interhemispheric synchrony. Subjects listening to Hemi-Sync tapes had increased synchrony scores, both frontally and posteriorly. Hypnosis did not noticeably increase synchrony scores per se. Awareness meditators practicing Vipassana meditation did increase their synchrony scores. Putting subjects through an EMDR protocol (Eye Movement Desensitization and Reprocessing) also increased the synchrony scores but did not have an overall frequency-changing effect like hypnosis, meditation, and corresponding Hemi-Sync tapes. EMDR is a new psychotherapy for clearing and detoxifying traumas. Subjects that got to experience both EMDR and Hemi-Sync said there were similar, but not identical, softening effects on disturbing memories.

In a mini-experiment using a beta tape, accumulated spectrographs over a 40-second period of time displayed together in what is termed a waterfall display were taken of a subject with mild dyslexia. When the subject was listening to the beta tape, there appeared to be more high-beta ridges during the tape, though there are other differences as well. The subject reported experiencing greater clarity and ease of reading while listening to the tape.

The last mini-experiment involved taking the EEG spectrograph of a Reiki practitioner during a session, then taking the spectrograph of the patient (suffering from arthritis). Reiki is a form of bioenergetic healing invoked by a shift of attention and consciousness on the part of the healer while placing hands on the patient. A Hemi-Sync tape was played during the session. The healer's spectrograph has been lost, but it showed a minor alpha ridge. The patient's spectrograph showed a very large ridge of alpha, theta, and delta. Interestingly enough, the healer moved her hands from one location to another during the 40 seconds of data collection for the waterfall display. When she moved her hands, the low frequency decreased in amplitude but did not normalize. When she replaced her hands on the new location, the high amplitude ridge returned. This seemed to indicate that some consciousness effects are correlated with the actual transmission of Reiki. The lower ridge may be ascribed to either continuing effects on consciousness of the Reiki or the Hemi-Sync tape or both.

In summary, the mini-experiments with EEG spectroscopy indicate that there are frequency shifts associated with hypnosis and meditation. Hemi-Sync can produce similar shifts but with increased amplitudes. Hemi-Sync can be used to speed up learning time in EEG biofeedback. Hemi-Sync is associated with increased interhemisphere synchrony, as are EMDR and Vipassana meditation. Hemi-Sync tones using higher frequencies may be associated with higher beta waves on spectrographs and, in at least some instances, with greater cognitive clarity experienced by the subject.

The findings of this chapter are not meant as proof but as suggestions of possibilities and as invitations to further investigation.

Note

The author would like to acknowledge the assistance of Alan Finkelstein, Ph.D., with technical assistance in the setup of the CAPSCAN equipment for these investigations. He also would like to acknowledge the additional assistance of Robert Gerardi, Ph.D.; Steven Nozik, Ph.D.; and Steven Flynn, B.A., in the investigations of EMDR. Steven Flynn also assisted in the meditation, guided imagery, and beta investigations.

Bob Monroe and TMI's Impact on Consciousness Literature
Stephen A. Graf, Ph.D.

Steve Graf received his doctoral degree in experimental psychology from Ohio State University and has been interested throughout his career in the use and extension of standard change charts. He has 35 years of experience teaching college students and is the author of three college textbooks. Steve conducts workshops nationwide on using fluency tools in training. He has been a member of the Professional Division since 1990 and has participated in the Dolphin Energy Club since its inception.

Since about 1970, many individuals around the world have gained insight and information into the realms of consciousness through contact with Bob Monroe's writings or programs at The Monroe Institute (TMI). One way of quantifying this impact involved a sample of:

• total pages by year of "consciousness" books

• pages by year written by or about Robert Monroe

• pages by year written about The Monroe Institute

What range of topics might one expect to be covered in books involving consciousness? The following list provides a sample:

• planet consciousness

• out-of-body experiences

- near-death experiences

- sleep and dreaming

- remote viewing

- contact with the unbodied

- spiritual healing

- self-searching

- alien abduction experiences

- future visions/predictions

The data were collected from:

- books in the personal collection of the author and associates

- books available in local public and university libraries

- books available for inspection in local bookstores

- books with index viewable on the Internet through online stores

A total of 162 books make up the current sample with copyright dates from 1965 to 2001.

Within these books, data consisted of the number of pages per year in each of three categories. The results of these counts provide the data for Figures 1, 2, and 3. The categories consisted of pages:

- in all the books

- on which Bob Monroe was mentioned

- on which The Monroe Institute or its technology was mentioned

Examples from The Monroe Institute include reference to:

- Institute staff

- Hemi-Sync

- mention of Focus levels

• program names or descriptions offered by the Institute

• research directed or carried out by the Institute

Not all the book titles found could be included in the sample. Omitted were titles whose page contents or index could not be inspected. When feasible, a page-by-page inspection occurred in the search for Monroe or TMI references. In cases where an index existed, it was often used as the source of number of pages involved. Bibliography sources and reference lists were included as counts.

Using charting technology, the "change" and "bounce" for each of the three figures provide information on trends present in the 162 books sampled. The present article avoids technical details involving the charting itself and instead focuses on presenting, summarizing, and discussing the findings. Background for this approach can be found in Graf and Lindsley's *Standard Celeration Charting,* 2002.

"Change" refers to the trend in yearly counts. It reports a factor by which the count data is increasing or decreasing over a five-year period. Its value is figured by the slope of the best-fit line through the yearly counts. It is seen as the middle line in Figures 1–3. The bigger the change, the higher the change value. If no change were occurring, the line would be flat.

"Bounce" predicts a top and bottom count range for any particular year. It helps to remind us that we're looking at a sample rather than a population. It reports a factor representing the distance between the highest count and lowest count for any particular year. It is seen as the combination of top and bottom lines around the change line in Figures 1–3. The bigger the bounce in a sample, the greater the variability. With no bounce, all the data would fall precisely on the change line.

Counts falling outside the bounce lines are deemed "outliers." These counts do not fit the overall pattern. The reason for their existence is sometimes clear and sometimes not.

Figure 1 shows that pages in the 162 consciousness books sampled have increased by a factor of times 1.3 every five years since 1965. To use an example: 1,000 pages were found in the sample for 1983. Five years later, in 1987, we would expect to find 1,300 pages in the sample (1,000 x 1.3 = 1,300). This is what a change of "times 1.3" means.

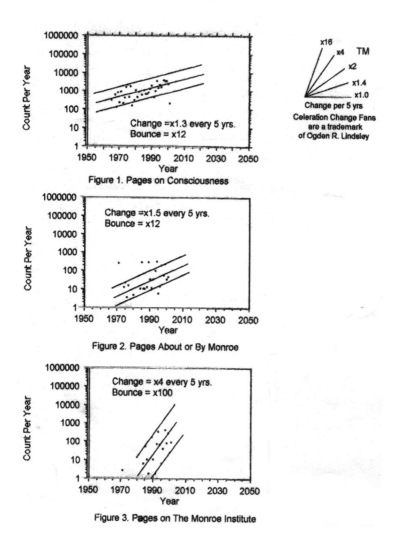

Figure 1. Pages on Consciousness

Figure 2. Pages About or By Monroe

Figure 3. Pages on The Monroe Institute

Figure 1 also shows a bounce of times 12. This indicates that for any particular year, the bandwidth of counts is a factor of 12. This can be seen as the vertical distance between the top line and the bottom line in Figure 1. As an example, in 1976 the bottom bounce line equals about 200 pages. A bounce of "times 12" means the top bounce line for 1976 would equal about 2,400 pages (200 x 12 = 2,400).

Two outliers occur below the bounce in Figure 1, in 1978 and 2001. In both cases only one book occurred in the sample.

Figure 2 shows that pages about or by Bob Monroe have increased by a factor of times 1.5 every five years since 1971, the first year any data occurred, with the publication of *Journeys Out of the Body*. Comparing this change line with Figure 1, it can be seen that based on this sample the pages about or by Monroe have grown faster than consciousness pages in general. What kind of a difference does this represent? Comparing the distance between the drawn change from the two figures in 1971, 120 pages of consciousness literature were estimated to exist for each page on Monroe. Some 30 years later, that difference is only one-third as much. Forty pages of consciousness literature are estimated to exist for each page on Monroe.

The bounce for Figure 2 is times 12, the same value as in Figure 1. This tells us that the bandwidth of these two samples is very similar.

Six outliers occur in Figure 2. Four of these are above the bounce and are easily identifiable. They represent the publication dates of Monroe's three books plus the biography of Monroe by Bayard Stockton in 1988, *Catapult*. The two outliers below the bounce occurred in 1972 and 1995. The 1972 case was a one-page reference to Monroe occurring in John Lilly's *The Center of the Cyclone*. Lilly's contact with Monroe was a personal one and not a reference to Monroe's first book. 1995 was the year of Monroe's death.

Figure 3 shows that pages about TMI have increased by a factor of times four every five years since 1984. This is more than triple the rate of growth of consciousness pages in general and more than double the rate of growth about Monroe himself, as measured by the sample.

The bounce for Figure 3 is times 100, which represents an eightfold increase over the bounce in Figures 1 and 2. This indicates a much greater instability of ups and downs in published pages per year for TMI compared to the consciousness field and Monroe the individual. The only outlier occurs in 1971 and comes from Monroe's own work published in that year.

Our background and beliefs may color our assessment of the impact of an individual or institution on knowledge or understanding within our culture. The charts of the sampled data described in this article allow one to easily see what changes are taking place. As additional data becomes available from books published in the past, the pictures we get from the charts can gain further clarity. Additional data in the future allows monitoring of continuing change. We would not expect, for example, that TMI pages would continue increasing by a factor of four every five years. If they did, they would overtake the whole of consciousness literature before 2010!

GALLIMAUFRY

These papers are not tucked away at the back because of any editorial value judgment but because each author deals with a topic not covered by anyone else. What they do have in common is each takes the reader into a very interesting area—an area where we escape from the limitations of space/time—well, that's one way of putting it!

Richard Werling is an explorer into those regions denoted by Monroe as Focuses 21 to 27. There, he is able to make contacts and bring back information of great interest. The paper gives only the briefest glimpse into his explorations and discoveries.

Carol Sabick refers to the magic that she has come across in her experience as a Monroe trainer and illustrates a particular occurrence. Lynn Robinson looks at another aspect of this "magic"—synchronicities. She describes what Monroe called a "ROTE"—a "thoughtball" that she received while on a course at the Institute and which she managed to unravel.

While this is one of the shortest chapters in this book, it may be that for some readers it could prove to be the most significant.

Healing by Retrieving the Shadow:
The Work of Richard Werling
Ronald Russell

For many years, to experience the state or phase of consciousness known as Focus 21 was the summit of achievement for those attending courses at The Monroe Institute. This was "the Edge of Here-Now," where the constraints of space and time cease to exist. We had, as it were, climbed the highest peak within our range. As we surveyed the scene, we could discern even higher peaks—but they were shrouded in mist, and we had neither guide nor map to enable us to explore them.

Then in 1991 Robert Monroe launched the Lifeline program. Here was the map we needed, and, as before, Monroe himself was the guide. The directions were precise. You could follow him through the dark lands of Focus 22, where those who were neither fully alive nor physically dead lingered until they were given the order of release, through the chaos of lost spirits awaiting rescue in 23, across the belief system territories of Focuses 24 to 26, and into the Park, that imaginal realm created by the thoughts and aspirations of countless generations, where spiritual healing, comfort, intelligence, and reconciliation were available to all. Subsequent programs, Exploration 27 and Beyond 27, took the explorer still further from the space-time continuum and nearer still to the Source.

To play chess or basketball, to follow a timetable or a road map, you observe the rules. But in the exploration of the further reaches of consciousness, there are no rules. Monroe's directions were useful, especially to those exploring the realms beyond Focus 21 for the first time. What happened, however, was that the explorers simply found what they found, and this was not always what they expected to find. For example, Lifeline participants were directed to make contact with a soul (or entity, spirit, or essence) lost in Focus 23 and guide this soul to the Park, where it would be befriended and counseled as needed. But some participants instead found lost parts of themselves languishing in Focus 23 and were able to reintegrate them, making themselves whole.

For Monroe himself, this was fine. His answer to anyone who asked him anything about what might happen or be discovered in any Focus level was, "Go find out and come and tell me what you find." So the reports on their return from those who journeyed to Focus 27 and beyond—and that is just about everyone who participated in these programs—were rich and varied. A sample of them may be found in Monroe's last book, *Ultimate Journey*.

Richard Werling is one of the explorers who in recent years has spent much time researching the areas of consciousness leading up to and including Focus 27. He holds two engineering degrees and a doctorate in public administration, and was a senior management consultant at Stanford Research Institute, where anomalous phenomena such as remote viewing are studied. Following several programs at The Monroe Institute, Richard was moved to redirect his interests. He has made certain discoveries about what he describes as "the little people who make up the 'Shadow'." To explain this, he quotes from Ken Wilber:

> The shadow is the personal unconscious, a series of "feeling-toned complexes." These complexes are images and concepts which become "contaminated" by the lower levels—in particular, the emotional-sexual—and thus are felt, for various reasons, to be threatening to the higher-order structure of the ego-mind. These complexes are thus split off from consciousness (they become a shadow), a process which simultaneously distorts the self-concept (the ego), and thus leaves the individual with a false or inaccurate self-image (the persona). If the persona and shadow

can be reunited, then the higher-order integration of the total ego can be established. (*Eye to Eye: The Quest for the New Paradigm*, Shambala, 2001)

Richard has developed a procedure for his research. He works with, or for, an individual (the subject) who has asked for help, or for whom help has been sought. A typical procedure begins by dedicating the session to the subject's Higher Self, with the understanding that the work is for use at an appropriate time, since it takes place outside the time-space continuum. He suggests that the Subject be aware of any "hitchhikers" who might want to join them as they move, using Hemi-Sync, into higher states of consciousness. These hitchhikers are parts or soul fragments that have been separated from the subject during past times of physical or emotional trauma. Such parts were typically formed when the subject was between two and six years of age, or from the teenage years. Often they are "shadow parts," long hidden, of which we are ashamed and which we do not want to acknowledge. They may also derive from accidents or severe emotional or physical trauma occurring at any age.

In Focus 27 they move to the "Healing Center," and especially to an area Richard describes as the "Hall of Light and Colors," where divine energy is available to merge and restore the separated parts into the subject's energy body and where additional healing energy is available to re-energize this energy body. Richard says that helpers or attendants are available in the Healing Center. These are often related to the subject's belief system—major biblical figures, for example. Others may also help with the subject's karmic lessons, relationships, and life plans, in consultation with the subject's Higher Self.

The subject's condition is then clarified and assessed. It may be necessary to take the subject into the "Hall of Forgiveness," where highly charged emotional experiences may be dealt with and energy thereby released. It may also be necessary for the subject's energy body to be partly rebuilt.

When the various procedures are completed, the subject can choose from three courses of action: to remain in his or her present body and continue with the present life, to take on some goals planned for "the next life" and continue with the present life, or to transition to death of the present physical body. Then, before returning, the subject expresses thanks to all those who have helped and spends some time with loved ones who are no longer living in physical bodies.

This is an example of the way Richard works. It is not always possible to express in words experiences that occur in these "higher" Focus levels, and much of what has been described above may be interpreted as metaphor rather than as a literal account. Many Lifeline graduates continue working within Monroe's directions, involved with retrieval of the souls of individuals who have difficulty making their transition. Some have developed their own means of providing this kind of help, while some prefer to work in groups to the same end. All would agree in expressing gratitude to Robert Monroe for introducing them to the concept of Focus 27—and all would agree that death is not the end.

The Magical Mix
Carol Sabick

Training Hemi-Sync programs, both residential and weekend Outreach courses, is very hard work, with long hours. There is a need to be grounded but also to stay in the flow of the session, often dealing with emotional upheavals or international participants with language difficulties, acting as surrogate mother (sometimes being blamed for what Mom did or didn't do), and being involved with things from roommate problems to phone cards, meal preferences to kundalini experiences . . .

It can be exhausting, but wow, what a lot of fun, satisfaction, and joy all in one package! It's always a lesson that everything is perfect, and that neither the Institute, nor the trainers, nor the participants know, or plan, the whole story. Somehow it seems to all be arranged by guides and/or helpers from another dimension, in conjunction with our own Higher Selves. It is the perfect group of people joined together in time, in a setting conducive to inner work, teaching, and learning from each other as each one needs in the moment.

Many participants are convinced that they already know each other when they arrive, that maybe they form part of the same spiritual group, or "I/There," as Robert Monroe would say. One incident that comes to mind illustrates this vividly. As the trainer for the Lifeline program to begin on the following Saturday, I was watching television while waiting for a leisurely and luscious dinner at a local bed and breakfast. A group of three people entered the room where I was sitting, a woman—we'll call her Linda—with a man on each side. As I looked up to greet them I noticed a look of surprise/concern/astonishment on Linda's face, and she immediately turned and ushered the two men outside.

I could only wonder if she didn't find watching TV to be proper before a spiritually oriented course, or if my deodorant had failed. When we were to be seated at the long table, I noticed that they waited to see where I would be sitting—and then took seats at the opposite end of the table. None of this overly concerned me, because I suspected they were participants in one of the programs starting the following day, and it's not uncommon to be in a strange state of mind beforehand. I theorize that it could be because, deep inside, a part of us knows that we will go home as different people, and no one really likes change, especially if you don't know what that change is going to be.

The following day I realized that the three were to be participants in the program I was training. But the mystery was to last a while longer. I believe they were even more surprised to see me as the trainer than I was to see they were in the program. During the first days, all went well, and no one mentioned the dinner incident. The three were from different parts of the United States and also re-encountered several other people they had known from previous programs.

On Tuesday, Linda sat by me at lunch and said that since she knew me a bit better by then, she would like to confide a strange incident. It seems that she and her friends had signed up for Lifeline in June but had decided to come to this one in August owing to a dream that Linda had experienced several months before. A lady came to her in the dream and said very clearly, and in no uncertain terms, that she and her friends were not to go to the program in June, but to wait a bit longer until the "entire group" could gather. She had no idea what that meant since her little group was already gathered. But since it was such a clear message, and for one of the others it was easier to come in August, they decided to change the date of their program to the end of summer.

They arrived a day early, and the first person they saw was the lady in the dream—me—looking exactly the same and wearing exactly the same clothes. When Linda first saw me she grabbed the other two to tell them in astonishment: "That's the lady in the dream! That's the one who told us to wait! What do you suppose she is doing here?"

They were all so rattled that their first line of action was avoidance. But now, after having spent a few days with the entire group, Linda had realized that there seemed to be a plan, and all 16 participants were helping each other in many ways unimaginable a few days prior. Coincidental remarks, synchronistic experiences during tapes, messages for each other, it all seemed to be magical. Many old and deep wounds were being healed by inner individual work combined with sharing and co-creating. It was a very sacred space for all.

This sacred space seems to be a cornerstone of every Monroe program. Feeling safe, people open in ways they are unwilling or unable to do in their own environments. Any group of people with common interests may open to share more than at home, but here we have another special ingredient, the technology. Hemi-Sync facilitates going deeper. It provides the support for adventuring into unknown territory of Self and exploring, finding out more about who we really are. It helps us to release old patterns of fear and emotions that no longer serve us well, accomplished in subtle and profound ways that open the gates for true change from within.

Step by step, the Hemi-Sync sounds and process guide us further and further from that part of us called the physical body to other dimensions of Self and beyond. Safely and surely we are guided to remember who we really are, to experience existence out of time, to open to and communicate with those who have already transitioned out of the physical space/time reality. Some of our beliefs are shed along the way, and others are converted into "Knowns."

We like to explain this process with the X-words:

• expand awareness

• experience more of your Total Self

• explore energy systems

• experiment with the new energies, and

• express more of your Total Self.

The energy of the group makes all this easier. And though groups don't always receive outward signs, like the dream in this case, that clearly underline the importance of very specific individuals coming together at a specific moment in time, every group is very special. The other participants, plus the trainers, are the ones who encourage us to experience more, join us in exploring and experimenting more, and listen as we take the first steps in expressing more of the Total Self.

The Monroe Institute programs are a conglomerate of many different ingredients, each in the proper measure, to make up the magical experience. According to research by Todd Masluk, this special mix brings about many positive long-term changes, including feeling more responsible for one's life, a greater sense of self-acceptance, living more in the present, an increased love for and desire to help humanity, a willingness to take more risks, acting more spontaneously and intuitively, and, last but not least, *knowing* one is more than a physical body.

Just in case you're wondering—as trainers we don't go around visiting people in their dreams. I, of course, was totally unaware of any of this and didn't even know who Linda was before the program. But a curious note—the clothes she recognized so well as being the ones I was wearing in the dream in March had been bought the day before the dinner, some five months after her dream. There is so much magic, so much we don't know, so much about consciousness still to explore, and where better to do it? As a recent participant said, "The Monroe Institute is the only place in the world where much of this work can be done."

The Intersection of Synchronicity and a Thoughtball

Lynn B. Robinson, Ph.D.

Lynn is a professor emerita of marketing, a consultant, an author, and more especially a wife, mother, and grandmother.

When you're living in the flow, things happen in titillating sequence. One thing leads to another, and you're in awe of the patterns that move you forward. That's what I want to tell you, how The Monroe Institute moved into my life and became woven into its larger fabric. The dates may not be exact, but they'll be close enough. Events occurred in a sequence and timing of their own, seemingly congruent with a larger pattern.

In 1990, I resigned from the university where I was a professor, had chaired a department, and had been director of graduate studies for the college of business. That move had not been part of my long-term strategy, but it's what I felt compelled to do. I took my consulting business into a home office.

About that time, a friend, who was corporate officer of a multinational chemical giant, told me of a profiling instrument they had used in their New York headquarters. He couldn't remember its name. He said, "Lynn, it's your kind of stuff. You'd love it." He described its approach and some of its content.

Shortly thereafter, I read a contemporary book with a chapter devoted to the Herrmann Brain Dominance Instrument. There was no doubt that this was the system my friend had described to me. Immediately, I ordered the hardback edition of *The Creative Brain* by Ned Herrmann and completed the complimentary profiling instrument included therewith. Early in 1992, I was in Lake Lure, North Carolina, the Herrmann headquarters, enrolled in an accreditation course for using the instrument. Once accredited, my company, Luminiferous, was licensed to use the instrument, the HBDI, now known as the Thinking Style Assessment.

At some time during my work with Ned Herrmann, he mentioned a workshop he administered for his organization using the facilities at The Monroe Institute. He found the environment there, its grounds and special living arrangements, especially conducive to his creativity training seminars. I was intrigued by Ned's descriptions and wrote for information about TMI programs. The information went into a filing cabinet with an intention to follow it up when my life and work permitted. Though I seriously wanted to go, the timing was not right.

My younger child graduated from college. I began mulling the possibility of writing a nonacademic book and took a noncredit creative writing course. I continued to do consulting work for my business clients. One of them requested that I read a book that was unavailable in the mobile public library or at the university here. A copy was ordered for me through a library loan service. When I went to pick it up, there was a display of new books near the checkout desk. I looked quickly at the brightly colored jackets and found myself catching one that fell from the top of the case into my hands. I was holding *Ultimate Journey* by Robert A. Monroe.

Years before, a similar thing had happened when a book about Findhorn, Scotland, had fallen into my hands. This was a mystical place that I later visited. Having had that and other similar experiences with books presenting themselves to me, I knew I had to take *Ultimate Journey* with me. Monroe talked about existence after death and where we go when we leave our physical bodies. I was even more committed to attending a program at the Institute. Learning about the availability of the Lifeline program added intensity to my intention. I thought that Lifeline could offer me a more disciplined approach to my natural proclivities, and I could offer my developing skills to the goals of Lifeline. I was excited by the possibilities.

By then, I was well into the writing of a book myself and had a commitment for its completion. However, the book refused to be finished until I wrote what became chapter 5, in which I was forthcoming about my personal experiences communicating with others no longer in physical bodies. Hitherto I had resisted coming that far out of my own "psychic closet," still protective of my professional reputation. The book, however, simply would not finish until I acknowledged those experiences. In July or August of 1994, I returned the bluelines to my publisher. The book was out of my hands.

As if completing the book removed all barriers between me and The Monroe Institute, in November of 1994, I attended the Gateway Voyage program. In the following month I attended Lifeline. In August of 1995, I attended Exploration 27.

During one of those programs, Bob's idea of catching a "thoughtball" was part of our discussions. As I understood it, a thoughtball was a fully formed concept that came into individual consciousness, a knowing so full and complete that to share it, one would have to unravel it, unwinding it to its core. Stated another way, as the thoughtball is absorbed into your mental and sensory processing, it expands, having been too much to grasp all at once. In *Ultimate Journey*, Monroe says, "I was filled, almost overcome, with a surge of enormous energy, an immensely powerful vibration of very high frequency. This I knew as a ROTE, short for Related Organized Thought Energy, a sort of ball of condensed thought and ideas."

I felt I knew exactly what that meant. In my work, I had also received full mental, conceptual constructs that shaped programs, speeches, and the like. They had come as full-blown ideas, zapped directly into my brain. However, I was unprepared for the larger thoughtball that came my way in October 1996.

I again chose to attend a learning event seemingly unrelated to my work. I was at the Living Enrichment Center in Wilsonville, Oregon, at the first meeting for the Society for the Universal Human. Mary Mannin Morrissey, Joan Borysenko, Leo Booth, Kathlyn and Gay Hendricks, Gary Zukav, Jean Houston, and Barbara Marx-Hubbard were all midwifing a shared vision. Caught up in the phenomenal energy of the birthing, I retreated from time to time for meditative rest. Most of us did. It was during one of those rests, or perhaps during theta-time as I moved out of sleep early one morning, that the thoughtball came fully formed into my consciousness.

Immediately, I reached for pen and paper so that I might capture its essence as best I could. The unraveling took on a pattern that Jean Houston had used in some of her presentations. Without the priming of Bob Monroe and the holistic structuring of Jean Houston, much might have been lost, perhaps totally. I might not have recognized the complexity or the enormity of what came fully formed and might have failed to write it down.

Here is the thoughtball as it was unraveled in October 1996. Brief basics: The Infant in the Elder, the Elder in the Infant, and They are all part of the One.

Level 1: Human Chronology

As we age, we carry with us the wonder and inquisitiveness of the newborn in continuing pursuit of survival. When we're born, we enter our humanity with creator/creative knowing, with cellular memory, and in natural pursuit of survival. Infants and eldermost-elders share a lesser physical capacity and greater dependence. There is wisdom in both states that we all need to honor and to learn to recognize, especially the elder in the infant. Accomplishing this will lead to greater appreciation of all living beings, regardless of age.

Level 2: Nature's Hierarchy

In the Judeo-Christian Western tradition, we've placed humanity in the position of the elder-one-up—more exalted, experienced, more evolved than minerals, plants, or animals. We've ignored our infant in the elder, that is, our dependence on those life forms we've classified as infant/lesser-developed. We've concomitantly failed to honor the elder in the infant of those "lesser" life forms—their inner direction, elegant simplicity of design, and contribution to our "elder" survival.

Level 3: Society/Culture

The one-ups in our culture traditionally have been the males, Caucasians, formally educated, urban, propertied. They have assumed the role of honored elder, ignoring the elder contribution of the societal infant (anyone or anything not having their elder characteristics). The failure to honor the elder in their designated infants has led to imbalance, distortion, disharmony, and the inability to be the Oneness inherent in the created pattern.

Level 4: Archetypal/Mythical

The great stories undergirding our culture are of hierarchies of gods/goddesses (infants) and super-gods (elders), of angels and archangels. Other cultures have their great stories about circles of life, webs of time and space . . . of Oneness. Our most repeated stories emphasize cause and effect. Only occasional reference is made to time without end, or to humans as though they are akin to drifting dawn mists forming dew on the fields, rising and gathering into a cloud and then falling down as rain . . . and they are One, humans, just as the mist, the dew, the cloud, the rain, all one in circular webs and stories of life.

Level 5: Mystical/Spiritual

Envision the infinity symbol. The point of intersection is a "jump-time," where the elder passes into the infant, circles around for the infant to cycle into the elder; where this passage is continuous and exists within and without time and space; where its multiplicity is perceptually available to only those with multi-sensory awareness. At the point of intersection, Creation reaches out to experience itself, brings its knowing back and through its center, then reaches out again, only to bring itself back through its center, so that all of its knowings know each other, first or last, infant or elder folding back into One. The elder in the infant, the infant in the elder, and they are One.

The meaning has expanded over time. I pondered how this knowing might be made useful. A program for honoring the wisdom of our infants, our children, began taking shape. I chose to use a commercial setting for application, where children seven and eight years of age became "consultants" to managers, catalysts for managerial change. In May 1998, a pilot program was completed, and a book began taking shape and is still in progress. I saw the familial, societal, and cultural ramifications. The meaning of the thoughtball was growing. Its expansion persisted, leading to ongoing work and expression.

Synchronicities continue. It won't be surprising to me if other intersections occur. My meeting the editors of this volume at a Monroe Institute Professional Division gathering might well be one. What I hope is that you, the reader, find your own intersection of synchronicity with the thoughtball that I received, that you bring meaning to its message in your own life and work. If that happens, then I may have been worthy of receiving it, and of having been prepared for it by two luminaries, Bob Monroe and Jean Houston.

If you choose to act upon its meaning, and then to share with me or others, then those who exist in nonphysical realities will have their work with us honored again and again. Together, those of us who are embodied and are in collaboration with others that are not in a physical body will be joined in the Union of One, "at the point of intersection," where Creation reaches out to experience itself, brings its knowing back and through its center, and reaches out again, only to bring itself back through its center so that all of its knowings know each other, first or last, infant or elder, folding back into One.

Thank you for considering the possibility.

IN-HOME TRAINING SERIES, MONROE PRODUCTS, AND RESIDENTIAL COURSES

The use of Hemi-Sync as an aid to access the inner self has resulted in the development of many series of home study programs aimed at helping the individual achieve diverse goals. These range from augmenting recovery during physical and mental health challenges to allowing easier access to the areas of human consciousness where personal growth can be most effective.

The Gateway Experience: People travel from all over the world to attend The Monroe Institute's six-day residential **Gateway Voyage** program. This renowned program has been adapted for in-home use in a series of six albums. Each album or Wave represents the waves of natural energy that one learns to navigate in the exploration of the greater self. A gradual step-by-step development of the participant's skills leads to profound experiences of expanded awareness.

The title of each Wave aptly describes the step that each represents in leading the participant to greater self-knowledge and experience of personal potential. Used sequentially, each Wave builds on the tools and techniques learned in the previous Wave. The pace is left to personal choice, and no time limits are set.

The Waves are titled: *Discovery, Threshold, Freedom, Adventure, Exploring,* and *Odyssey.* Each wave contains six exercises.

Going Home: A groundbreaking collaboration between Robert Monroe, Elisabeth Kübler-Ross, M.D., and Charles Tart, Ph.D. These well-known authors and researchers developed a series of exercises intended to help patients and their caregivers deal with the challenge of terminal illness. The exercises provide the opportunity to understand that death need not be feared and offer ways for participants to experience living more fully in the moment.

The series consists of two six-cassette albums, one intended for the patient or subject, and the other album for the support, be they family, caregivers, or professional hospice workers.

Opening the Heart: Developed from the Institute's residential Heartline Program, this series promotes the development of skills to deal with life and with other people from a more loving perspective. Unconditional love is one of the greatest challenges to achieve in our busy world, and this series supports us with exercises to release blocks and prejudices that impede our ability to enhance our relationships with each other.

Lucid Dreaming: The goal of this series of four exercises is learning to consciously participate in, and recall more completely, the nightly dream cycles. Our dreams come to us with powerful personal messages, which we cannot always easily understand. The language of the mind is symbolic, and the challenge is to be able to interpret the symbols and adapt them to daily life. The perspective, from a state of expanded awareness, makes it easier to explore and interpret the symbolic realms.

Opening the Way: The responsibility of bringing new life safely into the world is addressed in this practical series which deals with physical childbirth preparation as well as the emotional adjustments for new parents. Exercises also include tools for support during postpartum and nursing activities.

Progressive Accelerated Learning (PAL): Designed to provide high-powered exercises for optimizing the study and job performance skills needed in learning environments, as well as in the work place. Exercises provide the tools needed for dedicating information to memory, instant recall of information, and application of total attention to the task at hand. Especially useful to people challenged with attention and learning disorders.

The **PAL Student** series contains four exercises, and the expanded **PAL Executive** Package contains six exercises. The exercises are also available as single titles.

Positive Immunity Program: Strengthening the mind-body connection, this series is designed for those with immune system dysfunction as well as those looking to reinforce healthy immune defenses. The power of the mind/body connection and the role it plays in the resistance to, and healing of, existing disease has now been recognized by the scientific community. Doctors and researchers have confirmed the importance of positive emotional input for the well-being of the human body. This series is devoted to the support of that positive reinforcement.

Support for Stroke Recovery: As described above, utilizing the capacity of the body to participate in its own healing process, this series provides the tools to the patient for regaining lost motor and verbal skills. It is also recommended by doctors for patients recovering from head trauma. Frequently, the areas injured are the same as those affected by a stroke, resulting in the partial or complete loss of speech or motor abilities. As an adjunct to physiotherapy or continuation of in-home therapy, the Stroke Recovery exercises help support the healing process.

Surgical Support Series: As its title suggests, this product is for use prior to and during hospital visits for elective and emergency procedures. Doctors have been very open to the request by their patients to have the exercises playing over headphones while undergoing surgery. The series includes exercises to prepare the body for surgery, to participate with the surgical staff in the success of any procedure, and to return quickly from the effects of anesthesia after the operation is over. Relaxation exercises are highlighted, and positive input for the recuperation of full movement and activity after surgery is emphasized.

Cancer Support Series: This series was developed to help strengthen the mind-body connection and access inner resources to boost the immune system. It includes exercises for those undergoing chemotherapy and radiation therapy, and has four titles: *Chemotherapy Companion, Journey through the T-Cells, Radiation Companion* and *Sleeping through the Rain.*

Single Tapes/CDs

These fall into three groups:

Mind Food: This group includes several verbally guided exercises covering a wide variety of subjects, including pain control, energy building, relaxation, meditation, and sleep. There are also some non-verbal exercises for relaxation and sleep.

Human Plus: Thirty-six exercises of similar format with verbal guidance and cues (function commands) that allow you to re-create a desired effect when needed, covering a wide variety of purposes.

Metamusic: Metamusic combines musical selections with embedded audio signals. Many titles incorporate blends of very low frequencies to slow excess mental activity in order to facilitate meditation or relaxation, or to encourage sleep. Others employ predominantly beta frequencies for focused intent and concentration.

For a descriptive list of all Monroe Products, see *The Hemi-Sync Catalog,* available from Monroe Products, PO Box 505, Lovingston, VA 22949, phone 434-263-8692 or 800-541-2488 (toll-free), www.hemi-sync.com

Residential Programs

Gateway Voyage: This internationally renowned program is designed to provide tools that enable self-discovery, the development and exploration of human consciousness, and expansion of one's awareness.

The following residential programs are open only to graduates of the Gateway Voyage.

Guidelines: This program provides learning methods through which communication can be established with greater parts of one's self-awareness, providing an overview beyond our typical perception.

Lifeline: Offers training in states of consciousness beyond those explored in Gateway and Guidelines. Participants learn to contact those who have made the transition from physical reality and who need assistance in moving forward.

Exploration 27: Provides intensive investigation into uncharted nonphysical territories in order to obtain information and direct personal experience related to this different state of being. A week of pioneering, cutting-edge explorations open only to Lifeline graduates.

Heartline: Offers new approaches for removing the obstacles to the expression of love in our daily lives, as well as methods for exploring deeper levels of self; an invitation to the left-brain, rational self to open, allow, and welcome the heart feeling connection to come into balance.

Other Programs. The Institute offers other graduate residential programs than those detailed here and new programs are being designed and implemented on an ongoing basis. Please visit TMI's website for information on these programs as well as programs in French and Spanish.

Dolphin Energy Club

The Dolphin Energy Club (DEC) is a healing service offering a means for Hemi-Sync users to help themselves and others. Contact The Monroe Institute for further information.

USEFUL BOOKS

Atwater, F. Holmes. *Captain of My Ship, Master of My Soul*. Charlottesville, VA: Hampton Roads, 2002.

Bache, Christopher. *Dark Night, Early Dawn*. New York: SUNY, 2000.

Campbell, Don. *The Mozart Effect*. New York: Avon Books, 1997.

Carter, Gari. *Healing Myself*. Charlottesville, VA: Hampton Roads, 1993.

Coren, Stanley. *Sleep Thieves*. New York: Simon & Schuster, 1996.

DeMarco, Frank. *Muddy Tracks*. Charlottesville, VA: Hampton Roads, 2001.

Godwin, Malcolm. *The Lucid Dreamer*. Shaftesbury, Dorset: Element, 1995; Charlottesville, VA: Hampton Roads, 2001.

Greenfield, Susan. *The Human Brain*. London: Weidenfeld & Nicolson, 1997.

Kübler-Ross, Elisabeth. *The Wheel of Life*. New York: Simon & Schuster, 1997.

LaBerge, Stephen. *Lucid Dreaming*. Los Angeles: Jeremy Tarcher, 1985.

Lorimer, David, ed. *Thinking beyond the Brain*. Edinburgh: Floris Books, 2001.

———. *Wider Horizons*. Leven: Scientific & Medical Network, 1999.

Martin, Paul. *Counting Sheep*. London: Harper Collins, 2002

McKnight, Rosalind. *Cosmic Journeys*. Charlottesville, VA: Hampton Roads, 1999.

McMoneagle, Joseph. *Mind Trek*. Charlottesville, VA: Hampton Roads, 1993.

———. *The Ultimate Time Machine*. Charlottesville, VA: Hampton Roads, 1998.

———. *The Stargate Chronicles*. Charlottesville, VA: Hampton Roads, 2002.

Monroe, Robert A. *Journeys Out of the Body*. New York: Doubleday, 1972.

———. *Far Journeys*. New York: Doubleday, 1985.

———. *Ultimate Journey*. New York: Doubleday, 1994.

Russell, Peter. *From Science to God*. Novato: New World Library, 2003.

Russell, Ronald. *The Vast Enquiring Soul*. Charlottesville, VA: Hampton Roads, 2000.

Stockton, Bayard. *Catapult: The Biography of Robert A. Monroe*. Norfolk, VA: Donning, 1988.

Talbot, Michael. *The Holographic Universe*. New York: Harper Collins, 1991.

Tart, Charles. *States of Consciousness*. New York: Dutton, 1975.

———. *Open Mind, Discriminating Mind*. New York: Harper Collins, 1989.

———, ed. *Body Mind Spirit*. Charlottesville, VA: Hampton Roads. 1997.

Velmans, Max. *Understanding Consciousness*. London: Routledge, 2000.

ABOUT THE EDITOR

Ronald Russell has written and edited some 15 books published in the United Kingdom and United States, most recently *The Vast Enquiring Soul: Explorations into the Further Reaches of Consciousness.* He edited *Using the Whole Brain,* 1993, the predecessor of the present title. He is a graduate of Oxford University, served in the Royal Air Force, enjoyed a career in teaching, and has worked for several University examining boards. He lectures for Glasgow University from time to time on issues concerning human consciousness. He is a member of The Monroe Institute's Advisory Board and its Professional Division.

Hampton Roads Publishing Company

. . . for the evolving human spirit

Hampton Roads Publishing Company
publishes books on a variety of subjects,
including metaphysics, health,
visionary fiction, and other related topics.

For a copy of our latest catalog, call toll-free
(800) 766-8009, or send your name and address to:

Hampton Roads Publishing Company, Inc.
1125 Stoney Ridge Road
Charlottesville, VA 22902

e-mail: hrpc@hrpub.com
www.hrpub.com